Sacramental Preaching

SERMONS *on the* HIDDEN PRESENCE *of* CHRIST

Hans Boersma

BakerAcademic
a division of Baker Publishing Group
Grand Rapids, Michigan

© 2016 by Hans Boersma

Published by Baker Academic
a division of Baker Publishing Group
P.O. Box 6287, Grand Rapids, MI 49516-6287
www.bakeracademic.com

Printed in the United States of America

Library of Congress Cataloging-in-Publication Data
Names: Boersma, Hans, 1961– author.
Title: Sacramental preaching : sermons on the hidden presence of Christ / Hans Boersma.
Description: Grand Rapids, MI : Baker Academic, 2016. | Includes bibliographical
    references and index.
Identifiers: LCCN 2015045922 | ISBN 9780801097454 (pbk.)
Subjects: LCSH: Jesus Christ—Person and offices—Sermons. | Bible—Homiletical use. |
    Christian Reformed Church—Sermons. | Sermons, English—Canada.
Classification: LCC BT203 .B64 2016 | DDC 252/.057—dc23
LC record available at http://lccn.loc.gov/2015045922

In keeping with biblical principles of creation stewardship, Baker Publishing Group advocates the responsible use of our natural resources. As a member of the Green Press Initiative, our company uses recycled paper when possible. The text paper of this book is composed in part of post-consumer waste.

16 17 18 19 20 21 22   7 6 5 4 3 2 1

To
Bert & Wieke
Clary & Stacey
John & Wendy
Mike & Jacqui
Peter & Louise
Pim & Margreet

In gratitude for
Seeking Christ in the Scriptures
Sharing prayer and fellowship

Novum in vetere latet et in novo vetus patet.
(The New is in the Old concealed, and the Old is in the New revealed.)

—St. Augustine

Scripturae autem divinae sancta profunditas adeo communes sermones habet, ut eam universi incunctanter admittant. Sensus autem recondit veritatis arcano, ut in ipsa studiosissime vitalis sententia debeat indagari.
(Now the holy depth of divine Scripture is expressed in such common language that everyone immediately takes it in. But buried within it are hidden senses of truth, so that the vital meaning must be most carefully sought out.)

—Cassiodorus

Contents

Foreword

Sacramental Theology

The pulpit is ever this earth's foremost part; all the rest comes in its rear; the pulpit leads the world. . . . From thence it is the God of breezes fair or foul is first invoked for favorable winds. Yes, the world's a ship on its passage out, and not a voyage complete; and the pulpit is its prow.

—Herman Melville, *Moby-Dick*

I read those words while at university, and they took root in my imagination and eventually formed a strong sense of identity of myself vocationally as a pastor with a pulpit: *Yes, the world's a ship on its passage out, and not a voyage complete; and the pulpit is its prow.*

But in the fifty-five years that I have been a pastor, I haven't had many colleagues who share that conviction. What a delight to find a friend in Hans Boersma who does, who believes that the "pulpit is its prow" and is doing his best to make that believable. This book is evidence of his passion.

The Bible as a whole comes in the form of narrative, what I have come to think of as *incarnational* storytelling, God revealing himself in human form—"the Word became flesh . . . and we have seen his glory, glory as of the only Son from the Father" (John 1:14)—and what Hans Boersma designates *sacramental* storytelling.

Wallace Stegner, deceased but with a still alive reputation as one of our great contemporary storytellers, tells us: "if the forms are bad, we live badly." Our Holy Scriptures are a good and true form by which we live well. Storytelling creates a world of presuppositions, assumptions, and relations into which we enter. Stories invite us into a world other than ourselves, and if they are good and true stories, a world larger than ourselves. The story that is Holy Scripture invites us into a world of God's creation and salvation and blessing, God in human form in action on the very ground on which we also live, an incarnational *story*, that is, a flesh and blood story, a story worked out in actual lives and places (not in abstract ideas or programs or inspirational uplifting anecdotes), but a Jesus *story* in which we recognize the action of God in the everydayness of a local history in our stories, a *sacramental* story.

This idea of sacramental story is important, for a widespread practice in our postbiblical church culture is taking the story and eliminating it by depersonalizing it into propositions or "truths" or morals or ideas. The story is eviscerated of relationships and persons. Jesus, the center of the Christian faith, is depersonalized into an abstract truth, and men and women are depersonalized into problems to be fixed or resources to be exploited. Eventually there is no story left.

The distinctiveness of what we have learned to name *gospel* is that it brings the centuries of Hebrew storytelling, God telling his story of creation and salvation and blessing his people, to the story of Jesus, the mature completion of all the stories, in a way that is clearly revelation—that is, God's self-disclosing—a way that invites, more like *insists* on, our participation.

In some respects this is an odd kind of story, this Jesus creation/salvation/blessing story. It tells us very little of what ordinarily interests us in a story, and we learn virtually nothing about what we are really interested in. There is no description of Jesus' appearance. Nothing about his friends, his schooling, his childhood. Very little about what he thought, how he felt, or his interior struggles. There is a surprising and disconcerting reticence in regard to Jesus. We don't figure Jesus out, we don't search for Jesus, we don't get Jesus on our terms. If we stay with the story long enough, we recognize that Jesus and the life he embodies are not consumer items.

Immersion in this gospel world has always been the primary way Christians have developed a sacramental imagination. The first followers of Jesus saw this world take place in their company and before their eyes; they saw "the Word become flesh" in the humanity of Jesus and actually live among them. Peter was the first to name what they saw and heard as God took human form and over an extended period of time (three years) lived in their neighborhood. Subsequent generations searched the Old Testament, the Hebrew Scriptures, for implicit evidence of the incarnation, Jesus the Christ. But they did not arbitrarily put him there; they *found* him there. The New was always already present in the Old. "Christ himself is hidden in all of the Old Testament. The biblical text is a sacrament, and Christ is really present in it," is Dr. Boersma's summary conclusion.

Reynolds Price uses the term "narrative hunger" to call attention to our "need to hear and tell stories . . . second in necessity apparently after nourishment and before love and shelter. Millions survive without love or home, almost none in silence; the opposite of silence leads quickly to narrative, and the sound of story is the dominant sound of our lives."[1]

American poet Christian Wiman, exploring his newly realized Christian identity, says it like this: "I begin to think that *anything* that abstracts us from the physical world is 'of the devil.'"[2] Wiman adds, "Christ speaks in stories as a way of preparing his followers to stake their lives on a story, because existence is not a puzzle to be solved, but a narrative to be inherited and undergone and transformed person by person."[3]

So we are speaking of an incarnational imagination, a Jesus-soaked imagination, a sacramental imagination so that every truth becomes a lived truth, lived in the homes and workplaces that our congregations face us with every time we preach a sermon.

1. Reynolds Price, *A Palpable God* (San Francisco: North Point Press, 1985), 3.
2. Christian Wiman, *My Bright Abyss: Meditation of a Modern Believer* (New York: Farrar, Strauss and Giroux, 2013), 115.
3. Ibid., 88.

———✭———

Pastoral preaching is rooted in language: God speaks. When God speaks, things happen. Holy Scripture opens with the words "God said . . ." ringing out eight times. After each sounding we see, piece by piece, one after another, elements of heaven and earth coming into being before our eyes, and then climaxing in man and woman formed in the image of God. Psalm 33 compresses Genesis 1 into a single sentence: "For he spoke, and it came to be" (Ps. 33:9). This sets the stage for everything that follows in our Bibles, a profuse outpouring of commands and promises, blessings and invitations, directing and comforting that make up our Holy Scriptures.

As Jesus speaks, his words flourish into conversations and discourses with all sorts and conditions of people, conversations brief and lengthy, conversations pithy and elaborate, but *conversations*. Several times the conversations develop into discourses. But the conversational tone is always maintained. The Lord of language uses language not to "lord it over" anyone but to enter relationships of grace and love, creating community and bringing it to maturity from the pulpit and through person-to-person conversations that include the praying presence of Jesus.

In the final book of the canon, The Revelation of Jesus Christ, the risen Jesus Christ identifies himself to John alphabetically, "I am the Alpha and the Omega" (1:8)—that is, "I am the alphabet, all the letters from A to Z, the vowels and consonants out of which all words are made." Jesus speaks in such ways that the brokenness of the world and our experience develop into a dazzling holiness that evokes worship on a grand scale involving everything in heaven and earth, and concludes with a celebratory wedding banquet.

And here is something that never ceases to astonish me. Pastor John of Patmos knew his Bible inside and out. The Revelation has 404 verses. In those 404 verses are 518 references to earlier Scripture. But there is not a single quote; all the references are allusions. Here is a pastor who is absolutely immersed in Scripture and submits himself to it. He does not merely repeat, regurgitate, and proof-text. As he preaches, the Scriptures are re-created in him. He first assimilated the Scriptures and then lives and preaches these same Scriptures.

The Revelation is a thorough immersion in and the last word in what I have come to think of as lived theology, often designated as spiritual theology. It is the "one great poem which the first Christian age produced."[4]

My metaphor of choice for grasping what is involved in listening and meditating on God's Word is "eat this book." It occurs first in Jeremiah (15:16) and Ezekiel (3:3) in their role as prophets during the devastating Babylonian exile. It comes to unforgettable prominence in the final book of the Bible when the apocalyptic strong angel in the presence of John of Patmos took the cosmos for his pulpit, one foot planted in the ocean and the other on land, and held the Scriptures in his hand, ready to preach. The angel "called out with a loud voice, like a lion roaring" (Rev. 10:3). John was about to write what he heard. He grabbed his notebook and pencil, but a "voice from heaven" said, "do not write it down" (10:4). The words in the book had just been revoiced, taken off the page and set in motion in the air where they could enter ears. Writing them down would be like taking the wind out of the words and flattening them soundless on paper. The preaching angel had just gotten them off the printed page, and now John was going to put them back again. "No," says the heavenly voice, "I want those words out there, creating sound waves, entering ears, entering lives. I want those words preached, sung, taught, prayed—*lived*." The voice from heaven told John to ask for the scroll from the angel. The angel gave it to him and told him, "Take and eat it" (10:9). "Get this book into your gut; get the words of this book moving through your bloodstream. Chew on the words and swallow them so they can be turned into muscle and gristle and bone." And John did it; he ate the book: "I took the little scroll from the hand of the angel and ate it" (10:10). He preached the word of God.

What I eventually came to recognize in John as a preacher is this: Godtalk—depersonalized, nonrelational, unlistening, abstract language—kills. In the "land of the living" it is blasphemous, whether

4. Austin Farrer, *A Rebirth of Images: The Making of St. John's Apocalypse* (Westminster, MD: Dacre Press, 1949), 6.

spoken from pulpits or across the breakfast table. We pastors can't be too careful in the way we use language, this sacred language, this word-of-God language. When we enter John's language world, we soon realize that he was totally immersed in his Bible (which for him was the Old Testament) and in his seven congregations, their strengths and weaknesses, testings and difficulties. At the same time, he was mindful of the political and economic world in which they lived, the killing and suffering and evil. Then taking all of this into account, with his incredible sacramental, Spirit-formed imagination, he gathered his congregations into the great drama of salvation and provided them with an embracing story, a clear instruction and a dramatic poem that rocks with "Amens" and "Hallelujahs." And not a cliché anywhere to be found.

I have used this metaphor for much of my pastoral/preaching life as a way of focusing on and clarifying what it means to have these Holy Scriptures and how the holy community has learned to eat them, receive them in a way that forms us into Christian women and men created and saved and blessed by God the Father, God the Son, and God the Holy Spirit.

Eugene H. Peterson
Professor Emeritus of Spiritual Theology
Regent College, Vancouver, BC

Preface

Sermons are tied to particular times and places that shape them in countless ways. I would like to say a few words, therefore, about the places where I first preached the contents of this book. The most important context for these sermons is my local church—Immanuel Christian Reformed Church in Langley, British Columbia, where our family has worshiped for the past seventeen years. I preached each sermon in this collection first in this evangelical, Reformed church of about 350 members on Canada's west coast. The date at the heading of each sermon indicates the Sunday on which I first preached it in my home church. For this collection, I have changed the wording and sentence structure here and there, and the very public character of this collection required other changes and omissions (such as references to events in our congregation). For the most part, however, the changes are minimal, so the sermons as you find them here are not much different from how I preached them in my home congregation.

I also preached quite a few of these sermons in our Tuesday morning chapels at Regent College, an evangelical graduate school of theology in Vancouver, where I have been privileged to teach since 2005. Our chapels are well attended by students and faculty, comprising a group of about two hundred worshipers. Because of time constraints, I presented most of the sermons at Regent in abbreviated form. Although one might think that preaching for graduate theology students is quite different from preaching in a regular evangelical congregation, I have found that usually just minor adjustments for the sake of my Regent College audience suffice. I suppose the reason is that when we preach, we're meant not to come with "lofty speech or wisdom" but with "Jesus Christ and him crucified" (1 Cor. 2:1–2).

It remains for me to thank the people who have contributed to this book—most especially my home congregation and my students, for the sake of whose final happiness I wrote these sermons in the first place. I would also like to thank Kees van der Kooi, along with his colleagues at the Faculty of Dogmatics and Ecumenics at the Free University in Amsterdam, for inviting me to join them for several months as researcher-in-residence during the summer of 2014, during which time I was able to prepare several of the sermons as well as the Preacher's Notes accompanying each. I very much enjoyed their generous hospitality and support. I am also obliged to C. J. de Vogelstichting for providing me with additional funding for our stay in Amsterdam. The board and administration of Langley Christian School were most gracious in giving my wife a two-month leave of absence so that she could join me on our mini-sabbatical in Amsterdam. I am particularly grateful to the group of Regent College students who meticulously read through this entire book and gave up many of their Friday evenings to discuss its contents together. A very warm thank you, therefore, to Corine Boersma, Alex Fogleman, Kevin Greenlee, Kyle MacKenney, Brittany McComb, Becky Pruitt, and Tracy Russell, as well as to Matthew Thomas, who took time away from his doctoral studies in Oxford to painstakingly read through the whole manuscript. The efficiency and skill of my research assistant, Phillip Hussey, were a tremendous asset to the final stages of proofreading and of compiling the indexes. Alec Arnold is not just an excellent scholar but also a great artist, and I am indebted to him for the drawing of the ziggurat (fig. 2 on p. 156). Eugene Peterson's endorsement of this project in the form of the foreword to the book is deeply humbling, and I am most grateful to him for fueling the sacramental imagination with the Scripture story. It is my hope that this book will be a small but fitting continuation of his many years of faithful preaching, teaching, and writing, both for Regent College and the people of God more broadly. I would also like to thank

David Nelson and his fellow editors at Baker Academic for their support of this project. I am well aware that publishing sermons is a risky endeavor, and I am all the more honored by the trust they have shown in me by publishing these sermons. Finally, my wife, Linda, has not only listened to each of these sermons but has also been my most honest and faithful critic. I am most grateful to God for the happiness that you bring into my life.

Introduction

*T*hese sermons try to give an answer to a question I have often been asked over the years: Can we read the Bible today in the same way the church fathers did? Particularly, my students have repeatedly come to me with this question. Sometimes the question comes with a slightly skeptical undertone: surely, the allegorical flights of fancy that we see in the early church and Middle Ages have no lasting value. To adopt their approach to the Bible, and to interpret Scripture the way they used to do, must lead us down the garden path. More often, however, my students have asked me the question out of genuine interest. They have become intrigued with questions of interpretation—sometimes because they have encountered contemporary theoretical treatments of interpretive practices and as a result have begun to wonder whether patristic exegesis can shed light on the questions raised in these contemporary debates. Or in preparing for pastoral ministry, they have become intrigued with the profound depths of insight they are discovering in the church fathers. As a result, they ask themselves some basic hermeneutical (interpretive) questions. Almost invariably at some point the question comes up: What do we do today with patristic modes of exegesis?

My response comes as a compilation of sermons for at least three reasons. First, had I used some other format, it would have been possible to hide behind the rhetoric of a theoretical discussion regarding the importance of patristic interpretation. Sermons, by contrast, speak for themselves. Any reader can decide for himself or herself whether my sympathies with patristic biblical interpretation lead to fruitful results, and readers schooled in the early church's reading of the Bible can see for themselves where the points of continuity and discontinuity lie between premodern readings and the exegesis that lies behind these sermons. Second, I work with the conviction that the Bible is the book of the church. So it's best to test whether a particular exegetical or interpretive approach is viable, not through theoretical discourse (however valuable in itself), but in the church's preaching.

Third, the genre of sermon or homily reaches not just theology students but also a wider audience. I preached all the sermons in this book in my local church; no particular training is required, therefore, to read them. I hope and pray that the Spirit will use these sermons to allow people from a wide variety of backgrounds to see the face of Christ more clearly. For those learning how to preach or wanting to know more about what happens at the preacher's desk prior to Sunday morning, the Preacher's Notes following each sermon will hopefully be of help. These notes are of a somewhat "theoretical" nature. They explain in more depth what I believe it means to preach sacramentally as well as some of my exegetical choices and other matters of interpretive, pastoral, and homiletic interest. If you just want to read some sermons, skip the rest of this introduction and the Preacher's Notes.

The response I give to my students' question is not that they should simply imitate patristic or medieval exegetical approaches in their own exegetical work. Such an answer would clearly fall short. Throughout the tradition, there have been differing approaches to the biblical text. To regard patristic and/or medieval exegesis as a homogeneous whole would be obviously problematic. What is more, the sermons we preach today land in an audience whose horizons differ in important respects from people listening to preachers such as Gregory of Nyssa, Augustine, or Bernard of Clairvaux. More than anything else, the sense of history to which modernity gave birth sets today's listeners apart from those of the premodern period. Chronological progress, change, and development have become part of the modern consciousness in ways they simply were not for earlier generations.

While it may be a bit of a shortcut, it is not wrong to characterize this difference by saying that a vertical mind-set, a focus on eternal, timeless truths, has made room for a horizontal viewpoint, seeing truth as embedded in historical circumstance. Whatever the metaphysical convictions of the preacher, we cannot ignore the more horizontal and historical mind-set that our audience has likely absorbed. Preaching in the twenty-first century will of necessity be different from preaching in the fourth century.

But does it matter what kind of mind-set we have—a vertical or a horizontal one? We may want to give this metaphysical question some attention. If the more vertical understanding of reality assumed by earlier Christians has greater semblance to truth than the focus on history that we have inherited particularly through the eighteenth-century Enlightenment, then preachers cannot ignore the implications. It would mean, for instance, that the realities we encounter in time and space aren't as ultimate as many in our society tend to assume.[1] As a result, preachers will want to challenge the contemporary one-dimensional focus on the here and now (the physical realities of our sensible world) and also take seriously the spiritual and moral dimensions of reality. Paul Tyson helpfully characterizes the metaphysics of the Christian tradition as 3-D (three-dimensional), distinguishing it from the reductionism of the 1-D (one-dimensional) approach that tends to inform our basic stance in the modern period.[2] Patristic and medieval audiences worked with a 3-D metaphysics that took eternal, heavenly realities as its focal point; contemporary audiences lean toward a 1-D metaphysics that takes seriously only the things we can see and touch. Aware that this 1-D metaphysics has infiltrated their congregations, preachers have the task of guiding them to a more wholesome mind-set that takes seriously the upward thrust of the Christian faith.

1. Daniel J. Treier, in his helpful introduction to theological interpretation, rightly comments: "The Enlightenment and its aftermath finalized this metaphysical separation between history and God. Ever since, time and space no longer seem to participate in the divine but rather have 'natural' autonomy." *Introducing Theological Interpretation of Scripture: Recovering a Christian Practice* (Grand Rapids: Baker Academic, 2008), 27.

2. Paul Tyson, *Returning to Reality: Christian Platonism for Our Times* (Eugene, OR: Cascade, 2014), 16.

I have elsewhere characterized the metaphysics common among premodern listeners as sacramental.[3] By this I mean that this-worldly, created realities participate in the heavenly, uncreated reality of the eternal Word of God. Created being is merely derivative, and it receives its value from the divine "real presence" that gives it existence. To be sure, speaking of creation as "sacramental" in character has its dangers. When doing so, we should be careful not to undermine the qualitatively different sense of sacramentality that we encounter in Christ and in the church's sacraments, most notably baptism and the Eucharist. Kathryn Tanner's distinction between "weak" and "strong" participation, or we could say a weak and a strong sacramental presence, is important.[4] We don't want to lose the distinct salvific character of the church. Nonetheless, it seems to me that the Christian tradition has rightly worked with a sacramental metaphysics, assuming that the appearances of the physical realities around us not only point to, but also make present, greater and more significant realities than the appearances themselves.

Although there were numerous theological and homiletical differences among individual preachers in the premodern era, most would have agreed that some kind of "depth dimension" or mystery—a sacramental reality—underlies the created objects of time and space. Therefore, these preachers were keen to point to this depth dimension in their preaching. Convinced that created realities of time and space find their deepest truth in Christ himself, the Word incarnate, these preachers explored the biblical text primarily to locate Christ. Put differently, we can say that not only did they regard created objects, such as trees and dogs and stars, as in some sense sacramental; they also viewed the biblical text—particularly the Old Testament—as sacramental. They viewed both as sacramental because both point upward to Christ as the reality in whom all things hold together (Col. 1:17). It is this basic sacramental understanding of the Scriptures—as divine means of grace, making Christ present to us—that is also of value for us today. In this sense, we can still preach the same way the church fathers used to preach.

3. Hans Boersma, *Heavenly Participation: The Weaving of a Sacramental Tapestry* (Grand Rapids: Eerdmans, 2011).
4. Kathryn Tanner, *Christ the Key*, Current Issues in Theology 7 (Cambridge: Cambridge University Press, 2010), 11–12.

We see the same sacramental approach to the Scriptures in the cover image of this book. The painting is the last of a set of thirty-five known as the *Armadio degli Argenti* (*Silver Chest*), painted by Fra Angelico between 1451 and 1453. Each panel depicts an aspect of the life of Christ, and in each Fra Angelico portrays Christ's life as a typological fulfillment of the Old Testament. The final panel is known as the *Lex Amoris* (*Law of Love*), and a woman in the bottom left (not visible on the book cover) holds a shield that displays these Latin words. Fra Angelico, drawing on Thomas Aquinas, meant to juxtapose the New Testament as the law of love (*lex amoris*) to the Old Testament as the law of fear (*lex timoris*),[5] while at the same time recognizing their close connection.[6] Fra Angelico's concluding panel shows both aspects. On the one hand, the twelve prophets, each holding a scroll with a key prophetic verse, are juxtaposed with the twelve apostles, each holding a scroll containing a line of the Apostles' Creed. On the other hand, the central axis, rising up from the middle branch of a menorah, connects the two sides by going through the life of Christ (and the church) in twelve subsequent steps. The message is that Christ links the prophets of the Old Testament to the apostles of the New.

Thomas Aquinas underscores this close link between Old and New by insisting that the latter is contained (*continetur*) in the former. Similar to the way a species is present in a genus, a whole tree in a seed, and a kernel of corn in an ear, so also the New Law is contained in the Old.[7] Apparently, the law of love was already present—virtually, that is—within the law of fear. Thomas' description is extremely compelling. He seems to suggest that the truth or reality (*res*) of the New Testament is somehow present in the Old Testament. His "containing" language turns the Old Testament into a sacrament (*sacramentum*) of sorts, with the Old Testament types containing

5. Thomas Aquinas does so in the *Summa Theologica*, trans. Fathers of the English Dominican Province (New York: Benziger, 1948), I/II, q.107, a.1.

6. Lasse Hodne points out Fra Angelico's dependence on Thomas in "Reading and Viewing Words in Fra Angelico's Typological Paintings," in *Inscriptions in Liturgical Spaces*, ed. Kristin B. Aavitsland and Turid Karlsen Seim, Acta ad archaeologiam et artium historiam pertinentia, new series, 10 (Rome: Scienze e lettere, 2011), 243–63, at 251.

7. Thomas Aquinas, *Summa Theologica* I/II, q.107, a.3.

their New Testament antitype—which is their fulfillment in Christ and the church. Thomas wasn't particularly innovative in his claim that exegesis of the Old Testament is a sacramental practice. Nor did Fra Angelico's *Armadio degli Argenti* start a new trend by emphasizing the close link between the law of fear and the law of love. Sacramental reading is something that goes back to the church fathers—it goes back to the New Testament—and is something we need to recover in our preaching today.

It will be clear from the sermons that follow that I am not advocating a wooden adherence to the particularities of patristic exegesis. But it will also be obvious that I have learned a great deal from premodern exegesis and that I work on metaphysical assumptions that are no different from those that characterized this earlier tradition. Really, at bottom the homiletic implication is simply this: We always want to preach Christ. By preaching Christ we do not arbitrarily *impose* him on the text, even if we happen to preach from the Old Testament; we attempt to *find* him there, since he is the deepest real presence contained within the outward symbol of the biblical text. As an important aside, we should note this also means no gap exists between exegesis and application. Application is not something we do after we have finished our exegesis. Application is found by opening up the treasure of the text to see what's already inside: Christ himself, along with all the gifts he brings to us.

The sermons that I have selected for this book illustrate my conviction that for much of church history, theologians would have read the biblical passages under consideration not just at a historical level, but also at a spiritual level. That is to say, they would have looked for Christ as the sacramental mystery present in the text. These homilies attempt to follow the church fathers in their move from the surface level of the text, as the fourth-century preacher Gregory of Nyssa put it, to the deeper, contemplative level. In doing so, I try to retrieve a key aspect of patristic exegesis and show that the sacramental cast of exegesis isn't just an ancient relic but is still the key to Scripture reading. The outward sacrament still contains the reality of the inward mystery.

In one important respect, these sermons differ from many other sermons I have preached over the years. These sermons reflect on the nature of exegetical practice. More or less explicitly, each addresses the question of how we should read the biblical text and what it means to read the text sacramentally. In other words, I encourage the congregation to consider what we do when we move from the letter to the spirit in exegetical practice. Each of the sermons in this book doesn't simply *practice* a theological hermeneutic, but also *consciously reflects on* this practice of spiritual interpretation. Obviously, not every sermon should do this, and usually my sermons don't. But since I want to deal with the viability of patristic and medieval exegesis, I thought it would be helpful to address this question not just by example (i.e., by pointing out the christological depth behind the letter of the text) but also by reflecting on the hermeneutical questions more directly in the contents of the sermon. As a result, you will find in these sermons not only a deliberate engagement with the sacramental, christological depth of the biblical text, as each sermon moves from the historical to the spiritual level, but also hermeneutical discussions on how we move sacramentally from the letter to the spirit of the text.

The move from the historical to the spiritual is, as I have indicated, a vertical or upward move from the temporal sacrament to its eternal reality. One of the insights I have gained from St. Gregory of Nyssa is that this interpretive move in our (or the preacher's) biblical exegesis corresponds to a spiritual move in readers (or the audience); they increasingly ascend so as to enter further into the life of God as revealed in Christ. It is this ascent that gives us the happiness of Christ—both the happiness that comes *from* Christ and the happiness that *is* Christ. First, true happiness comes only from Christ. As Robert Wilken puts it in his reflections on Gregory of Nyssa's sermons on the Beatitudes: "Happiness is possessing Christ. The beatitudes are not simply moral maxims, but invitations by Christ to his disciples 'to ascend with him' that they might enjoy 'fellowship with the God of all creation.'"[8] Second, Christ himself is the very definition of happiness. As we see more of him on our upward journey, we realize more and more that growing in Christ means growing in happiness. Christ himself is the happy ending to which these sermons point.

8. Robert L. Wilken, *The Spirit of Early Christian Thought: Seeking the Face of God* (New Haven: Yale University Press, 2003), 278.

xxivIntroduction

I have deliberately resisted the temptation to surrender using the term *happiness* in favor of *blessedness*. The latter term does have an advantage: it doesn't convey that our purpose is simply a fleeting, subjective emotion, which is central to the common use of *happiness*. However, the large majority of Christian theologians have understood our aim in life to be happiness, that is, the eternal possession of Christ as our greatest good.[9] Thus *happiness* is a term worth reclaiming in the service of Christian doctrine.

This upward or anagogical move (from the Greek *anagōgein*, meaning "to lead upward") to Christ as our happiness is reflected in the four-part structure of this book. Part 1, "Sensed Happiness," deals with passages that help us to reflect on the role of the physical senses and the created realities they access. In part 2, "Pilgrim Happiness," we move to the Christian life as a journey to the Promised Land. The sermons in part 3, "Heavenly Happiness," refer to heaven as the reality behind the objects of the senses and as the destination of the journey. Finally, since we aim for contemplation of God in the heavenly beatific vision, part 4, "Unveiled Happiness," asks questions about the contents of our eternal bliss or happiness. The four parts of the book deliberately ascend step by step into the heavenly realities and mirror the move from sacrament to reality that unfolds in each sermon. As a result, every sermon individually, and the book as a whole, conveys the significance of the sacramental character of biblical preaching.

The fourfold structure of the book should not be taken to imply that those listening to the last sermon have advanced further on their spiritual journey than those listening to the first. Although genuine spiritual progress is possible, no spiritual elitism is either meant or implied. After all, each individual sermon takes us from sacrament to reality. Nor should these sermons be taken to imply that the created realities of time and space are negative and should be escaped as we move from material to spiritual realities. To be sure, the anagogical ascent asks for practices of discipline and renunciation, and the Christian vision regards spiritual union with God as a higher aim than material pleasure. At the same time, however, in a sacramental vision

9. See ibid., 274.

the realities of time and space participate in the life of God, which gives them genuine value. The tension this implies runs throughout the tradition and is one that we should not attempt to resolve, either by lapsing into crass materialism or into gnostic escapism. Nor are these sermons meant to imply that only at the summit of the journey (Unveiled Happiness) do we see God. Although the Christian journey moves in stages, we truly do see God every step of the way—though in more indirect and veiled ways in earlier stages than in subsequent ones. The created realities of time and space convey the presence of God, so they can function as theophanies—divine appearances. We need to recognize their theophanic character so that we strain forward (Phil. 3:13) to enter more deeply into the life of God and ever more clearly see his face in Jesus Christ.[10] So, on the one hand, the various stages of the Christian life correspond to varying degrees of participation in the life of God. On the other hand, we genuinely participate in the being of God at every stage and already share in the final hope of eternal happiness. Even our sensed happiness—the basic satisfaction we derive from material goods—is in some small way a participation in the supernatural heavenly happiness for which we aim.

10. I am currently working on a long-term project on the beatific vision of God in the hereafter, which I hope will result in a publication in due time.

1

Why Join the Chariot?

Acts 8:26–35

Acts 8:26–35

²⁶Now an angel of the Lord said to Philip, "Rise and go toward the south to the road that goes down from Jerusalem to Gaza." This is a desert place. ²⁷And he rose and went. And there was an Ethiopian, a eunuch, a court official of Candace, queen of the Ethiopians, who was in charge of all her treasure. He had come to Jerusalem to worship ²⁸and was returning, seated in his chariot, and he was reading the prophet Isaiah. ²⁹And the Spirit said to Philip, "Go over and join this chariot." ³⁰So Philip ran to him and heard him reading Isaiah the prophet and asked, "Do you understand what you are reading?" ³¹And he said, "How can I, unless someone guides me?" And he invited Philip to come up and sit with him. ³²Now the passage of the Scripture that he was reading was this:

> "Like a sheep he was led to the slaughter
>   and like a lamb before its shearer is silent,
>   so he opens not his mouth.
> ³³In his humiliation justice was denied him.
>   Who can describe his generation?
> For his life is taken away from the earth."

[34] And the eunuch said to Philip, "About whom, I ask you, does the prophet say this, about himself or about someone else?" [35] Then Philip opened his mouth, and beginning with this Scripture he told him the good news about Jesus.

Sunday, July 27, 2014

Christians are people of the book. Adam and Eve, Abraham, Moses, David, Jesus, Paul—they are key figures in the book. The mere mention of their names calls to mind the things they did and the stories to which they belong. Knowing the people, knowing their stories, we nonetheless go back to them again and again. The reason is that we are deeply aware that the people of these stories aren't buried in the rubble of history. Even today they shape our lives and give us our identity. Therefore, even today each of these characters in the biblical narrative lives on in our lives. This is why as Christians we are people of the book. This book—its people and its stories—makes us who we are.

The Ethiopian eunuch and Philip both know that the biblical stories make us who we are today. Recognizing the shaping power of the ancient Scriptures for his life, the eunuch has been reading Isaiah 53. Encouraged by the Holy Spirit, Philip soon joins him in the chariot, and together they explore how the ancient story is supposed to shape their lives. You and I too want to join the chariot. We too want to read along with the eunuch and with Philip. This morning, therefore, all of us are traveling from Jerusalem to Gaza. All of us are reading yet again the well-known Servant Song of Isaiah 53.

Why? Why join the chariot? Why doesn't Philip just leave the Ethiopian eunuch reading on his own? And why don't we leave these two Bible readers alone while we do our own thing without getting all hung up about this chariot? "Why join the chariot?" is the question we're going to put front and center this morning.

The most immediate answer to the question is, of course, that we've been *asked* to join the chariot. We read in Acts 8:31 that the eunuch *invites* Philip to come up and sit with him. The reason for the invitation is that the eunuch *needs* Philip to explain to him what is going on in the Bible passage that he's reading. All by himself, the eunuch doesn't get it. "Do you understand what you are reading?" Philip asks (8:30). "How can I," is the response, "unless someone guides me?" (8:31). Both Philip's question and the eunuch's answer are instructive. "Do you understand what you are reading?" "Understanding" and "reading" are the two key words in the question, and they are not the same. Sometimes they look as though they are the same, and in Greek the two sound almost the same: "to read" is *anaginōskein*, and "to understand" is *ginōskein*. On the surface, there is very little difference. But merely to read, to sound out the words, is not yet to understand. We all know that sometimes reading leads to *mis*-understanding rather than to understanding. The eunuch realizes he needs someone else with him in the chariot to guide him in understanding the Scripture.

We shouldn't think, though, that the Bible—and we have to think here of the Old Testament—was a completely foreign book to the eunuch. We know he made the trek all the way from Ethiopia, south of Egypt, to Jerusalem, and that he was on his way back home via the coastal city of Gaza. The reason for his long journey up to Jerusalem, we read, was to worship (8:27). This prominent official at the court of Candace, the Ethiopian queen, worshiped the God of the Jews. We don't know exactly what caused this remarkable situation—the Ethiopian minister of finance worshiping the God of Israel. One way or another, however, this man came under the spell of the stories of Israel's people. They shaped him. They made him into a different person. They formed his identity. Somehow, I suspect, this was not the first time this man read Isaiah 53.

Yet he remains puzzled—something that no doubt bothers him. He wants not just to read but also to understand, for he knows from experience—especially from his conversion to the God of Israel—that reading with understanding will allow him to become the person he is meant to be. Confronted with Philip's question, he therefore readily acknowledges that he doesn't get the meaning of the passage: "How can I, unless someone guides me?" The eunuch's deepest desire is that these words from God would chisel and mold him.

In a remarkable way, God enters into this spiritual journey. The event is marked both beginning and end by God's activity: in the beginning, Acts 8:26, "Now an angel of the Lord said to Philip, 'Rise and go toward the south,'" and also verse 29, "The Spirit said to Philip,

'Go over and join this chariot'"; in the end, verse 39, "the Spirit of the
Lord carried Philip away, and the eunuch saw him no more, and went
on his way rejoicing." It is an angel of the Lord, and it is the Spirit of
the Lord, who enter into this man's search for God and ensure that
Philip joins the chariot. In a real sense, it isn't just Philip, but it is the
Lord himself who joins the chariot. He doesn't leave us traveling on
our own when, hearts burning, we read the stories yet again.

Luke wants us to note that it is the Lord who meets up with the
eunuch in his chariot. After all, the ascended Lord himself is on a
mission and has been on a mission since the beginning of the story.
In Acts 1:1, Luke tells us that in his first book, his Gospel, he "dealt
with all that Jesus began to do and teach." If Luke's Gospel tells us
what Jesus *begins* to do and teach, then the implication is that the
book of Acts tells us what Jesus *continues* to do and teach. He may
have ascended into heaven, but Jesus is still doing things and teaching
things. He pours out his Spirit in Acts 2, and it is the Spirit of the Lord
who from that moment directs the mission, beginning at Jerusalem and
moving from there via Judea and Samaria "to the end of the earth"
(1:8). The Ethiopian eunuch's story, then, is part of a larger narrative.
With persecution scattering the church from Jerusalem "throughout the
regions of Judea and Samaria" (8:1), Philip, one of the seven appointed
as deacon back in chapter 6, "went down to the city of Samaria" to
preach the word (8:4–5). Thanks to Philip's work, "many villages of
the Samaritans" had the gospel preached to them, we read in 8:25.

What's happening in our passage is that the Spirit of the ascended
Lord is telling Philip to keep the mission going. When the eunuch
becomes a disciple of Jesus, for the first time in the story, the gospel
moves past the boundaries of Judea and Samaria into gentile territory.

This mission, on the forefront of our minds, shapes the way we
read the story of the Ethiopian eunuch. It guides us as we move from
reading to understanding. Later tradition fills us in on some of the
details of this story. It reports that the eunuch's name was Indich.
Once back in Ethiopia, Indich preached the gospel and converted
Queen Candace and many other people to the Christian faith.[1] Much

1. Nicephorus 2.6; taken from Paton J. Gloag, *A Critical and Exegetical Commentary on the Acts of the Apostles* (Edinburgh: T&T Clark, 1870), 1:310.

of this story is probably apocryphal. But it nonetheless reminds us of something important. The book of Acts is about mission. Philip is a link in that mission. The eunuch too is a link in that mission. Everyone who joins the chariot becomes a link in that mission. The links continue, just as the mission continues. These missional links make up a long tradition. After all, we still read the Scriptures; we still read Isaiah 53. One way to read the Scriptures well—to move from *anaginōskein* to *ginōskein*, from reading to understanding—is to ask, how does our reading fit our mission?

If still today our Lord is on a mission—if still today he uses the same Scriptures to pass on the good news—then that mission is *our* mission, and much like the eunuch and much like Philip, we learn to read the Bible in a way that serves the mission. To understand the Bible's meaning well, it's crucial to know its purpose. Its purpose is missional. After all, we're reading the Bible on our journey, traveling together in the chariot. The characters of the biblical story—Adam and Eve, Abraham, Moses, David, Jesus, Paul (and also Philip and the Ethiopian eunuch!)—do not lie buried in the rubble of history. They continue to help us on our journey. They still guide us on our mission. Whatever other reasons we may have to read the Bible, the overall purpose is always this: to join the mission of our Lord.

To join the chariot is not only to join the *mission* of Christ; it is also to join the *church* of Christ. Again, this is of central importance to Luke. The Feast of Pentecost in Acts 2 is also the feast of the beginning of the church. It is when the twelve apostles are "all together in one place" (2:1) that the Spirit is poured out. The entire book of Acts is about the church. It's about the church's origin. It's about the church's growth. It's about the church's mission. The church is the context, the framework, within which we read the Bible. So the eunuch's response, "How can I [understand], unless someone guides me?" (8:30), implies that we need the church's guidance to read the biblical story well.

The eunuch knows he'll never figure out the meaning of Isaiah 53 as long as he's alone in the chariot. He needs Philip, led by and filled with the Spirit of God, with him in the chariot. Philip—or we could perhaps say the chariot—stands for the church. Reading together in the chariot means that we read the Bible in line with the way the church has read it in the past. Bible reading has to do with both the future and the past. We have already seen how the Bible takes us to the future, that Bible reading is missional in purpose and direction, and that the end point is the gospel being preached to the ends of the earth. But the Bible also takes us to the past. Reading the Bible makes us want to stand in line with the eunuch, with Philip, and with all the others who follow in that long chain, that long tradition of Bible readers—all those people who joined the chariot long before you and I did.

We don't like others telling us what to do. We are a fiercely independent lot. But if we want to move from reading to understanding, from *anaginōskein* to *ginōskein*, then we need to recognize that our reading of the Bible happens between the future, the mission of the church, and the past, the tradition of the church. And in our reading, we are bound to both. We can't understand the Bible properly if we forget the missional purpose of reading. Neither is it possible to get the fullness of what Scripture means if we go it alone without the guidance of Bible readers who have gone before us.

Reading the Bible is kind of like playing jazz piano. There's a lot of freedom in how you go about it and a great deal of creativity in your own performance. But as every jazz pianist knows, when you refuse to play by the basic ground rules of the musical tradition, or when you're unfamiliar with the skills involved in playing jazz, the result will be people closing their ears as soon as you put your fingers to the keys. Playing jazz implies that you have learned to take your place within the bounds of the proper rules for playing jazz. Reading the Bible is similar. It implies that we have learned to take our place within the long tradition of the church and that we read the Bible in line with the way others in the church have read it before us. To understand the Bible, we need to take our place inside the chariot.

There's one final point. So far, I've talked about mission as the future purpose of our reading, and I've spoken of tradition as the past starting point for our reading. But we haven't done the actual reading yet. Sure, we've perused Acts 8 in some detail, but we haven't yet looked at Isaiah 53. And that's the passage Philip is explaining to the eunuch in the chariot.

> Like a sheep he was led to the slaughter
> > and like a lamb before its shearer is silent,
> > so he opens not his mouth.
> In his humiliation justice was denied him.
> > Who can describe his generation?
> For his life is taken away from the earth.
> > (Isaiah 53:7–8 as quoted in Acts 8:32–33)

Note that the eunuch asks a specific question about Isaiah: "About whom, I ask you, does the prophet say this, about himself or about someone else?" (Acts 8:34). The question takes us to the heart of the passage from Isaiah. It's a question of identity: Who is this about?

Now, I would like us to do a thought experiment. Imagine you didn't know the gospel. Imagine you didn't know the story of Jesus, of his silent suffering, of his humiliation, and of his death. Imagine that none of this is familiar to you. And now you read Isaiah 53. How would you read it? Who do you think the prophet is talking about here? Could it be himself? Could it be someone else? The eunuch's question is an entirely sensible one. It's a question any ordinary reader would wonder about.

When we do a thought experiment like that, we realize that the question can be answered in different ways. You and I know the prophet is speaking about Jesus. We've learned that from Philip: "Then Philip opened his mouth, and beginning with this Scripture he told him the good news about Jesus" (8:35). Philip tells the eunuch plainly that the prophet is talking about Jesus. But let's stick for a moment with our thought experiment. How would we respond to Philip's claim that Isaiah is talking about Jesus? "Jesus?" we might ask. "Who is that? Tell me more about him. Why do you think Isaiah is talking about Jesus? How do the events of Jesus' life pattern onto this passage of Isaiah?" We don't know how the conversation between Philip and the eunuch continued, and we don't read the exact questions the eunuch asked Philip. But it's hard to imagine that the eunuch would not have asked questions much like these.

Do you see what Philip is doing? He is not just preaching the gospel all by itself, talking about Jesus' death and resurrection. Nor is he simply explaining Isaiah 53 all by itself, ignoring the gospel of Jesus in the process. No, instead he *begins* with the gospel about Jesus, taking what he knows about Jesus and fitting it back into Isaiah 53. Then he says to the eunuch, "See how well the gospel fits? Isn't it clear now that these words of Isaiah 53 speak of someone who would come much later?" From the outset, then, Philip takes as a given that this passage speaks about Christ. Philip teaches us that if we want to move from reading to understanding, from *anaginōskein* to *ginōskein*, we have to move from the words on the page to the person of Christ. Christ is the true meaning of the Scriptures. Whether we're reading about Adam and Eve, about Abraham, about Moses, or about David, it doesn't matter. At its profoundest depth, the meaning of the Scriptures is always about Christ. The reason is this: Christ is the treasure hidden in the field; Christ is the sacrament hidden under the surface of the text. As long as we haven't yet seen Christ in the Scriptures, we haven't yet moved from reading to understanding.

I would love to have been a fly on the wall, listening in on the conversation between Philip and the eunuch in the chariot. I wonder how Philip would have read Isaiah 53 as being all about Jesus. What links would he have seen between Isaiah 53 and the life and death of Jesus? Or, to go back to the music analogy, what would the jazz have sounded like with Philip playing the piano? We don't know. But we do have examples from later in the Christian tradition. For instance, when Augustine reads Isaiah 53:7 about the sheep led to the slaughter and the lamb without a voice in the presence of his shearer, he asks the same question the eunuch asked: "Who is this?" Augustine believes the next verse, 53:8, gives us a clue. When Isaiah says that in his humiliation the Servant's "judgment" is taken away and that nobody can explain his generation, Isaiah must be talking about the judgment that Christ has as eternal king and about the Son's eternal generation from the Father. The lamb, therefore, is at the same time the lion of Judah (Rev. 5:5). Augustine then waxes eloquent about this Savior who is lamb and lion at the same time:

> Who is this, both lamb and lion? He endured death as a lamb; he devoured it as a lion. Who is this, both lamb and lion? Gentle and strong, lovable and terrifying, innocent and mighty, silent when he was being

judged (cf. Mark 15:5), roaring when he comes to judge. . . . Why a lamb in his passion? Because he underwent death without being guilty of any iniquity. Why a lion in his passion? Because in being slain, he slew death. Why a lamb in his resurrection? Because his innocence is everlasting. Why a lion in his resurrection? Because everlasting also is his might.[2]

Did Philip link the life of Jesus back to Isaiah 53 exactly the way Augustine did? I have my doubts. I rather suspect Philip and Augustine each had his own interpretation of Isaiah 53. Good jazz pianists all create their own performances. But both Philip and Augustine opened up the prophet to the new reality that is Jesus.

Why join the chariot? When we join the chariot, we become part of a mission, a mission involving Philip, the eunuch, and everyone else who takes as his or her purpose the mission of Christ. Why join the chariot? When we join the chariot, we join the church; we link up to tradition reaching back as far as the Feast of Pentecost. Why join the chariot? When we join the chariot, we recognize Christ whenever we open the Scriptures. Traveling home in the chariot, we move from mere reading to understanding. Between the past and the future, between the church's tradition and the church's mission, Christ is the content of all our understanding. He is the good news from beginning to end.

Preacher's Notes

This first sermon is the most straightforward in this collection in asking the question head-on: Is it possible for us meaningfully to read biblical texts that were written thousands of years ago, many of them long before the coming of Christ? Preaching always touches on the relationship between what the text *meant* and what it *means*. The book of Acts deals with preaching and contains a number of sermons. This passage highlights a specific instance of gospel preaching as Philip preaches the good news to the Ethiopian eunuch.

2. Augustine, *Sermon* 375A.1–2, as quoted in Robert Louis Wilken, trans. and ed., *Isaiah: Interpreted by Early and Medieval Commentators*, with Angela Russell Christman and Michael J. Hollerich, The Church's Bible (Grand Rapids: Eerdmans, 2007), 427.

It is not my primary purpose in this sermon to expound the entire pericope. The passage runs from Acts 8:26 to 8:40, and I cut it short at verse 35, omitting the eunuch's baptism, the Spirit's carrying Philip away to Azotus, and his subsequent preaching. My choice of verses 26–35 was determined by the overall aim of the sermon (also the aim of this whole book): to see what the passage teaches about how to interpret the Scriptures. So I made the sermon topic the question of what makes for proper interpretation, the question of hermeneutics. This choice introduces a potential tension between the central message of the passage and the hermeneutical question I want to address in these sermons. My preaching is hardly ever topical, so as a result I generally don't deal with this kind of tension in my preaching. In writing the sermons collected in this book, however, I found the tension to be a fruitful one. As long as the preacher is careful not to impose a topic on a text in ways that are clearly contrary to the overall intent of the passage, I think it is possible to reflect on a given topic, such as the question of how to read Scripture, while at the same time bringing to the fore one or more of the key aspects of the text.[3]

Topical preaching often goes wrong by abstracting certain timeless principles or gleaning practical messages from a biblical text. One way to counter these problems is to draw attention to the context of the passage and indicate how the context is integral to the meaning of the text. In this sermon, I do this especially in the sections dealing with the future aim (mission) and the past backdrop (tradition) of biblical interpretation. The overall context of the book of Acts is obviously missional, and the Spirit's shaping of the church over time is also central to the book. As both mission and tradition are important to the book of Acts, they properly enter into our understanding of this passage. These topics are also of theological importance since the apostolicity of the church—highlighted particularly in Acts 1, but also at several subsequent major junctures in Luke's narrative—speaks both of the church's apostolic origin and character (tradition) and of

3. Eugene H. Peterson has a keen sense that we ought to combine spiritual reading with careful exegesis. While advocating a personal, participatory reading of the text, he also comments, "Exegesis is the discipline of attending to the text and listening to it rightly and well." *Eat This Book: A Conversation in the Art of Spiritual Reading* (Grand Rapids: Eerdmans, 2006), 50.

the church's task (since the Greek *apostellein* means "to send forth"). Therefore, in this sermon, I deliberately try to deconstruct any kind of opposition between the importance of tradition and mission.

In the sermon I use several rhetorical strategies to add to the persuasive character of what I have to say. It is key that listeners find themselves not just engaged by the sermon but also recognize they have a place in it. To facilitate this understanding, it is often helpful to place listeners in the position of one or more of the narrative's characters. In this case, the listeners could find themselves in the story when they were invited to join the eunuch and Philip in the chariot. Because they had a place in the chariot, the listeners faced the same questions and issues as the eunuch and Philip. As a result, they too had to struggle with the question of how to read Isaiah 53.

Also, by speaking of the move from reading to understanding (Acts 8:30) as a transition from *anaginōskein* to *ginōskein*, I am not trying to put my own knowledge of Greek on display (always a bad thing to do in a sermon). Instead, I am indicating that the difference between reading and understanding may seem rather small, only three letters in Greek, but is in reality an important issue. Rhetorically, the centrality of that difference, which not all listeners may immediately recognize as serious, was highlighted by repeatedly alluding to the Greek terms *anaginōskein* and *ginōskein*.

I am not a great fan of telling stories, either to introduce a sermon or to illustrate key points. Such stories can insult the listeners' intelligence, and while stories initially have the advantage of being easy listening, after a while the congregation tends to be anesthetized to their effect and ends up being troubled, whether consciously or not, at being patronized. In the long run, sporadic use of illustrations keeps people engaged and makes the illustrations more effective. In this sermon, I use two extrabiblical sources in part for rhetorical purpose. First, I briefly relate the idea that the eunuch (named Indich) preached the gospel in Ethiopia. Second, I explain how Augustine reads Isaiah 53 christologically. As a rhetorical *ploy*, the latter obviously contributes to the sermon's contents more substantially than the former.

Let me briefly elaborate on the christological point. Underlying the sermon is the conviction that Old Testament narrative functions as a sacrament that contains Christ as its real presence. Christ is the reality to which the Old Testament narrative points and which it makes present. Put differently, the Old Testament narrative is the outward sacrament of which Christ is the true meaning and reality. This in no way renders genre, context, or historical backdrop insignificant. In this sermon, as well as others in this book, I reflect on a variety of these aspects, but always with the purpose to illuminate the central christological point I am trying to make in the sermon. Christ is the center, and historical issues should not supplant the spiritual purpose of the text.

In this sermon we are dealing with a prophetic passage that the church has always read as pointing toward Christ. In some sense, then, I make things (overly) easy for myself as a preacher, because in a prophetic passage the christological meaning may be more obviously present for my listeners than in other Old Testament texts. Still, the question of whether Isaiah 53 is properly read messianically and prophetically speaks of Christ is much under debate among contemporary scholars.[4] Generally, I think it best to avoid referencing contemporary scholars and debates in sermons because they tend to be far removed from most people's experience. Therefore, I do not address the academic question of whether to read Isaiah 53 messianically. Instead, I assume that—regardless of the passage's initial intent—we are to read it as a messianic text since the New Testament does (apart from the fact that every Old Testament passage, prophetic or not, should be read christologically). A sermon does its job when it moves from sacrament to reality—that is to say, when Christ is preached.

4. See John Goldingay and David Payne, *A Critical and Exegetical Commentary on Isaiah 40–55* (Edinburgh: T&T Clark, 2007), 2:284–88.

Part I

Sensed Happiness

What is the proper Christian attitude toward the senses? How ought we to treat realities that we access through taste, touch, smell, hearing, and sight? How should we treat enjoyment that comes from food and drink, from sexuality, from family life? The basic stance of these sermons is that the blessings of time and space are sacramental gifts. That is to say, in provisional ways they make present to us the heavenly reality of the Christ-shaped, divine life. Christians value such gifts, seeing as they are sacramental blessings, but refuse to view them as ultimate or as having the greatest significance in life.

Therefore, the starting point of the next four sermons is that the *sensed happiness* of time and space gives us only a foretaste of the supernatural reality of God's happiness that comes to us in Christ. The sermons reflect on various ways in which the Old Testament opens up to us the mystery of Christ in and through sacramental gifts of this-worldly time and space. Time is framed around the new reality introduced by Christ (Exod. 12). In Scripture's bleak description of a life of vanity we can detect Christ inviting us to reach out for his wisdom (Ecclesiastes). Christ is the lover sacramentally present in erotic love (Song 4); Christ is also the child who comes to us in and through the blessing of the children of Israel (Exod. 1).

2

First Things First

Exodus 12:1–12

Exodus 12:1–12

¹ The Lord said to Moses and Aaron in the land of Egypt, ² "This month shall be for you the beginning of months. It shall be the first month of the year for you. ³ Tell all the congregation of Israel that on the tenth day of this month every man shall take a lamb according to their fathers' houses, a lamb for a household. ⁴ And if the household is too small for a lamb, then he and his nearest neighbor shall take according to the number of persons; according to what each can eat you shall make your count for the lamb. ⁵ Your lamb shall be without blemish, a male a year old. You may take it from the sheep or from the goats, ⁶ and you shall keep it until the fourteenth day of this month, when the whole assembly of the congregation of Israel shall kill their lambs at twilight.

⁷ "Then they shall take some of the blood and put it on the two doorposts and the lintel of the houses in which they eat it. ⁸ They shall eat the flesh that night, roasted on the fire; with unleavened bread and bitter herbs they shall eat it. ⁹ Do not eat any of it raw or boiled in water, but roasted, its head with its legs and its inner parts. ¹⁰ And you shall let none of it remain until the morning; anything that remains until the morning you shall burn. ¹¹ In this manner you

shall eat it: with your belt fastened, your sandals on your feet, and
your staff in your hand. And you shall eat it in haste. It is the LORD's
Passover. [12] For I will pass through the land of Egypt that night, and I
will strike all the firstborn in the land of Egypt, both man and beast;
and on all the gods of Egypt I will execute judgments: I am the LORD."

Sunday, October 9, 2011

In about 180 or 190, a major controversy was brewing in the church.
It was only a century and a half after Christ's death on the cross,
and already the unity of the church was in danger. The issue was the
following: On what date should we celebrate Easter? The Jews, as we
know from Exodus 12, celebrated Passover every year on the night
of the fourteenth day of Nissan. It was a full-moon festival during
springtime held in accordance with God's command in Exodus 12.
Every Jew knew that the night of the fourteenth of Nissan was the
evening to celebrate God redeeming his people, setting them free
from the oppressive power of Egypt. The early Christians, of course,
weren't just remembering Israel's redemption from Egypt; they were
recalling the church's redemption from sin. They weren't just celebrating the defeat of Pharaoh; they were rejoicing in the defeat of Satan
and death. They weren't just interested in the sacrifice of a literal
lamb; they had in mind the sacrifice of Christ on the cross. In other
words, Christ's death and resurrection was something so radically
new, early Christians recognized it had to affect even the way they
were to read and understand the Passover story in Exodus 12.

Everyone agreed: first things first! Christ offers us a new beginning
in every way. All of life looks different now that Christ has come. Certainly, the way we look at the Passover feast of Exodus 12 is different
in light of the Paschal mystery of Christ. First things first! That means
Christ's death and resurrection is the starting point of everything. But
while everyone agreed on this basic principle—that Christ was the
beginning of something markedly new—it wasn't always immediately
clear what this meant in practice. One issue that wasn't instantly
obvious was on what day the church should celebrate Easter. Many
people, especially in the East (modern-day Turkey and elsewhere),
acknowledged: yes, first things first! Everything is new with Christ.

But that didn't mean they had to change the date. They could continue to celebrate Passover on the fourteenth of Nissan. The *contents* of the celebration changed—it was now all about Christ—but the *date* could stay the same. Others, however, weren't so sure. The bishop of Rome, someone by the name of Victor, was convinced that people in the East had it all wrong. If first things were first, then not only the *contents* of the Passover were new, but the *date* had to be changed as well. Think about it. On which day of the week had Christ been raised? Was it not Sunday? Wasn't Sunday the day of resurrection? Well, the fourteenth of Nissan could coincide with any old day of the week. Some years it fell on Monday, other years on Tuesday, yet other years on Saturday. Much as with our calendar, so with the ancient Jewish calendar: in different years, the same date would fall on different days of the week. So if Christians were to fix Easter on the fourteenth of Nissan, they would celebrate it only occasionally on a Sunday. For the bishop of Rome—and for many others in the West—this just couldn't be. The resurrection had to be celebrated on a Sunday. The only way to ensure this was to break with the regulation of Exodus 12, say good-bye to the Jewish calendar, and not celebrate Easter every year on the fourteenth of Nissan.

As I said, this disagreement about when to celebrate Easter nearly tore the church apart. The bishop of Rome was ready to excommunicate those Quartodecimans (or "fourteeners") in the East who weren't willing to celebrate the resurrection on a Sunday. Thankfully, cooler heads prevailed. One of the great church fathers, Irenaeus, wrote a letter to the bishop of Rome and told him to calm down, which he evidently did. People agreed to disagree, which kept the church united. And time healed the wounds the disagreement had inflicted. More than a century later, in 325 at the great Council of Nicaea, the entire church adopted the practice of celebrating Easter on Sunday morning. From then on, it was first things first all around: not only the *contents* of Easter but also the *date* of Easter was based on the great, new thing that God had done in the suffering, death, and resurrection of Christ.

When we look back on the Quartodeciman controversy of long ago, it's easy for us to shake our heads at those benighted people of the second century: Didn't they have anything better to argue about? But this morning I want to say something in defense of these early

Christians—not to try to stir up an old controversy. We're not going to redo a second-century controversy in the twenty-first century. However, we need to keep in mind: *we* have a long history to go by, and that makes it a matter of course for us that we celebrate Easter on Sunday. If someone were to suggest changing Easter to a Wednesday or a Thursday, my hunch is many of us would have something to say about that! But these people lived at the beginning of the Christian tradition. What were they to use as their yardstick? Was Exodus 12 still authoritative? Did they *have* to celebrate Easter on the fourteenth, regardless of what day of the week that happened to be? Or was the fact that Christ had risen on Sunday morning authoritative? So did they have the right, perhaps even the duty, to change the regulation of Exodus 12? These weren't easy questions to answer—not when you were still trying to come to grips with how to read Exodus 12 now that you had become followers of Jesus Christ. What is more, if you wanted to be faithful to God's will, you were going to take these difficult questions very seriously. After all, there's nothing as important as worshiping God the way he wants to be worshiped. First things first, after all! So the issue was difficult, and everybody rightly sensed the great importance attached to it: this was about celebrating the most central feast of the entire Christian year!

While I'm glad Irenaeus calmed down the bishop of Rome, we shouldn't underestimate the importance of what is going on here. What does the first verse of our chapter say? "The Lord said to Moses and Aaron in the land of Egypt, 'This month shall be for you the beginning of months. It shall be the first month of the year for you'" (Exod. 12:1–2). Note two things. First, there's a divine command here. God is not leaving this issue to Moses and Aaron to decide for themselves. God is the one determining the calendar of the Israelites. Now, that is important. I don't mean just the fact that God sets the *calendar*, though that too is important. The Christian calendar lies at the very heart of who we are as a church—but that's not what I'm thinking of here. I mean that *God* is the one who sets the calendar. When you read through the whole passage, you cannot but be impressed with God's care for detail and with how *he* determines all those details. *God* says there is to be a lamb for every household (12:3). *God* says the lamb should be a one-year-old male without blemish (12:5). *God* says select the lamb on the tenth of the month and slaughter it four days later at twilight (12:3, 6). *God* says put blood on the two doorposts and on the lintel of the frames with a bunch of hyssop (12:7, 22). *God* says roast the lamb in its entirety and finish it off completely (12:9–10). *God* says don't break any of its bones (12:46). *God* says only circumcised people are allowed to eat the lamb (12:43–45). *God* says eat it with your cloak tucked in, your sandals on, and your staff in your hand (12:11). *God* says eat bitter herbs with the lamb (12:8). *God* says remove all the yeast from the house and eat unleavened bread for seven days (12:15). The details of these divine commands are unmistakable. The Israelites don't decide for themselves the way things are to be done in worship, especially not the way things are to be done at Passover. Our text says, "The LORD said to Moses and Aaron" (12:1). He is the one who frees the Israelites from slavery; he is the one they are to follow from now on.

Second, note the command: "This month shall be for you the beginning of months. It shall be the first month of the year for you" (12:2). The exodus from Egypt was such a momentous event that from then on, God says, the Israelites were to start the calendar on this date. He says in effect, "This month is the month I defeated your enemy. This month is the month I gave you your freedom. This month is the month you became an independent nation. Time itself is going to be framed around this new reality of the redemption that I have worked for you." These words, "This month shall be for you the beginning of months. It shall be the first month of the year for you," hold some important clues for us. With the birth of Christ, we all know what happened to the calendar: we started counting time all over again. Any mention of a particular year—say, 2000 or 2016—causes our minds to go back, implicitly at least, to the birth of Christ. His birth was an event of such monumental significance that time itself has been framed around this new reality. Also with the resurrection of Christ, we all know what happened to the calendar: we changed the day of rest from Saturday to Sunday. What this says is that in the resurrection of Christ, we find our rest; his new life is the beginning of our new lives. His resurrection was an event of such radical significance that time itself has been framed around this new reality. First things first! The birth of Christ and the resurrection of Christ determine the course of history.

With two closely linked words—*beginning* and *first*—our text draws attention to the fact that we have a new beginning here. The month of Nissan is the first month not just in a chronological sense, as if Nissan just happened to be the first month of the year and Passover just happened to be celebrated in the first month of the year. No, Nissan starts a new beginning. It holds a place of priority, and therefore it comes first. The Israelites' identity, their sense of who they are, was to be determined by the day that marked their departure from Egypt. The feast of freedom stands at the beginning of everything they do from this moment onward. Even the setup of the calendar is determined by this new beginning. Time itself gets a different shape when God acts to set his people free.

With Christ's death and resurrection, the New Testament authors recognized: From now on we have to read Exodus 12 differently. From now on, this chapter is about Christ. Remember all those detailed divine commands? All of a sudden, the apostles realized what they were for. The one-year-old male lamb without defect? Well, Peter says in 1 Peter 1:19, Christ is "a lamb without blemish or spot." None of the bones of the lamb were allowed to be broken? Well, St. John says in his Gospel, that's why the soldiers didn't break Jesus' legs, but instead pierced his side to check if he had died (John 19:33–36). The blood of the lamb that had to be smeared on the doorframes with hyssop so that the firstborn Israelites would not be killed but redeemed? Well, Peter says in 1 Peter 1:17–19, you who believe in Jesus have also been ransomed or redeemed with the blood of the Lamb. The unleavened bread, showing that the Israelites were in such a hurry leaving Egypt that they couldn't wait for the bread to rise? Well, Paul says in 1 Corinthians 5, *you*, the believers, are the new lump, the new batch of dough. And I don't want there to be any yeast mixed in with you. Instead, I want you to be pure. "For Christ, our Passover lamb, has been sacrificed. Let us therefore celebrate the festival, not with the old leaven, the leaven of malice and evil, but with the unleavened bread of sincerity and truth" (1 Cor. 5:7–8). In other words, malice and wickedness are the yeast that belongs in Egypt. That's what we have to get away from; we don't want that Egyptian trash infecting the pure dough, the "bread of sincerity and truth." What is happening in the life of Jesus, and of the church that belongs to him, can be seen already in Exodus chapter 12. With the new reality of Christ's death and resurrection, this chapter suddenly opens up for us. All at once we realize why the Lord gave Moses all these detailed commands. Hidden inside them are the much greater New Testament realities that were to come.

First things first. That certainly counts when we read Exodus 12. We first look for Christ in the text. Christ, our Passover Lamb, comes first. And because he comes first, we read Exodus not just as a story about what happened to the Israelites long ago. We read it also as a narrative about what Christ has done and what God is still doing in our midst. This holds not just for chapter 12, but it holds for all of Exodus and for all of the Old Testament. It's never just about historical events from long ago. No, with Christ, time itself is framed around the new reality that he brings. Christ himself, and we the church, are present in those very stories from long ago. They are stories about Christ; they are stories about us. Christ himself is hidden in all of the Old Testament.

One of those second-century Christians engaged in the debate about when exactly to celebrate Easter was Melito of Sardis. He preached a homily about Easter in which he beautifully explained that Christ is the reality hidden in the story of the exodus:

> This is the lamb slain,
> this is the speechless lamb,
> this is the one born of Mary fair ewe,
> this is the one taken from the flock,
> and led to slaughter.
> Who was sacrificed in the evening,
> and buried at night;
> who was not broken on the tree,
> who was not undone in the earth,
> who rose from the dead and resurrected humankind from the
>   grave below.[1]

First things first. Christ, Melito is saying to us, is the one with whom we start. He is the beginning and the end, the Alpha and the

---

1. Melito of Sardis, *On Pascha: With the Fragments of Melito and Other Material Related to the Quartodecimans*, trans. and ed. Alistair Stewart-Sykes (Crestwood, NY: St Vladimir's Seminary Press, 2001), no. 71.

Omega. Along with the story of the Passover, the entire Old Testament is all about him.

Whenever we worship with the church above and the church below, time is framed around the new reality that is ours in Christ. We celebrate the Passover yet again. We share in Christ's sacrifice yet again. And yet again, we are in the heavenly places with the Lamb who looks "as though it had been slain" (Rev. 5:6). Every time again, the Lamb offers himself to us. Word and Table, they give us Passover redemption; they give us Passover freedom. The Passover meal in Egypt, the death of Christ on Calvary, the future hope of heavenly glory, they all join together as the heavens open up in worship. "First things first!" Christ says to us as he gives himself to us. "First things first. I myself will take care of everything else for you."

Preacher's Notes

The sermon title, "First Things First," contains a *triple entendre*. At its most obvious, literal level, the title alludes to the month of Nissan as the "beginning of months" and the "first month of the year" in Exodus 12:1. The title thus indicates that in the sermon I deal with the institution of the Passover in the month of Nissan, which is the first and foremost month of the year. At a deeper, allegorical level, the title refers to the Paschal mystery of Christ's death and resurrection. Christ makes a new beginning, and as Alpha and Omega, he stands at the beginning of all things. The implication is that historical and natural realities cannot be understood on their own terms. They need to be read through the lens of the newness of the Christ event. The christological depth of history requires that we take the Paschal mystery as the starting point in our reading of the Old Testament, including the Passover narrative in the book of Exodus.

Finally, at the moral or tropological level, "First Things First" means that we regard ourselves as included in Christ, so that we take the worship of God as the starting point for our lives. In the sermon I do not deal with this moral element in detail—though I make the point that Christ's new life is the beginning of our new lives. The assumption here is that a reconfiguration of time has occurred in and through him, so that his heavenly time is now the determining factor of our earthly time. "First Things First" alludes to the fact that the historical progression of this-worldly temporality is secondary to the eternal or heavenly reality of God's providence.

This sermon is based on the conviction that, in the Christian understanding of reality, the chronological character of historical events is not ultimate. My broader underlying assumption here is that all sublunar human experience—everything in the world of the senses—is penultimate at best. Much of modern culture assumes the precedence and priority of both history and sense experience. (This is closely linked, as we will see in the next few sermons, to the primacy of pleasure in our cultural mind-set.) This reordering of priorities by the historicism and materialism foundational to the contemporary outlook has gone hand in hand with a flattening of our interpretation of Scripture, at times reducing it to an archaeological enterprise. I attempt to draw my listeners into the recognition that a move from the surface of the text to its deeper, christological content is plausible and necessary. In doing so, I lay the groundwork for the message that neither the temporal unfolding of events nor the material realities of this-worldly existence are primary in the claims they lay on us.

Focusing on the first verse of Exodus 12 allows me to zero in on this time reference. That is to say, I turn a contextual item—the time reference in Exodus 12:1—into the central point. In all sermon preparation, what one decides to focus on within a larger context has obvious ramifications for how the sermon is going to connect with the passage, and it is important to keep this in mind. In this sermon, while I focus on the time reference of Exodus 12:1, the contextual reference to time (the first month of the year) needs to be linked to the main point of the chapter: God (through Moses) giving instructions to the Israelites on how to structure their Passover celebration, both on this occasion and in the future. (Brevard Childs rightly points out that the narrator does not distinguish between the first and subsequent Passover celebrations.)[2] The result is that I focus on the relationship between time, mentioned in Exodus 12:1, and redemption, the central theme of the broader context.

2. Brevard S. Childs, *The Book of Exodus* (Philadelphia: Westminster, 1974), 198.

The question of the nature of time, and in particular of its link with redemption, is an important one. I have argued elsewhere in some detail that time is sacramental in character.[3] That is to say, chronologically distinct historical events are linked and become simultaneous inasmuch as together they participate in the *higher time* of God's eternity. If it is true that the Christ event determines all history—both that which follows *and* that which precedes it—then Christ is the great model or antitype on which the earlier, Old Testament types are modeled. The Paschal events of Christ's death and resurrection are not modeled on the Passover instructions of Exodus 12; rather, the Passover instructions are patterned on the later Christ event. We may go even further and say that the Christ event is genuinely linked to—really present in—the ancient Jewish celebrations of the Passover. Speaking of the real presence of Christ in the Passover implies a sacramental understanding of the events described in Exodus 12: the earlier type is a sacrament of the later antitype. And the fact that the type already contains the antitype as its deepest reality or meaning implies that time itself is opened up by the Christ event. The centrality and all-determining character of the Paschal mystery means that we should not regard earlier Passover celebrations simply as historically or chronologically separate from the later Christ event. In and through Christ's Passover mystery, time comes to participate in eternity; put differently, eternity comes to be present sacramentally in time. This radically deepens the relationship between otherwise seemingly disparate moments in time.

In the sermon, I do not deal with the Eucharist at length. Still, the implications of this sacramental understanding of time are also significant for the way we understand what happens during Communion. In the conclusion of the sermon, I briefly allude to the fact that in our liturgical worship the heavens open up, and we get to share in Christ's sacrifice as the Lamb offers himself to us in our celebration of word and sacrament. It has become my conviction that time and

3. Hans Boersma and Matthew Levering, "Spiritual Interpretation and Realigned Temporality," in *Heaven on Earth? Theological Interpretation in Ecumenical Dialogue*, ed. Hans Boersma and Matthew Levering, Directions in Modern Theology (Malden, MA: Wiley-Blackwell, 2013), 1–10. See also Hans Boersma, *Heavenly Participation: The Weaving of a Sacramental Tapestry* (Grand Rapids: Eerdmans, 2011), 120–36.

space are reconfigured through Christ—or as I put it in the sermon, time itself is framed around the new redemption that is ours in him. It is not only the act of the ritual killing of a lamb in the Jewish Passover that participates in the sacrifice of Christ; the eucharistic celebration too takes on a sacrificial character. This doesn't mean that Christ is sacrificed all over again in the Lord's Supper. However, it does mean that the once-for-all sacrifice of Christ is made present again in our congregational worship on Sunday morning.[4]

In the first sermon of this book, I made the point that all Old Testament interpretation needs to be christological. In this second sermon, on the nature of time, I try to explain in more detail what gives shape to such christological exegesis. If temporally distinct events are linked in and through Christ, and if the antitypical reality of the Paschal mystery is the deepest reality of the types that foreshadow it, then the Old and New Testaments relate to each other as sacrament (*sacramentum*) and reality (*res*). The historical narrative of the Old Testament needs to be read as the outward sign of the inward grace that is ours in Christ. Interpretation of the Old Testament, therefore, isn't first and foremost a matter of reconstructing events to which the text alludes. Nor is it primarily a matter of figuring out what the author or authors initially meant. Exegesis is first and foremost searching for the reality of Christ.[5] When we find the mystery of his presence in the pages of the Old Testament, we have begun to move from reading to understanding.

In sermon preparation we need to give careful attention to both the moment and the manner of introducing the christological or sacramental depth of the Old Testament text. The move from the sacrament to the reality—from the historical to the spiritual—is one that the modern mind-set tends to resist. Almost any congregation or audience will tend to think of historical events as unrelated and chronologically separate. The contemporary Western mind-set in

4. For further discussion, see Hans Boersma, *Eucharistic Participation: The Reconfiguration of Time and Space* (Vancouver: Regent College Publishing, 2013).

5. Perhaps no one has done as much to draw attention to the sacramental character of the interpretive process as the twentieth-century French patristic scholar Henri de Lubac. See especially his accessible book, *Scripture in the Tradition*, trans. Luke O'Neill (New York: Crossroad, 2000).

particular is historically minded: we don't typically think of historical events as participating in greater spiritual realities. Whereas Melito of Sardis and other church fathers could point to the sacramental presence of Christ without startling their listeners, preachers today will often have to make homiletical moves from the historical to the spiritual in circumspect fashion, since such moves may easily come across as artificial and arbitrary. There is wisdom, therefore, in suggestively and obliquely introducing the notion of the christological or spiritual depth as already genuinely present in the Old Testament narrative.

However, in this sermon there is nothing suggestive or oblique about the way I introduced the christological starting point. The reason is that the New Testament itself already does much spiritualizing of the exodus—for example, in the texts referenced in the sermon (John 19:33–36; 1 Cor. 5:7–8; 1 Pet. 1:18–19)—so listeners will likely be more open to it in this case than they might otherwise be. This New Testament spiritualizing makes it easy for the preacher who wants to point to the deeper reality contained in the Old Testament narrative. The direct contrast between the historical (the sacrament) and the spiritual (the reality) in the sermon introduction gives me an advantage throughout the remainder of the sermon; I build on this and draw out the implications of the newness of the Christ event for our understanding of time.

3

Eat, Drink, and Be Merry?

Ecclesiastes 2:24–26; 3:12–13, 22;
5:18–20; 8:15; 9:7

Ecclesiastes 2:24–26

24 There is nothing better for a person than that he should eat and drink and find enjoyment in his toil. This also, I saw, is from the hand of God, **25** for apart from him who can eat or who can have enjoyment? **26** For to the one who pleases him God has given wisdom and knowledge and joy, but to the sinner he has given the business of gathering and collecting, only to give to one who pleases God. This also is vanity and a striving after wind.

Ecclesiastes 3:12–13, 22

12 I perceived that there is nothing better for them than to be joyful and to do good as long as they live; **13** also that everyone should eat and drink and take pleasure in all his toil—this is God's gift to man. . . .

22 So I saw that there is nothing better than that a man should rejoice in his work, for that is his lot. Who can bring him to see what will be after him?

Ecclesiastes 5:18–20

[18] Behold, what I have seen to be good and fitting is to eat and drink and find enjoyment in all the toil with which one toils under the sun the few days of his life that God has given him, for this is his lot. [19] Everyone also to whom God has given wealth and possessions and power to enjoy them, and to accept his lot and rejoice in his toil—this is the gift of God. [20] For he will not much remember the days of his life because God keeps him occupied with joy in his heart.

Ecclesiastes 8:15

[15] And I commend joy, for man has nothing better under the sun but to eat and drink and be joyful, for this will go with him in his toil through the days of his life that God has given him under the sun.

Ecclesiastes 9:7

[7] Go, eat your bread with joy, and drink your wine with a merry heart, for God has already approved what you do.

Sunday, October 24, 2010

We may as well be up front about it right at the outset: the book of Ecclesiastes is enough to drive us to despair. "Vanity of vanities, says the Preacher, vanity of vanities! All is vanity" (Eccles. 1:2). When we look for the word "vanity" (*hevel* in Hebrew), and we find it coming up about thirty-eight times in a row, the conclusion seems obvious. Everything is nothing but a breath, nothing but mist, nothing but vapor, and we could easily conclude that life is pointless, futile, vain, meaningless. The Preacher of Ecclesiastes, so it would appear, tells us that my life and yours is exactly like that of Abel—a name that comes directly from the same Hebrew word, *hevel*. Genesis 4 already seems to tell us that life is brief, and it's pointless. Ecclesiastes simply reinforces the message and could easy drive us to depression and despair.

A ray of hope, however, shines from this seemingly gloomy book. But we won't see that ray as long as we're stuck at the surface of the text. It is when we look beyond the letter of the text and instead ask deeper questions that a bright perspective opens up from these words about vanity. After Cain murders his brother Abel, God says to Cain,

"The voice of your brother's blood is crying to me from the ground" (Gen. 4:10). Abel's blood calls for revenge. Even though Cain has cut short Abel's life, his blood continues to speak. That little detail, that Abel's blood continues to speak from the ground even after his death, is something that Hebrews picks up on: "Through his faith," we read in Hebrews 11:4, "though he died, he still speaks." In the next chapter, we read that "the sprinkled blood [of Jesus] speaks a better word than the blood of Abel" (12:24). Hebrews, in other words, looks at the name *hevel* (Abel, futility) and completely flips things around. Now that Jesus with his blood enters the picture, things are no longer what they look like on the surface. Abel's name, *hevel*, no longer has the last word: no more mist, no more pointlessness. Everything takes on new meaning through the blood of Christ.

Today we are going to ask: What happens when we read Ecclesiastes no longer just in terms of the words on the page? What do we do with the letter of the text if it's true that it takes on new meaning through Jesus' blood? If pointlessness comes from the letter, or the surface of the text, how do we find the point that lies hidden *under* the surface? If vanity shows up as the letter of the text, how do we find the usefulness that the Spirit conveys *through* the letter? If futility appears as long as Christ is silent in the text, how do we find the purpose that our greatest Preacher and Teacher wants to show us *beyond* the text? Today we are going to look for what difference it actually makes when we no longer just read the letter of the text. Specifically, we are going to see what difference it makes for a life of pleasure and enjoyment. If we are no longer just looking at the letter of the text, but if Christ shows up in our reading, what does that mean for all the talk about pleasure in this book?

I don't need to say much about the relevance of this topic. I think it's obvious. In our culture, we tend to hoard. We're after pleasure, and we aim to satisfy the senses. In some way, this is quite understandable. The world around us is astonishingly beautiful. When we smell, when we taste, when we hear, when we see, when we touch—the pleasure that follows can be overwhelmingly powerful. But pleasure is not the purpose of our lives. The purpose of our lives is sacrifice: it is to offer back to the Creator every one of the gifts he gives us, as a sacrifice of praise. When we think of the ultimate purpose of life—giving back

God's gifts to him—we recognize how deeply troubling it is to focus instead on gratifying the senses. Yet much of our economic system functions because you and I will do what we can to satisfy our senses. The pursuit of pleasure is a powerful drive; it shapes in detail the way we structure our day-to-day life. But whether it's an appetite for food, desire for possessions, urge for sex, or obsession with entertainment, the appeal is to our bodily, material passions, and that means we are reduced to what we have in common with animals. This reduction of who we are as human beings to animal status, living by instincts to satisfy our desire for pleasure, gives us a quality of life that we can describe only as pointless, futile, and meaningless. When we no longer treat bodily and material goods as gifts to offer back to God, they lose their point and no longer have a purpose.

But then what about Ecclesiastes? Don't those six passages that make up our text recommend that we eat, drink, and be merry? Don't they tell us that in the end we are all pleasure-seeking animals? Well, yes, they do. But remember they have more than one level of meaning. The surface, the words on the page, is simply what we *start* with. It is not the final meaning of the text. After all, if we listen to Jesus' parable of the rich fool (Luke 12:13–20), it is pretty clear that we cannot take the advice of Ecclesiastes at face value. It is a fool, after all, who hoards possessions and says to himself, "Relax, eat, drink, be merry" (12:19). God sharply rebukes him for his pleasure-seeking attitude: "Fool! This night your soul is required of you, and the things you have prepared, whose will they be?" (12:20). The life of eat, drink, and be merry has nothing to commend itself. It is only the letter of the text that *seems* to tell us that we might as well become pleasure-seeking animals. But the letter isn't all there is. If we look for Christ underneath the surface, Ecclesiastes tells a rather different story about what it means to eat, drink, and be merry.

To get to that point, we do need to *begin* with the letter of the text and go back for a moment to the first chapter. Look at Ecclesiastes 1:3: "What does man gain by all the toil at which he toils under the sun?" Note that last expression, "under the sun." Then go to verse 9, "What has been is what will be, and what has been done is what will be done, and there is nothing new *under the sun*," and verse 14, "I have seen everything that is done *under the sun*, and behold, all is vanity and a striving after wind." I could go on. The expression "under the sun" shows up twenty-nine times in the book. In addition, several more times we find the expression "under heaven," which basically means the same thing. It is one thing to find the same expression used twice. By coincidence we might perhaps find the same expression used three or four times. But twenty-nine times? This *must* be deliberate! When the Preacher talks about things "under the sun" or "under heaven," what exactly is he talking about? Well, he is talking about the things that we can see, that we can feel, that we can touch, that we can smell, that we can hear. We are talking about the things that we can access with the senses. We are talking about material, bodily, created realities. These make up life under the sun.

Ecclesiastes takes the same daring step our culture has taken. Imagine if all we had were life under the sun. Imagine if all we had were the things we could see, feel, touch, smell, and hear. What would life be like? To be sure, there's a difference—a *huge* difference—between Ecclesiastes and our culture. Ecclesiastes looks at this reduction to nothing but life under the sun as just a thought experiment. Our culture makes this same reduction a reality: all we have, certainly in our public life together, is life under the sun. We don't deal with the question of God in public life. We certainly don't allow Christian convictions to infiltrate public policy. A colleague of mine at Regent College, Craig Gay, has an excellent book, *The Way of the (Modern) World: Or, Why It's Tempting to Live As If God Doesn't Exist.*[1] Ecclesiastes, on the surface, is about living as if God does not exist. The modern world tells us to live as if God does not exist. But what Christ, the true Preacher of Ecclesiastes, says to us is this: Let's try a thought experiment. What do you think it would look like if we lived as if God did not exist? What would it look like if all we had was life under the sun?

So let's follow the Preacher's scary thought experiment and have a look at life under the sun; let's see what life would look like if God did not exist. Six passages of Ecclesiastes talk about this—about what life would look like if God did not exist. Six times the Preacher comes

---

1. Craig Gay, *The Way of the (Modern) World: Or, Why It's Tempting to Live As If God Doesn't Exist* (Grand Rapids: Eerdmans, 1998).

to the conclusion that if all we have is this life of the senses, this life under the sun, the best thing to do is to eat, drink, and be merry. But we need to take note of what, in each case, leads up to this conclusion. The first time we get the advice to eat, drink, and be merry is in 2:24: "There is nothing better for a person than that he should eat and drink and find enjoyment in his toil." What could possibly justify such remarkable advice? So far in the book, the Preacher has taken on the role of Solomon and played the wise man. And what are his conclusions about wisdom? "For in much wisdom is much vexation, and he who increases knowledge increases sorrow" (1:18). "For of the wise as of the fool there is no enduring remembrance, seeing that in the days to come all will have been long forgotten. How the wise dies just like the fool!" (2:16). Even the life of wisdom, the very life the Preacher is unpacking for us in this book, is pointless. What he is actually saying is, "I might as well not write this book, because wisdom is meaningless. This very book is meaningless." Talk about depressing! What then about working hard so you get lots of money and in the end have time to relax? That one's a no-brainer for the Preacher: "Then I considered all that my hands had done and the toil I had expended in doing it, and behold, all was vanity and a striving after wind, and there was nothing to be gained under the sun" (2:11). When you die, he says a little later, you leave everything to someone else, "someone who did not toil for it" (2:21). So you see, the conclusion that everything you do is futile makes the Preacher declare in 2:24 that you might as well eat, drink, and be merry.

The same thing happens, and we come to the same conclusion, in 3:12: "There is nothing better . . . than to be joyful and to fare well as long as they live."[2] Again, it's a counsel of despair. Leading up to this, we have a monotonous list of things that happen under heaven: "a time to be born, and a time to die; a time to plant, and a time to pluck up what is planted; a time to kill, and a time to heal," and so on (3:2–3). Time moves on, and all kinds of things happen in life—weeping and laughing, mourning and dancing, loving and hating. There is no way anybody is going to make sense of a life

2. In place of the ESV's "do good," I follow James L. Crenshaw's translation of "fare well." *Ecclesiastes: A Commentary*, Old Testament Library (Philadelphia: Westminster, 1987), 98–99.

marked by such opposites. There's no way we can fathom such an existence. Life is a roller coaster that willy-nilly carries us along. We may as well eat, drink, and be merry. We are like animals anyway: we die, just like animals do! Who knows what's going to happen after we die? Are we going to be better off than the animals? Who knows! "So"—the last verse of chapter 3—"I saw that there is nothing better than that a man should rejoice in his work, for that is his lot. Who can bring him to see what will be after him?" (v. 22). We might as well enjoy the ride.

The next time we get one of these conclusions about eating, drinking, and being merry is 5:18. Again, if we look at what leads up to this conclusion, we find it's much of the same. Poor people are oppressed; rulers take advantage of their subjects; and in the end, every single one of us dies, rich and poor alike. "Just as he came," says 5:16, "so shall he go, and what gain is there to him who toils for the wind?" We may as well eat and drink and enjoy it, because in this situation, that's simply the best thing left for us to do.

On we go to 8:15, which is much the same: "I commend joy, for man has nothing better under the sun but to eat and drink and be joyful." What is the reason for this advice? Go back one verse, to 8:14: the righteous get what the wicked deserve, while the wicked get what the righteous deserve. There is no justice in this world. You never know what's coming your way. You may as well enjoy life while you can.

And, finally, 9:7: "Go, eat your bread with joy, and drink your wine with a merry heart." Why? It hardly gets more crass than this. Verses 3–5 insist we're all going to die. At least as long as we live, we still have hope. If we live we know that one day we will die, but the dead don't even know that! So being alive is still better than being dead. We may as well eat and drink and live it up.

So far, the thought experiment of the Preacher has presented what life under the sun is like, which is the way of the modern world. Briefly put, the argument is this: without God, everything is pointless; and if everything is pointless, we may as well just become pleasure-seeking animals. To be sure, it's not that God is *completely* out of the picture. If you've followed along in these passages, you may have noticed that even the pleasure-seeking animal appeals to God a number of times. Here and there he adds a pious phrase, pulling God into the picture:

God is the one who gives us our pleasures (5:19); God favors what we do (9:7); and so on. So, yes, it's true. Even people who live strictly under the sun, who live as if God did not exist, still appeal to God when they need him. But, really, their appeals to God are nothing but excuses covering up their own selfish life of pleasure.

So how do we live in a culture that consistently tells us we are simply pleasure-seeking animals? Certainly we do well to keep our eyes wide open so that we actually see the many ways we are tempted to adopt the same pleasure-seeking lifestyle that people all around us take for granted. Certainly on numerous occasions Christians are called to say no to the relentless pursuit of the passions of our sensory, bodily existence. But the Christian faith is not first of all reactive. We are not people who simply say "no" to a culture that focuses on eating, drinking, and being merry. Instead, we are people with a positive aim that we look forward to and that guides us on how to live. After all, if everything in Ecclesiastes tells us that life under the sun is pointless, if everything in Ecclesiastes tells us that life without God turns us into nothing but pleasure-seeking animals, then what is the implication? Isn't the implication that there is *more* than life under the sun? Isn't the implication that death is *not* the end? Isn't the implication that the resurrection allows us to look *beyond* the sun, as it were?

The reason you and I find it easy to cave in to a pleasure-seeking lifestyle is that a life of pleasure satisfies the senses: we satisfy our eyes, our touch, our ears, our smell, our taste. But if what the Christian faith maintains is true—that death does not have the last word, that there really is a resurrection—then what are we to do? Wouldn't the resurrection become our very aim in life? Wouldn't it transform the purpose of the work we do? Wouldn't it shape the way we treat our food? Wouldn't it affect the way we deal with sexuality? Wouldn't the bodily senses change to fit the resurrection life? Many in the Christian tradition have talked about how the deeper meaning of our bodily senses lies in the spiritual senses. Our eyes change, for now we long to see God face-to-face. Our sense of touch is transformed, for now we want to touch the cloak of Jesus. Our ears pick up different things, for now it is the gospel call that invigorates us. Our smell gets attuned differently, for now we ourselves turn into the aroma of

Christ. Our taste buds are no longer the same, for now we long for
heavenly manna, for Christ who is our food and drink. Indeed, our
passionate desires are transformed and turn upward—toward the
heavenly Groom.

St. Paul puts it this way in 1 Corinthians 15:32: "If the dead are not
raised"—note how he starts—"If the dead are not raised, 'Let us eat
and drink, for tomorrow we die.'" If the dead are not raised—that is
the Preacher's daring thought experiment in Ecclesiastes. But, Paul
says, the dead *are* raised. Because there is a resurrection, the entire
pleasure-seeking culture in which we live stands condemned. Because
there is a resurrection, we are not merely pleasure-seeking animals.
Because there is a resurrection, it is the resurrection life for which
we long with the most passionate desire. No more *hevel*. No more
vapor. No more futility. Christ has risen from the dead!

Preacher's Notes

About halfway through this sermon, I surreptitiously smuggle in
the identification of Christ as the Preacher of Ecclesiastes: "What
Christ, the true Preacher of Ecclesiastes, says to us is this: Let's try
a thought experiment." This identification is unlikely to startle the
congregation, both because the sermon doesn't draw attention to it
and because Christ has already been introduced earlier as speaking
in and through Ecclesiastes. Still, some kind of justification for the
identification seems to be required. I first preached this sermon as
the second in a miniseries on Ecclesiastes. The first sermon deals
explicitly with the identity of the Preacher, and I explain that the
Preacher places himself in the position of Solomon. The Preacher is
"the son of David, king in Jerusalem" (Eccles. 1:1; cf. 1:12). Much as
Solomon's wisdom and proverbs were renowned, so the Preacher is a
king who offers proverbial wisdom (Eccles. 1:13, 16). Moreover the
Preacher, much like Solomon (1 Kings 10:21, 27; 11:2), acquires silver,
gold, and a harem (Eccles. 2:8). Though probably written about seven
hundred years after Solomon's death, Ecclesiastes appears to present
the Preacher in the position of Solomon as he engages in Solomonic
experiments, trying to determine the meaning of life.

Many in the history of interpretation have seen in the "son of David" the one who in wisdom claims to be "greater than Solomon" (Luke 11:31). Here is what the fourth-century Cappadocian mystical theologian Gregory of Nyssa says about the identity of the Preacher: "Who else would he be but the true King of Israel, the Son of God, to whom Nathanael said, *You are the Son of God, you are the King of Israel* (John 1, 49)?"[3] Evagrius Ponticus, an ascetic monk who lived much of his life in Egypt around the same time, argued equally strongly: "The *Preacher* is the Christ."[4] Christ's identity as "wisdom from God" (1 Cor. 1:30), as well as the son of David, along with the fact that God's eternal wisdom comes to us in the pages of Ecclesiastes, all point in the direction of the patristic identification of the Preacher both as Solomon, the surface meaning, and as Christ, the deeper, allegorical meaning.

The overall message, as well as the structure and (lack of) consistency of Ecclesiastes, is much debated.[5] Suffice it to say here that my exegetical approach shows especially the influence of James Crenshaw, who argues that Ecclesiastes presents us with a rather bleak overall outlook.[6] This leaves me with a dilemma: How can Christ be the book's Preacher if the overall message is despondent and almost despairing? This is where the "thought experiment" comes in. It seems to me that by placing himself in the position of Solomon, experimenting on the basis of strictly human wisdom ("under the sun"), the Preacher points us to the truth that we are left with pointlessness when we try to enjoy created goods for their own sake. Implicitly then he points to the fact that only God is to be enjoyed for his own sake. In other words, the Preacher (Christ) points his readers to himself as the object of genuine happiness.

3. Gregory of Nyssa, *Gregory of Nyssa: Homilies on Ecclesiastes: An English Version with Supporting Studies: Proceedings of the Seventh International Colloquium on Gregory of Nyssa (St. Andrews, 5–10 September 1990)*, ed. Stuart George Hall (Berlin: de Gruyter, 1993), 34 (emphasis original).

4. Evagrius Ponticus, *Selected Scholia on Ecclesiastes*, trans. Luke Dysinger, no. 1. See www.scribd.com/doc/22487142/Evagrius-Ecclesiastes (emphasis original).

5. See Iain W. Provan, *Ecclesiastes, Song of Songs*, NIV Application Commentary (Grand Rapids: Eerdmans, 2001), 23–42; Tremper Longman III, *The Book of Ecclesiastes*, New International Commentary on the Old Testament (Grand Rapids: Eerdmans, 1998), 21–39.

6. Crenshaw, *Ecclesiastes*, 23–28.

The recognition of such a dilemma in the biblical text can be ex-
egetically fruitful. We may take our cue here from the third-century
theologian Origen, who argues in *On First Principles* that the Logos
has purposely placed "obstacles" in the text to force the reader to go
beyond the surface level by means of spiritual or allegorical exegesis.[7]
Contemporary scholars often critique this notion of divinely arranged
obstacles. And perhaps Origen's approach is somewhat mechanical.
In my view (and I think Origen would largely agree), the primary
reason for spiritual exegesis is not the presence of obstacles as such,
but that the biblical narrative functions as a sacrament in which the
reality of Christ lies hidden. Nonetheless, the move from history
to spirit does proceed at times by way of obstacles—or as I put it,
dilemmas—and Ecclesiastes gives us an example.

This sermon's message centers on the moral implications of Ecclesiastes. These implications are not the only thing to which this
book draws our attention, but the verses that make up the sermon
text do have the moral life as their central theme. My exegesis assumes that Ecclesiastes does not want us to take the injunctions to
"eat, drink, and be merry" at face value. Accordingly, this sermon
takes a relatively antithetical stance in relation to our culture's focus
on this-worldly pleasure. The result is an inevitable one-sidedness
in terms of how Christians are to approach material and bodily
goods. We do well to remember that our good Creator God made
the world so that "everything created by God is good, and nothing is
to be rejected if it is received with thanksgiving" (1 Tim. 4:4). Since
some people in the congregation will likely think about this other
side of the coin, I give several nods in this direction, such as the comment, "The purpose of our lives is sacrifice: it is to offer back to the
Creator every one of the gifts he gives us, as a sacrifice of praise."
This comment acknowledges that bodily and material created goods
are God's gifts—even though they point beyond themselves. However, on my reading the text highlights the problem of taking sensible reality (selfishly) as one's ultimate end, so the sermon's main

7. Origen, *On First Principles*, trans. G. W. Butterworth (Gloucester, MA: Smith,
1973), IV.2.9, 285. Cf. Peter W. Martens, *Origen and Scripture: The Contours of the
Exegetical Life* (Oxford: Oxford University Press, 2012), 60; Joseph W. Trigg, *Origen*
(New York: Routledge, 1998), 33–34.

point needs to be that such a focus makes one's life pointless or futile.

Not only is this approach to sensible reality in line with the message of Ecclesiastes, but also it allows me to draw attention to the rich Christian tradition of ascetic theology and the theology of the spiritual senses. Many theologians in the tradition have regarded the physical senses as God-given abilities that point beyond themselves to the spiritual senses.[8] This focus on the spiritual senses comes to fruition particularly in the theology of the beatific vision—seeing God face-to-face in the hereafter. But a theology of the spiritual senses is not only about the vision of God (*visio Dei*); many have also explored the other four senses to see how they point to a spiritual apprehension of God. The five bodily senses all need to be transformed so that we may be fitted for the resurrection life. After all, it is in the resurrection that as human beings—body and soul—we will be taken up in the eternal exchange of mutual self-giving between the Triune God and the creatures whom he graciously assumes into his own eternal life.

8. See especially Paul L. Gavrilyuk and Sarah Coakley, eds., *The Spiritual Senses: Perceiving God in Western Christianity* (Cambridge: Cambridge University Press, 2012).

4

Virgin Mother

Song of Solomon 4:16b–5:1a

Song of Solomon 4:16b–5:1a

SHE
¹⁶ Let my beloved come to his garden,
and eat its choicest fruits.

HE
¹ I came to my garden, my sister, my bride,
I gathered my myrrh with my spice.

Sunday, December 2, 2007

Christians are people taken over by desire. "Come, Lord Jesus, Maranatha," we exclaim (1 Cor. 16:22; Rev. 22:20). We long for Christ to come into our lives. This desire has always been the deepest drive of those who look to God. "Behold, I am the Lord's servant. Let it be to me according to your word," Mary says (Luke 1:38). "Let my beloved come to his garden," says the bride of the Song of Solomon (4:16). We all long for our Lord to come to us. He is our Groom; we want to be his bride. So again this morning, with the words of our text, we give ourselves to him: "Let my beloved come to his garden." With the words of the Virgin Mary, we yield ourselves to him: "Let it be to me according to your word." We long for our beloved; that is to say, we want Jesus in our lives. We want to be his, and his alone.

But Jesus coming into the garden of our lives presents us with a difficulty, the difficulty of the virgin birth. In the virgin birth two things come together, two elements that in every other situation consistently exclude each other. The two are virginity and motherhood. Virginity is one thing; motherhood another. Never, one would think, do the two come together. Obviously, if she wants to become a mother, a woman must first lose her virginity. Just as obviously, if she wants to remain a virgin, she will not experience motherhood. But in the incarnation, we experience the mystery of a paradox. The paradox is this: in Mary, virginity and motherhood combine.

It is not always easy for us to appreciate this paradox. Our culture doesn't help us any. A mystery, so our culture teaches us, is a puzzle to be pieced together. Once we've put the various pieces where they belong, we are in control; we are now able to manage things. But the mystery of the virgin birth isn't a problem that we can solve. No matter how deeply we think about it, virginity and motherhood in one remains a paradox. What it means for virginity and motherhood to come together in Mary, and what it means for us as a church to share in this virginity and motherhood, is something we can never fully grasp. The mystery of the virgin birth always remains exactly that—a mystery. The combination of virginity and motherhood is not a puzzle we can solve; it is a mystery we must adore.

It is not only the mystery of the virgin birth that proves difficult for us, and it is not just the paradoxical combination of virginity and motherhood that has us stumped. Even if we looked at the two separately, we'd still have our issues. After all, both virginity and motherhood have a low place on the totem pole today. If we take an honest look at ourselves, we are forced to admit that we often tend to be self-seeking. We don't want others cramping our style. And that, of course, is something that virginity and motherhood have in common: both cramp our style. Opting for virginity means we cannot have sexual pleasure; choosing motherhood means a little child demands our time while our career may be on hold. Who wants virginity? Why choose motherhood? Our culture and, more important, our self-seeking attitudes teach us that both virginity and motherhood cramp our style. And if each by itself presents an obstacle, why would anyone look for the paradox of having both at the same time?

But such openness to mystery is exactly what Mary displays. Perplexed by the paradox—virginity and motherhood at the same time—she asks the angel, "How will this be, since I am a virgin?" (Luke 1:34). Now, Mary's reaction is an interesting one. Think of what we might say instead: "Me be a virgin? But surely I can at least have the pleasure that comes before all the hard work!" Or we might say, "Me be a mother? But I'm not ready for that. I've got far too many things I want to do before I can start thinking about motherhood!" Mary simply expresses her amazement, her bewilderment, at the divine mystery of the angel's words: "How will this be, since I am a virgin?" Then when she hears that the Holy Spirit will come upon her, Mary simply and obediently accepts the coming of the Son of God: "Behold, I am the servant of the Lord; let it be to me according to your word" (Luke 1:38); "Let my beloved come to his garden" (Song 4:16).

The question that we need to struggle with today is this: How can Mary's response become ours as well? Is there a way for you and me to echo those words: "Let my beloved come to his garden"; "Behold, I am the servant of the Lord; let it be to me according to your word"? I am convinced that the answer is yes. We can make Mary's words our own. All of us, men and women, can make these words our own. But I need to be up front with you. For all of us—not only for women but also for men—the Song of Solomon presents us with quite a countercultural message. If we want to affirm for ourselves the combination of virginity and motherhood, it will require of us some serious soul-searching and a willingness to look at things that we think may cramp our style.

The first potential obstacle comes with the very reading of our passage. When you read through the Song of Solomon, you get this sense of a teasing sensual dialogue that keeps going back and forth between Solomon the king and this poor but gorgeous Shulamite shepherd girl. She's certainly bold in the presence of the king. She is the one who starts off the conversation and gets right to the point in 1:2: "Let him kiss me with the kisses of his mouth! For your love is better than wine. . . . Draw me after you; let us run. The king has brought me into his chambers." This girl is infatuated with the king, and it becomes clear from the ongoing dialogue that the amorous feelings very much run both ways. There's direct invitation, suggestive portrayal of physical beauty, expressions of erotic desire, and even allusions to sexual union. And all that starts right in the very first verses with this simple girl suggesting that the king go to bed with her.

The whole poem goes on and on like this. Encouraged by a chorus of friends cheering from the side, as it were, the lover and the beloved play this cat-and-mouse game in which they sexually stimulate and arouse each other nearly the entire time. You can see why the church father Jerome advised one of his female disciples not to give this book to her daughter too quickly. He suggests that she first give her daughter Psalms, Proverbs, Ecclesiastes, Job, the Gospels, Acts, the Epistles, the Prophets, the five books of Moses, Kings, Chronicles, Ezra, and Esther. "When she has done all these," Jerome says, "she may safely read the Song of Solomon."[1] Jerome was obviously more than a little nervous about what this book might do to young minds.

Indeed, it's hardly just the young who are liable to misuse this book. Most of us, if we know ourselves a little, have to admit that we don't need much stimulation before our minds go wandering into places they shouldn't go. We don't need to be prudes to recognize the need for certain limits and safeguards in our lives. So what do we do when the Song of Solomon just keeps going on? Just before our text, the lover tells the beloved how with one glance she stole his heart; he confesses that she has completely intoxicated him: "How much better is your love than wine" (Song 4:10). She is just the sweetest, most precious, most alluring beauty: "Your lips drip nectar, my bride; honey and milk are under your tongue; the fragrance of your garments is like the fragrance of Lebanon" (4:11).

What do we do with this Song of Solomon, this back-and-forth love song between the king and his Shulamite? One can certainly

1. Quoted in Tremper Longman III, *Song of Songs*, New International Commentary on the Old Testament (Grand Rapids: Eerdmans, 2001), 31.

understand Jerome's reservation. Isn't it sort of like standing in front of the magazine rack by the checkout counter with your kids? Or like watching TV with them, and all of a sudden being confronted by some sexually suggestive scene? Why is this book even in the Bible? And how can we possibly think of virginity and motherhood when we find ourselves in such a sexually hyped atmosphere? What in the world did Christians in previous centuries do with this book?

Actually, this is where things get interesting. When we look at the way people read the Song of Solomon in the past, we notice a fairly radical break in about the mid-1800s in the way people understand the Song. In other words, in the modern period people fairly suddenly started interpreting this book differently. And this is perhaps one instance where we need to do some honest self-reflection. You see, regardless of St. Jerome's fears, apart from the book of Psalms, the Song of Solomon was by far—and I mean *by far*—the book most preached on during much of church history. All this time, for the first 1,800 years of the Christian faith, people read this love song about Solomon and the Shulamite as an allegory, a picture of the relationship between Christ and his church. Since Scripture teaches that Christ is the Groom and we are his bride, people felt, surely that's also what *this* book is all about. I'll say a bit more about that in a moment. Strangely enough, during the past 150 years or so, a commentary that takes this same approach has become almost rare to find. Today, almost everyone reads this song simply as a love story, and if we're lucky, one that has certain implications for married life.

Now, I hardly need to tell you that when we see a clear break in the way people interpret a book, something has happened in the cultural mind-set. It's not like people all of a sudden got that much more clever or that much more ignorant in the 1800s. We all recognize that something else is happening. Indeed, in this period following the Enlightenment, God was removed to the far recesses of the sky and we—and the inclinations of the human will—took center stage. This drastic shift in cultural sensibilities could not but affect our reading of the Song of Solomon. In the Song we now see human beings taking center stage. We recognize in the erotic descriptions the human will with its desires. We find it much more difficult than before to see in the story the God who longs for us.

Every time we open the Bible, we need to ask ourselves one crucial question: What does this passage tell us about Christ and about the church? No matter what we read in the Bible, Old or New Testament, the first question is always this: What does this passage tell us about the relationship that we have with God in and through Jesus Christ? Even a book like the Song of Solomon, simply because it is part of the Christian Scriptures, is a book that speaks to us about Christ and his love for us. So he says to you and me this morning, "I came into my garden, my sister, my bride" (Song 5:1).

Once we recognize our heavenly Lover in these words, we begin to hear in them the words of Gabriel to Mary, don't we? The well-known twelfth-century preacher St. Bernard of Clairvaux thought so too. As a result, he preached on this book during Advent. Actually, he preached no fewer than eighty-six sermons on it, and he still hadn't gotten further than 3:1! His sermons are beautiful depictions of God's love for us in Christ. In one of his first sermons, St. Bernard writes about "the burning desire with which patriarchs longed for the incarnation of Christ." When Bernard thinks about that desire of the Old Testament saints, he says,

> I am stung with sorrow and shame. Even now I can scarcely restrain my tears, so filled with shame am I by the lukewarmness, the frigid unconcern of these miserable times. . . . Very soon now, there will be great rejoicing as we celebrate the feast of Christ's birth. But how I wish [this rejoicing] were inspired by his birth! All the more therefore do I pray that the intense longing of those men of old, their heartfelt expectation, may be enkindled in me by these words: "Let him kiss me with the kisses of his mouth."[2]

When together with the long tradition of the church, we do read the Song of Solomon in this way, new perspectives open up. "Let my beloved come to his garden" (4:16)—we may cringe as we hear these words. After all, was it not common for the Lord God to walk with Adam and Eve "in the garden in the cool of the day" (Gen. 3:8)?

2. Bernard of Clairvaux, *The Works of Bernard of Clairvaux*, vol. 2, *Song of Songs I*, trans. Kilian Walsh, intro. M. Corneille Halflants, Cistercian Fathers Series 4 (Kalamazoo, MI: Cistercian Publications, 1971), 8.

When we read in this love song, "My beloved is mine, and I am his; he grazes among the lilies" (Song 2:16), are we not reminded of the garden of Eden? Is paradise not a picture of intimacy with God, an intimacy that we have betrayed? "Let my beloved come to his garden," we read. But after eating from the tree, Adam and Eve were hiding from the Lord (Gen. 3:8). "Do *not* let him come into his garden" was their only thought. Isn't it ours as well when we sin against our Beloved? In Scripture, idolatry and adultery are nearly the same thing. The reason is that when we sin against God by serving other gods, we betray our husband. Idolatry is adultery.

Time and again in the Old Testament we read about this idolatry, this adultery. Let me give you just one example from Ezekiel 16. Here we read how the Lord found Israel as a little infant, and how she then matured into a beautiful woman: "You grew up and became tall and arrived at full adornment. Your breasts were formed, and your hair had grown; yet you were naked and bare" (16:7). Next we read how God adorned his bride, Israel, with jewelry and perfumes. "You grew exceedingly beautiful and advanced to royalty" (16:13). Then, however, comes the startling betrayal. Israel begins to commit adultery by going after other gods: "You also took your beautiful jewels of my gold and of my silver, which I had given you, and made for yourself images of men, and with them played the whore" (16:17). "Adulterous wife, who receives strangers instead of her husband!" (16:32). The Old Testament contains a number of stories like this. Sadly, Israel has a lengthy history, full of adultery.

But these stories are precisely what make the Song of Solomon such a ray of sunshine in the darkness of the Old Testament. There's no betrayal here, no idolatry, no adultery, no fear of God's jealous anger bursting out. Instead we read, "Let my beloved come to his garden, and eat its choicest fruits" (Song 4:16). What we find in the Song of Solomon is a church burning with desire and the Lord responding with the story of the annunciation: "I have come to my garden, my sister, my bride" (5:1). What we find in the Song of Solomon is the promise of a new covenant: "I will be their God, and they shall be my people" (Jer. 31:33; Heb. 8:10).

To be sure, it is a very daring analogy. To compare the union between the eternal Word and human flesh in the incarnation to the sexual union between a lover and his beloved is an amazing thing. You and I wouldn't dare do it if Scripture itself didn't do it first. But sexual union is, of course, what these verses *do* talk about. The garden doesn't just remind us of paradise. The garden or the vineyard is also a picture of the body of the beloved. The Shulamite is kind of coy about her beauty, saying in 1:6 that she knows her hard labor out in the sun has darkened her skin. While taking care of the vineyards, she says, she has neglected her own vineyard. That is to say, she has neglected her body. As a girl from a working family, she hasn't had the opportunity to pay attention to her looks. This girl, the king also claims, is a garden. We read it in 4:12, "A garden locked is my sister, my bride." Of course, by the time we get to our text at the end of chapter 4, the garden is no longer locked up. The smells of her perfumes have reached her beloved by way of the winds blowing from the north and the south, and she has managed to intoxicate him: "Let my beloved come to his garden, and eat its choicest fruits. I came to my garden, my sister, my bride" (4:16–5:1)—a daring image for the paradox that takes place in the annunciation, when the Virgin Mary says, "Let it be to me according to your word" (Luke 1:38).

There's a purity in Mary's response that is hard to grasp, a spiritual purity that corresponds to her physical virginity. One of the things I did in preparation for this sermon was to read a short book by the fourth-century author St. Gregory of Nyssa titled *On Virginity*. Gregory defends virginity, saying that marriage isn't the only option and that virginity is a special calling. He has some important insights that a pleasure-seeking culture focused only on the here and now tends to overlook. One of those insights is that life and death are always and inevitably connected. Motherhood implies the grief of death. St. Gregory doesn't just mean that sometimes parents go through the pain of losing their children. Instead he means that *all* of life at some point comes to an end. Birth always leads to death. There's only one way to fully prevent death, and that is virginity. Life in the flesh inevitably leads to death. Only the life of virginity avoids bringing death into the world. Death, Gregory insists, "started with every new-born child and accompanied it to the end." But in virginity, death ran up against a barrier that it could not get past.

So when death came up to Mary, the mother of God, Gregory says death "dashed against the fruit of virginity as if against a stone," so that death came to nothing in the virgin birth.[3]

We are all called to virginity. We are all called to live the life of Mary. Of course, that doesn't mean that all of us should avoid getting married, though I do believe the option of sexual renunciation can function as a powerful witness in a sex-crazed world. But there is a sense in which we all need virginity. We all need the pure desire for our heavenly lover that the Song of Solomon speaks about. Doesn't the mystery of the incarnation speak about Christ being born in each of us? The lyrics of "Joy to the World"—do they not say, "Let every heart prepare him room"? In another Christmas carol, "O Little Town of Bethlehem," do we not sing, "O holy Child of Bethlehem! / Descend to us, we pray; / Cast out our sin and enter in, / Be born in us today"?

It all boils down to this: Do we long for Christ to be born in our lives? Do we long for Mary-like virginity? Do we live from this deep desire, "Let my beloved come to his garden"; "Let it be to me according to your word"? It is Mary-like virginity that allows us to live no longer "according to the flesh" but instead to live "according to the Spirit" (Rom. 8:4). It is Mary-like virginity that changes the patterns of our desires so that we "make no provision for the flesh, to gratify its desires" (Rom. 13:14). Fleshly existence is weak. St. Paul insists that it's so weak, it always leads to death (Rom. 8:13; Gal. 6:8).

We know the death-dealing effects of our weaknesses, don't we? We know of them from experience. Many of us still live with the grief and pain that result from the weakness of the flesh. But St. Paul holds out good news to us. Virginity is there for us, no matter our past. The Spirit can overshadow us, no matter our loneliness. The Holy Child of Bethlehem can be born in us today, no matter our barrenness. Let's set our every desire on this fruit, on the presence of Christ. Let's focus all of our longing on this fruit of the overshadowing Spirit. It is the fruit, Paul tells us, of "love, joy, peace, patience, kindness, goodness, faithfulness, gentleness, self-control" (Gal. 5:22–23). Every one of

---

3. Gregory of Nyssa, *On Virginity*, in *Saint Gregory of Nyssa: Ascetical Works*, trans. Virginia Woods Callahan, The Fathers of the Church 58 (Washington, DC: Catholic University of America Press, 1967), 49.

those virtues is a picture of Christ. Every one of those virtues is a
fruit that virginity yields. Friends, our God longs for you and me to
be virgin-mothers. He wants Christ to be born in us.

Christians are people taken over by desire. We long for Christ to
come into our lives. If we stick with the biblical imagery of the Song
of Solomon, we may even say, without misunderstanding, that as
Christians we are animated by a kind of erotic desire. The human
heart that opens up to the presence of God knows of a longing that
is stronger than any other desire in the world. It is the love of desire,
the desire to be united with the God who gives us eternal life. It is
the only desire that is stronger than death. So the lover says, "Love is
strong as death, jealousy is fierce as the grave. Its flashes are flashes
of fire, the very flame of the LORD" (Song 8:6). "Whom have I in
heaven but you?" the psalmist sings. "And there is nothing on earth
that I desire besides you" (Ps. 73:25).

Virginity and motherhood—they do go together, don't they? When
we place ourselves alongside the Blessed Virgin, and our deepest desire is to let our lover come into his garden, isn't it then that Christ
is formed in us (Gal. 4:19)? When we place ourselves alongside the
Holy Virgin and our true passion is to let it be to us according to
God's word, do we not all become mothers of Israel who bear fruit
for the kingdom of God?

Virginity and motherhood free us to enter into the great mystery of the annunciation. That's true for physical virginity and for
physical motherhood. Neither is an easy calling, but there is no way
they *really* cramp our style. The very opposite is true: they speak
of the Spirit overshadowing us with his love and grace. Virgins and
mothers have always had a special place in the church. They both
remind us of Mary's words, "Let it be to me according to your
word" (Luke 1:38).

But it's true also that *spiritual* virginity and *spiritual* motherhood
bring us into the mystery of the annunciation. What greater longing,
what purer desire, than that of Mary? What deeper union than with
our heavenly spouse? So aim for virginity. Aim for motherhood. Aim
for the mystical reality of Mary's prayer, "Let my beloved come to
his garden." And our Lover will surely say, "I *came* to my garden,
my sister, my bride."

Preacher's Notes

This is the third sermon in this section on "Sensed Happiness." As such, I deal with what is perhaps the most delicate topic connected to matters of sense experience: erotic desire. Few topics are as significant in our sex-obsessed culture as that of erotic desire. Interestingly, the Christian tradition has a great deal of wisdom for properly channeling erotic desire. In this sermon, I turn to how the Song of Solomon was read in the past to find resources for appropriating a Christian theology of desire that draws listeners into loving union with Christ.

I do not use the term *happiness* in the sermon, though the reality to which the term refers is obviously present. The bride longs for happiness through union with her groom. I don't discuss in detail the happiness that people derive from marriage and conjugal union, though such sensed happiness has a legitimate role to play. Thomas Aquinas famously distinguishes between natural and supernatural happiness.[4] He rightly doesn't deride natural happiness. However, he subordinates it to supernatural happiness. What is more, natural happiness has a proper place only as it serves supernatural happiness. Thomas has it exactly right. Whereas our culture seeks ultimate happiness in sensed happiness, Thomas insists that sensed happiness is always subordinate to the happiness of union with God in Christ—and in this Thomas simply follows the broad stream of the Christian tradition. This position asks for a positive view of renunciation and asceticism, a view that can go hand in hand with an appreciation of sensed happiness in a subordinate place.

If the greatest happiness is to be united with God in Christ—to see God face-to-face—it shouldn't surprise us that many in the Christian tradition looked to human sexuality and the desire it evokes to interpret our relationship to God. That Scripture repeatedly places God in the position of husband and Israel in the position of his wife has made the husband-wife and bride-groom metaphors particularly attractive (cf. Isa. 54:5; 62:5; Jer. 3; Hosea 2; Ezek. 23; Eph. 5:31–32).

4. Thomas Aquinas, *Super Boetium De Trinitate*, q.6, a.4 ad 3; Aquinas, *Summa Theologica*, trans. Fathers of the English Dominican Province (New York: Benziger, 1948), I, q.62. Cf. Rudi te Velde, *Aquinas on God: The 'Divine Science' of the* Summa Theologiae (Burlington, VT: Ashgate, 2006), 155–60.

This is not to say that desire for God is erotic in the straightforward sense of the term. The language of sexual desire is merely analogous. But this does not mean that it is bereft of meaning. There is good reason why so many theologians and preachers have found the language of erotic desire and sexual union particularly suitable for expressing our relationship with God. Sexual desire, as the most intimate of human longings, comes perhaps closer than anything else to describing God's desire for his people and vice versa.

In this context, the traditional allegorical readings of the Song of Solomon seem only natural. Allegorical readings of this biblical book stem from Judaism, which typically saw the relationship between God and Israel reflected in it.[5] Preachers in the early church followed this Jewish line of interpretation and almost universally regarded the book as speaking of the relationship between God or Christ and the church (or Mary or the individual soul). That the church was comfortable having the Song of Solomon in the canon is hardly surprising considering the universally accepted allegorical meaning of the book.

It will be clear at this point that when the church fathers allegorized the Song of Solomon, they didn't arbitrarily impose an alien meaning on the book. They took their cue from the overall scriptural teaching on the relationship between God and Israel, as well as from earlier Jewish modes of reading. More important, perhaps, their reading of the Song wasn't arbitrary because it was christological in character. It is not as though *any* identification of the lover and the beloved would be equally acceptable. It was always important for Christian readers that Christ be discerned in the Old Testament. Once we have accepted the need for christological exegesis, it becomes almost inevitable that we discern the relationship between Christ and the church as present—albeit only sacramentally present—in the Song of Solomon.

This is not the place to present a lengthy discussion of the more refined or detailed allegorizing of the Old Testament that we find in Bernard of Clairvaux and other premodern preachers. Briefly put, most exponents of the tradition employed detailed allegorizing on the following grounds. First, their starting point was a basic christological

5. Longman, *Song of Songs*, 24–26.

reading of the text—justified along the lines I have just explained—in which they would look at how related details in the text could be filled in allegorically. Second, they operated on the basis of a realist epistemology, which held that objects of sense experience lie anchored in the reality of the eternal, heavenly Word of God. As a result vertical, and hence allegorical, relationships seemed more important to them than horizontal relationships and historical categories. The late medieval break with a realist epistemology lies at the basis of the loss of allegory.[6]

Third, Christian readers were convinced of the providential guidance of God throughout history. So they would be more likely to regard similarities between various events reflected in different biblical passages as the result of God's faithful character rather than as mere historical coincidence.[7] This recognition of divine providence would then justify linking various biblical passages allegorically because these passages all reflect—each in a unique manner—the ways in which God typically acts. Fourth, Christian readers were more interested in the *use* of the text (and the usefulness of the text for the church) than they were in authorial intent. Theologians such as Gregory of Nyssa constantly hammer on the usefulness of particular texts.[8] Fifth, they generally were not working with the notion that the aim of exegesis is determining the one (literal) meaning of the text. Instead, they were open to multiple readings of the text, so that differences in allegorical meaning were not considered problematic. Augustine, along with other biblical readers, often places various interpretive possibilities alongside one another. Finally, the unity of the biblical canon means that, for most Christians, the interpretive aim was not just to secure the meaning of a passage within the context of a particular Bible book, but also to look for similarities—often verbal similarities—across the biblical canon. Premodern Bible readers typically display a love for the words on the page. When interpreting

6. For more detail on this assertion, see Hans Boersma, *Heavenly Participation: The Weaving of a Sacramental Tapestry* (Grand Rapids: Eerdmans, 2011), 150–53.

7. Cf. Matthew Levering, *Participatory Biblical Exegesis: A Theology of Biblical Interpretation* (Notre Dame, IN: University of Notre Dame Press, 2008), 18–25.

8. See Hans Boersma, *Embodiment and Virtue in Gregory of Nyssa: An Anagogical Approach* (Oxford: Oxford University Press, 2013), 68.

a particular term in an Old Testament passage, they frequently turn to the use of the same term elsewhere, particularly in the New Testament, to interpret the passage at hand.

Each of these aspects seems to me worthy of careful consideration. At the same time, a quick comparison between my sermon and the sermons of preachers such as Bernard of Clairvaux will make clear that the christological allegorizing of my sermon is more restrained. Bernard—along with many other preachers on the Song—used allegorical tools to fill in many of the details. I wouldn't dare stand in judgment over such practices, and it seems better to reserve our strongest censure for readings that fail to recognize any christological and allegorical elements. Nonetheless, we preach in a context in which most of our audiences will have absorbed a cultural antipathy to allegorizing, and it is more important to enable people to see Christ in the Song of Solomon than to suggest allegorical details that may be more or less fruitful.

5

The Blessing of a Child

Exodus 1:1–2:10

Exodus 1:1–2:10

¹These are the names of the sons of Israel who came to Egypt with Jacob, each with his household: ²Reuben, Simeon, Levi, and Judah, ³Issachar, Zebulun, and Benjamin, ⁴Dan and Naphtali, Gad and Asher. ⁵All the descendants of Jacob were seventy persons; Joseph was already in Egypt. ⁶Then Joseph died, and all his brothers and all that generation. ⁷But the people of Israel were fruitful and increased greatly; they multiplied and grew exceedingly strong, so that the land was filled with them.

⁸Now there arose a new king over Egypt, who did not know Joseph. ⁹And he said to his people, "Behold, the people of Israel are too many and too mighty for us. ¹⁰Come, let us deal shrewdly with them, lest they multiply, and, if war breaks out, they join our enemies and fight against us and escape from the land." ¹¹Therefore they set taskmasters over them to afflict them with heavy burdens. They built for Pharaoh store cities, Pithom and Raamses. ¹²But the more they were oppressed, the more they multiplied and the more they spread abroad. And the Egyptians were in dread of the people of Israel. ¹³So they ruthlessly made the people of Israel work as slaves ¹⁴and made their lives bitter with hard service, in mortar and brick,

and in all kinds of work in the field. In all their work they ruthlessly made them work as slaves.

[15] Then the king of Egypt said to the Hebrew midwives, one of whom was named Shiphrah and the other Puah, [16] "When you serve as midwife to the Hebrew women and see them on the birthstool, if it is a son, you shall kill him, but if it is a daughter, she shall live." [17] But the midwives feared God and did not do as the king of Egypt commanded them, but let the male children live. [18] So the king of Egypt called the midwives and said to them, "Why have you done this, and let the male children live?" [19] The midwives said to Pharaoh, "Because the Hebrew women are not like the Egyptian women, for they are vigorous and give birth before the midwife comes to them." [20] So God dealt well with the midwives. And the people multiplied and grew very strong. [21] And because the midwives feared God, he gave them families. [22] Then Pharaoh commanded all his people, "Every son that is born to the Hebrews you shall cast into the Nile, but you shall let every daughter live."

[2:1] Now a man from the house of Levi went and took as his wife a Levite woman. [2] The woman conceived and bore a son, and when she saw that he was a fine child, she hid him three months. [3] When she could hide him no longer, she took for him a basket made of bulrushes and daubed it with bitumen and pitch. She put the child in it and placed it among the reeds by the river bank. [4] And his sister stood at a distance to know what would be done to him. [5] Now the daughter of Pharaoh came down to bathe at the river, while her young women walked beside the river. She saw the basket among the reeds and sent her servant woman, and she took it. [6] When she opened it, she saw the child, and behold, the baby was crying. She took pity on him and said, "This is one of the Hebrews' children." [7] Then his sister said to Pharaoh's daughter, "Shall I go and call you a nurse from the Hebrew women to nurse the child for you?" [8] And Pharaoh's daughter said to her, "Go." So the girl went and called the child's mother. [9] And Pharaoh's daughter said to her, "Take this child away and nurse him for me, and I will give you your wages." So the woman took the child and nursed him. [10] When the child grew older, she brought him to Pharaoh's daughter, and he became her son. She named him Moses, "Because," she said, "I drew him out of the water."

Sunday, January 16, 2011

The first chapter of Exodus sets the stage for a long journey. The title of the book, Exodus, means "going out" or "departure." This is the story of Israel going out, departing, from Egypt. It is the story of God redeeming his people, setting them free. "I am the Lord your God, who brought you out of the land of Egypt, out of the house of slavery," says the Lord to his people just before he gives them the Ten Commandments (Exod. 20:1–2). Today's story, from the first few chapters of Exodus, places us back in Egypt. It places us back in the house of slavery.

Perhaps we don't usually think of ourselves as being there. We prefer to think of ourselves as free people, as people who have already made the great trek and have arrived in the Promised Land. But we do well to remember St. Paul's almost sarcastic comment to the Corinthians, who also thought they had arrived: "Already you have all you want! Already you have become rich! Without us you have become kings!" (1 Cor. 4:8). It is true in an important sense that in Christ we have indeed arrived; it is equally true that we often return to the fleshpots of Egypt. We often end up enslaving ourselves all over again to the "worthless elementary principles of the world," as Paul puts it to the Galatians (4:9).

We need to know about our slavery, because liberation makes sense only to people who are oppressed. That's what today's story is about: God is going to set his people free. He is about to take us out of Egypt. And the way he will do it is through the birth of a child, a child born in our own backyard. The way God sets us free is by entering our very lives. The Son of God becomes the Son of Man. He identifies with us not just in our humanity; he becomes one with us in our *lost* humanity. He comes to us not just in Bethlehem; he also visits us in Egypt. Matthew's Gospel is quite clear on that: Joseph takes the child and his mother to Egypt to prevent Herod from killing the child. They stay in Egypt until Herod's death. We then read, with a quotation from Hosea 11:1, "This was to fulfill what the Lord had spoken by the prophet, 'Out of Egypt I called my son'" (Matt. 2:15). Jesus joins us even in our slavery in Egypt.

God calls his children out of Egypt. These words of Hosea go back all the way to the story that we're looking at. It's the story of the birth of Moses, the birth of the child who will redeem his people out of Egypt. These same words of Hosea also speak about Christ. And these words are true also of you and me. We too know what it means to be in Egypt. We too are God's sons and daughters, and the words of the prophet speak also of you and me: "Out of Egypt I called my son."

There is a crucial lesson to be learned here. It is because Christ traveled down to Egypt, entered into our oppression and our slavery, that he can set us free. After all, it is *in* the Son that we may call God "Abba, Father" (Rom. 8:15; Gal. 4:6). It is *with* him that we leave Egypt behind. It is *in* Christ that God takes us on a journey. It is *united* to him that we go back to the Promised Land. It is Christ's entry into Egypt that makes this story of the exodus also about us, about our daily lives. The book of Exodus is about us because it is a book about Christ. It is a book about how God comes to us and sets us free in Christ. That is why I've chosen "The Blessing of a Child" as the title for this sermon. For that is what this book is all about. It is about the blessing of a child. The child is Moses. The child is also Christ, and the child is you and me, belonging to Christ.

In some sense, it's obvious that today's passage is about children, and especially about one child, Moses. We read about Moses toward the end of the story. Because you and I know the rest of the book, we know that this story merely sets the stage for a much longer story, that of the exodus. Because we know the rest of the book, we know that the birth of Moses in this story is the birth of a redeemer, the birth of the one who is going to set God's people free from slavery. This story is obviously about the blessing of a child. Moses is going to be a great blessing to the people of Israel.

But we should not jump ahead too quickly, for this story is not only about the blessing of *a* child, Moses; it is also about the blessing of *many* children. The story begins with lots of talk about lots of children. When famine drove Jacob to Egypt, where Joseph had become second in command, we read that seventy children and grandchildren came along with Jacob. Seventy is the number we read in Exodus 1:5 (cf. Gen. 46:27), a number that in Scripture speaks of wholeness, of perfection.

What happened when these seventy people passed the torch on to the next generation? "The people of Israel," says Exodus 1:7, "were fruitful and increased greatly; they multiplied and grew exceedingly strong, so that the land was filled with them." Note what it says. It doesn't just say, as a matter of fact, that the people were fruitful. No, the text really highlights the myriad of kids among the Israelites: "They were *fruitful* and *increased greatly*" and "grew *exceedingly strong* [or *numerous*], so that the land was *filled* with them." Notice all the different words used to describe what was happening. The English doesn't quite show this, but in the Hebrew are seven different words all highlighting the amazing blessing that unfolds in the land of Egypt.[1] You could say that the seventy people are blessed sevenfold. The blessing of kids is front and center in this chapter. What an increase! Joseph was in Egypt first. His name means "increase." Joseph is obviously true to his name. Beginning with this one person who traveled to Egypt as a slave, we now have a whole clan, with a sevenfold blessing for seventy people. And all this talk of children leads, of course, to the birth of *the* child, the birth of Moses, in chapter 2. We can see how, from the outset, God has in mind the birth of the redeemer child. Everything in this first chapter makes us look to the coming of the child who is going to set his people free. Everything makes us look to Christ. "Out of Egypt I called my son" (Matt. 2:15).

But it isn't just this first chapter, with all its talk about many children, that prepares us for the blessing of *the* child, the redeemer. No, the *whole* story—from much further back, from the very beginning—is a story about children. When God begins something new in history, he seems to do it through little ones. The story of creation, Genesis 1:28: "God blessed them. [Note the blessing!] And God said to them, 'Be fruitful and multiply and fill the earth.'" Then right after the flood, we see a new creation in Genesis 9:1: "And God blessed Noah and his sons [again, we're talking blessing] and said to them, 'Be fruitful and multiply and fill the earth.'" Now passage number three, Exodus 1:7: "The people of Israel were fruitful and increased greatly; they multiplied and grew exceedingly numerous, so that the land was filled with them." The blessing of Adam and Eve and the blessing of Noah come to a proper end here in Egypt. The story of Genesis finds its aim in the story of Exodus. In other words, it's not just the first chapter of Exodus that prepares us for the child. It's the entire book that comes *before* Exodus that from *its* very first chapter

1. See Umberto Cassuto, *A Commentary on the Book of Exodus*, trans. Israel Abrahams (Jerusalem: Magnes Press, 1951), 9.

leads us to this moment of salvation and that calls out for the Christ child to be born.

I would like us to pause here for just a moment. If it's true that Exodus 1 connects back all the way to Genesis 1—and the echoes in today's chapter deliberately remind us of the creation story—then there are huge implications here for the way you and I structure our lives. Genesis and Exodus are not two different stories. True, they're not quite one and the same either. But Exodus *builds* on Genesis. The story of salvation from Egypt ("Out of Egypt I called my son") *builds* on the story of creation ("Be fruitful and multiply"). The gift of grace (the birth of the child) *builds* on the gift of nature (the birth of *many* children). And the hope of the resurrection *builds* on all of history. This is also why, in the past, Christians often referred to Sunday as the eighth day. Sunday is the day of resurrection; it's the day that finishes and perfects the seven days of history, much like eternal life is going to finish and perfect everything that has happened throughout time (Eph. 1:10). Genesis is meant for Exodus. Creation is meant for redemption. The many children are meant for the one child. The seven days of the week are meant for the eighth day. All of our lives are meant for eternity.

That perspective changes everything. It means that from the moment we open our Bibles, we think of the child. Everything in the Bible, everything in history, from the first moment of creation, is stamped with the imprint of the child. The blessing of the child, after all, is God's purpose for the overall story. This means that nothing in the story of our lives is any longer strictly our own, to do with as we like. It's like the Heidelberg Catechism puts it: "I am not my own, but belong—body and soul, in life and in death—to my faithful Savior Jesus Christ." Everything in my story, everything that I am (body and soul, life and death), belongs to the Christ child. The whole week that makes up our life—all seven days—looks forward to the eighth day, the day of our resurrection. It's only when we get to the resurrection, the eighth day, the exodus, that the other seven days truly make sense. Without the eighth day of eternity, the seven days of our life would be a meaningless, and in many ways cruel, sequence of events.

I remember once visiting a pastor on his deathbed. He mentioned that he didn't know how much longer it would be before he would die. It could be sooner or later. It could be six days or six years, he told me. I remember him commenting that he would be at peace either way. Then he mentioned the Catechism—that in life and in death, we belong to Christ. Regardless of how much time we have, we belong to him. We are called upon to run the race and to run it to the end. That, he said, was all he was concerned about, that he would run faithfully to the end. I think he was exactly right. Our seven days here on earth are meant for the eighth day of heaven. The book of Genesis is meant for the book of Exodus. The many children are meant for the one child.

This first chapter of Exodus is in many ways a horrible chapter, reflecting the terrible things that often happen in our lives. It's a chapter in which Pharaoh acts like Herod. He acts "shrewdly," verse 10 reads, much like Herod was shrewd when he secretly called in the magi (Matt. 2:7). Pharaoh begins with forcing the Hebrews as slave labor to build the store cities of Pithom and Raamses (Exod. 1:11). But when God's blessing of children proves too strong for him—"the more they were oppressed, the more they multiplied and the more they spread abroad" (1:12)—Pharaoh digs in his heels and makes the Israelites' lives "bitter with hard service," working them "ruthlessly" (1:14).

Then Pharaoh moves from forced labor to slaughter of the innocents. With wicked genius, he even tries to get the Hebrews to kill their own children. To the *Hebrew* midwives he says, "When you serve as midwife to the Hebrew women and see them on the birthstool, if it is a son, you shall kill him, but if it is a daughter, she shall live" (1:16). But again, God's love for life proves stronger than Pharaoh's culture of death. The midwives don't cooperate (1:17). Like the magi tricking Herod with an alternate route home from seeing the Christ child (Matt. 2:16), the midwives trick the Egyptian king. When Pharaoh calls them to account, they mockingly tell him that Hebrew women are stronger than Egyptian women; they're so quick to give birth that the midwives always arrive too late to kill the child (Exod. 1:19). Then, lovely irony of ironies, "because the midwives feared God, he gave *them* families" (1:21). Kids enter into the story left, right, and center. Pharaoh's death-dealing plan, which is really *Herod's* death-dealing plan, is simply no match for God's loving plan

of new life. But, as you know, God's blessing of children serves only
to enrage Pharaoh. Just like Herod finally exploded and openly "sent
and killed all the male children" (Matt. 2:16), so Pharaoh finally had
enough and "commanded all his people, 'Every son that is born to
the Hebrews you shall cast into the Nile'" (Exod. 1:22).

Everything in this story—and, as we saw, everything in the book
of Genesis—prepares the way for the blessing of the child. The problem is that the culture of Egypt is a culture of death. Egypt's culture
does not welcome children; it is a culture that will go to great lengths
to prevent new life. We do well to hold up this story as a mirror to
ourselves. Life is a gift to be treasured. Life, from the very outset, is
a treasure in need of protection and care. We need to stand alongside the Hebrew midwives and recognize, cherish, and protect God's
blessing of new life. We may like to think the shrewd Pharaoh isn't
around anymore, but maybe he still is. We may sometimes act as
though Herod's wicked genius has disappeared, but perhaps that is
not quite the case. Their character, after all, was simply a reflection
of the serpent himself who, Genesis tells us, was "more crafty than
any other beast of the field" (Gen. 3:1). Pharaoh and Herod are still
around for the simple reason that the serpent is still around. Scripture
cautions us already in Genesis 3:15 that the serpent will bruise the
heel of the woman's offspring. It's good, therefore, to ask ourselves:
does the mind-set that we know from Pharaoh and Herod shape us
in some ways too? Remember, if there is anything the serpent hates,
it is the blessing of a child.

Thankfully, the gospel message from today's passage tells us that
the serpent, no matter how crafty, doesn't get his way. We see this
from the sudden turn of events in Exodus 2:1: "Now a man from the
house of Levi went and took as his wife a Levite woman." It's like
we get the story of Mary and Joseph suddenly thrown into Exodus.
Indeed, the story of the birth of Moses follows; the story of the
redeemer; the story of the child. Seven times we read about "the
child" in the first ten verses of chapter 2.[2] The mother puts the *child*
in a basket (2:3). When Pharaoh's daughter sees the basket—note the

2. Cassuto, *Exodus*, 21. In addition, the passage speaks once of "one of the Hebrew's children" (2:6), using the plural of the same Hebrew word.

exquisite irony of the culture of death defeating itself—she sends one of her young women, who opens it and sees the *child* (2:6). At this point sister Miriam jumps up from behind the reeds and asks, "Shall I go and call you a nurse from the Hebrew women to nurse the *child* for you?" (2:7). She indeed goes to fetch "the *child's* mother" (2:8), at which point Pharaoh's daughter makes the request, "Take this *child* away and nurse him for me, and I will give you your wages" (2:9). So the mother takes the *child* and nurses him (2:9). And when the *child* grows older, she brings him to Pharaoh's daughter, who then adopts him as her own (2:10). Seven times in these first ten verses, we read about the child. It's like the introduction of the child opens us up to the vistas of salvation. It's like victory is being announced: God's grace does finish and does perfect creation after all.

The birth of the child isn't something Pharaoh or Herod can prevent. The eternal day of eternal salvation isn't up for grabs. True, Satan does try mighty hard. The woman, pregnant and crying out in pain, is about to give birth, Revelation 12:1–4 tells us, when an enormous "red dragon, with seven heads and ten horns, and on his heads seven diadems" appears, ready to devour the child the moment he is born. Isn't it obvious that Pharaoh, in the way he goes about things, is simply a mirror image of his father, the devil (cf. John 8:44)? The dragon of Revelation 12 is the same dragon we see in Pharaoh; it's the same dragon we see in Herod.

Perhaps our shrewd opponent scares us. Maybe we are afraid for our kids when we look at the death-dealing culture in which they grow up. Or perhaps, as we listen to this morning's sermon, we have to admit to ourselves that the serpent has grabbed hold of certain aspects of our lives. But let's not be afraid. There's no need to be intimidated. It's not the serpent's intrigues that have the final say: the blessing of the child does. After all, we know the story line. Pharaoh has been tricked; there's a child in a basket. Herod has been tricked too; there's a child in a manger. Even the devil has been tricked: the child, Revelation 12:5 tells us, "was caught up to God and to his throne." With that child on the throne, no doubt remains about our final exodus. With that child leading us on, we know that the eighth day is just around the corner. There's only one thing to remember while we're still in Egypt and Pharaoh is still breathing violence: the

seven days of our earthly life do not belong to him. They belong to
the child. We are not our own but belong—body and soul, in life and
in death—to our faithful Savior, Jesus Christ.

Preacher's Notes

How people interpret the Bible, particularly the Old Testament, says
a great deal about how they understand the nature-grace relationship.
The narrative of Exodus 1–2 about the birth of Moses could be read
in an isolated fashion, simply as the founding story of the people of
Israel, a story that leads to God's people traveling through the desert
and subsequently entering the Promised Land. This story would then
be followed by stories of Davidic kingship, of national breakup, and
of exile to faraway lands. It is not as though such telling of the story
is illegitimate. It is just that it is incomplete because it omits the most
important element: it becomes a story at the historical (natural) level
that fails to reach its heavenly (supernatural) perfection. Narrating
the story of the exodus without speaking of the Christ child is like
organizing your daily life without concerning yourself with your
heavenly destiny.

The sermon comments: "The gift of grace (the birth of the child)
builds on the gift of nature (the birth of *many* children)." The assumption underlying this statement is that Christ's work of grace perfects
God's work of creation. In the sermon I try to bring to the fore this
intimate link between nature and grace in several ways. I mention not
only the birth of the many children climaxing in the birth of the one
child, but also Genesis leading to Exodus, the seven days leading to
the eighth day, and our earthly lives here and now leading to resurrection life in the future. In other words, creation and redemption
are not at odds. Rather, as the second-century church father Irenaeus
knew well, they belong together.[3] The one inexorably gives rise to the
second. Grace perfects, rather than destroys, God's good creation.

Grace does not obliterate nature, and the preacher cannot ignore
this passage's emphatic insistence that children are a natural blessing

3. Irenaeus, *The Scandal of the Incarnation: Irenaeus against the Heresies*, ed.
Hans Urs von Balthasar, trans. John Saward (San Francisco: Ignatius, 1981), 53–67.

from God. It leaps off the page. Nor would it be right to be silent about Pharaoh's radical opposition to God's gift of life among the Hebrews. The preacher must do justice to this oppositional logic of the passage. Both the insistence on children as a blessing and the acknowledgment of an antithesis between church and world give the sermon a countercultural feel. To my mind, this is something the preacher should not shy away from, perhaps for fear of giving offense. At the same time, good preaching tries to persuade. Thus I try to persuade by grounding the sermon solidly in the biblical text itself. When we let it speak, we helpfully avoid making ourselves and our opinions the focal point of the sermon.

The imagery of one child being born among the numerous children of Israel implies a close link between the many children and the one child. Though it is true that grace comes to us from the outside—that is to say, from God who infinitely transcends the created order—this grace is not alien to our natural world. Incarnation means that God genuinely takes on human flesh and, in Christ, comes down to our houses of slavery and makes them his own. Therefore, from the outset, the created order aims at our perfection in Christ.

Theologians have differed on the question of whether the incarnation would have happened if the fall into sin had not occurred. In some ways, this is a speculative question. The fall *did* happen, and perhaps our "what if" questions display needless curiosity. But underneath the hypothetical question lies an important theological point that has to do with the purpose of the created order. Does creation from the outset have as its aim perfection in Jesus Christ? Put differently, is the supernatural perfection of Christ the purpose for which we were made, right from the start? If this is the case—and I think it is—then God has made all human beings in such a way that we have a natural desire to grow toward happiness. It means that the link between nature and grace is so close that our ultimate, heavenly purpose, our *telos*, is genuinely fitting to the way we have been made. By the very fact that we are human beings, we are fitted for eternal life with God.

In the sermon, I do briefly mention the nature-grace relationship explicitly and allude several times to God's grace finishing and perfecting creation. It will be clear, however, that I avoid a detailed doctrinal discussion of the nature-grace relationship. My sermons purposely shy away from elaborate theological exposition. The task of the preacher is to proclaim God's saving work in our life in Christ and through the Spirit and to appeal to people's longing for God, in order to draw them more deeply into Christ and so into fellowship with God. The biblical narrative is crucial for this purpose; it cannot be left behind or bypassed. At the same time, theological background questions inevitably shape and color the character of a sermon, and it is important that preachers be aware of the kinds of theological assumptions they bring to bear on their exegetical work.

The recent rise of so-called theological exegesis has my warm support, and this book of sermons reflects this trend. There is a sense, however, in which the use of the term "theological interpretation" obscures things: *all* biblical interpreters engage in theological exegesis, whether or not they are aware of it and acknowledge it. This is an important point because those who consciously try to eschew theological interpretation, as though it were the latest fad, mistakenly assume that their literal or historical readings of Scripture are *not* impacted by theological considerations. The reality is that these theologians merely end up hiding their theological presuppositions. When we refuse to allow the newness of the Christ event to enter into our reading of the exodus narrative and when we view correct exegesis merely as the result of following the appropriate technical steps, we isolate nature from grace. Regardless of what we may think of such an approach, to claim that it is not theological is to hide from view what is actually going on. Since theology is queen of the sciences, whether she is recognized as such or not, our reading of the Bible too is theological, whether we are aware of it or not.

To underline that nothing in life is strictly autonomous vis-à-vis God's grace to us in Christ, I mention the Heidelberg Catechism (1563) several times in the sermon. My insistence that Christ's claim on us extends to our every aspect—"body and soul, in life and in death"—echoes the emphasis of the earlier tradition that we ought to keep nature and grace together. My use of this confessional statement is meant to highlight that God's gracious purposes in Christ come prior to the creation of the world. Though I could have used other examples from the tradition to make the same point, the Heidelberg

Catechism is particularly useful in this regard since I preach in a Christian Reformed Church where this confessional document has taken deep root. The homiletical point is that connecting with the congregation's theological background is important. A congregation rightly expects the preacher to link up with who they are, spiritually and theologically. Making connections with the church's lived theological experience determines in good part the trust that the preacher will obtain within the congregation and thus also the ability to speak into people's lives.

My use of the theology of the eighth day may seem a somewhat alien imposition on the text. The passage, after all, doesn't mention the days of the week. Still, the reference to the eighth day likely didn't confuse my listeners. The reason is at least twofold. First, the text itself plays with the number seven. The term "child" (*yeled*) is mentioned seven times, or eight times if we count the plural in 2:6.[4] It is not illegitimate to see in this number an allusion to fullness, so that the question of perfection, indicated by the number eight, naturally arises. Second, by going back to Genesis 1:28 and 9:1, this passage deliberately draws our attention to the perfecting of the created order by means of the Christ child. Therefore, when writing the sermon, I had to pay attention to the relationship between creation and redemption. One way to do this is by speaking of the relationship between the seven days of creation and the eighth day of perfection.[5] My use of the eighth day does not mean to suggest that the theme itself is explicitly mentioned in the passage; it merely draws out an important theme that is implicitly present in the text.

---

4. As Cassuto points out, also the words "midwife" (*yalled*) and "daughter" (*bat*) both occur seven times each (*Exodus*, 15, 17).

5. The *eighth day* was a popular trope in the early church, particularly in the theology of Gregory of Nyssa. See the fine discussion in Jean Daniélou, *The Bible and the Liturgy*, Liturgical Studies 3 (Notre Dame, IN: University of Notre Dame Press, 1956), 262–86.

Part 2

Pilgrim Happiness

*T*he previous four sermons have, in various ways, explored the life of the senses. While we derive some happiness from the embodied life of the senses (Sensed Happiness), these sermons nonetheless emphasized that we are to use the physical senses to train the spiritual senses. We find our ultimate destiny and enjoyment not in anything on this side of the Creator-creature divide. Our aim, true happiness, lies in God. The objects of the physical senses, therefore, awaken in us a growing desire to find God as the ultimate object of our spiritual desire.

By implication, the Christian life is one of pilgrimage. Many theologians in the Christian tradition have used the images of two paths, the narrow path versus the wide path, and of a ladder to depict the Christian journey toward God. By definition, Christians are on a pilgrimage, and they find enjoyment or happiness in anticipation of their destiny. Since the destiny is God himself, the pilgrimage is not only a journey that takes us to the end of time; it is also one that leads us upward. The ancient term *anagogy* (leading upward) gives expression to the Christian recognition that the destiny of the pilgrim lies in heaven. The next three sermons take us out of Egypt (Matt. 2), up the hill of Mount Zion (Ps. 24), and into the rest of the Promised Land (Heb. 3–4). These images speak to us of our spiritual pilgrimage toward the rest that God offers to us in Christ.

6

Out of Egypt

Matthew 2:13–21

Matthew 2:13–21

¹³ Now when they had departed, behold, an angel of the Lord appeared to Joseph in a dream and said, "Rise, take the child and his mother, and flee to Egypt, and remain there until I tell you, for Herod is about to search for the child, to destroy him." ¹⁴ And he rose and took the child and his mother by night and departed to Egypt ¹⁵ and remained there until the death of Herod. This was to fulfill what the Lord had spoken by the prophet, "Out of Egypt I called my son."

¹⁶ Then Herod, when he saw that he had been tricked by the wise men, became furious, and he sent and killed all the male children in Bethlehem and in all that region who were two years old or under, according to the time that he had ascertained from the wise men. ¹⁷ Then was fulfilled what was spoken by the prophet Jeremiah:

> ¹⁸ "A voice was heard in Ramah,
>   weeping and loud lamentation,
>   Rachel weeping for her children;
>   she refused to be comforted, because they are no more."

¹⁹But when Herod died, behold, an angel of the Lord appeared in a dream to Joseph in Egypt, ²⁰saying, "Rise, take the child and his mother and go to the land of Israel, for those who sought the child's life are dead." ²¹And he rose and took the child and his mother and went to the land of Israel.

Sunday, January 2, 2011

Today I want to reflect with you on what it means when we say that God calls us. Matthew 2:15 tells us quite emphatically, "Out of Egypt I *called* my son." Our God is a God who calls. At times, it is easy to lose sight of that. When difficulties come our way, life may seem like a dark labyrinth, and we don't know where to go to escape the darkness and find the light at the end of the maze. In our disorientation, it is easy to lose our direction. As Christians, we need to take careful note of this danger of losing our way. And the good thing is that the Lord particularly *wants* us to have a clear sense of direction. Today he provides us with nothing less than a GPS to navigate our way through the labyrinths of our confusion. He says to us, "If you feel as though you've ended up in a labyrinth, if you have the sense that there's no way out, let me give you some directions." On the GPS that he gives us are three points, three locations, that I want us to take special notice of. The three locations are Bethlehem, Egypt, and Israel. If we keep our eyes on these three places that we see on our GPS—Bethlehem, Egypt, and Israel—we're going to be okay. We'll safely arrive at the end of our journey.

One of the first things that strikes us in this chapter of Matthew's Gospel is all the traveling. First are the magi. They come all the way from the East to Jerusalem to worship the baby. When King Herod's top theologians tell the magi that, in line with Micah 5, the baby will be born in Bethlehem, we read in Matthew 2:9 that "they went on their way," with the star showing them where to go. When a dream warns them not to report back to Herod, the magi, we read in verse 12, "departed to their own country by another way." After an angel warns Joseph in a dream about Herod, we find Joseph taking the child and his mother on a journey, in the middle of the night, to Egypt (2:14). This is followed in verse 21 by Joseph—again acting on angelic instructions—taking the child and his mother and returning to the land of Israel. God does a lot of calling in this chapter. God calls, and people start traveling.

As we travel along, let's make a pit stop at the first location on our GPS, the town of Bethlehem. What kind of town is Bethlehem? When the magi first arrive in Jerusalem and visit King Herod, he calls together the chief priests and the scribes. He asks them where the Christ is to be born. "In Bethlehem of Judea," they reply, "for so it is written by the prophet" (2:5), and then they turn to the Scriptures and quote Micah 5:2. Bethlehem, they know from their Bibles, is the town in which the Messiah will be born. Now, there is nothing particularly significant about Bethlehem. It is a tiny little town just south of Jerusalem, which by all accounts has little going for it. People estimate that when Herod tried desperately to prevent the birth of the Messiah by sending in his soldiers to kill all the baby boys aged two and younger, he massacred perhaps fifteen or twenty children. Bethlehem wasn't much. Micah *emphasizes* the insignificance of Bethlehem. It says in 5:2, "But you, O Bethlehem Ephrathah, who are too little to be among the clans of Judah." Bethlehem is a tiny little backwater town south of Jerusalem.

What, then, is so special about Bethlehem? Well, nothing in and of itself. We cannot alter the facts. God does not call people because of who they are or because of what they have done. God calls people out of grace. But what is so special about Bethlehem is precisely that Bethlehem is the place where God calls people. Bethlehem is the place to which God sent the prophet Samuel: "Fill your horn with oil, and go. I will send you to Jesse the Bethlehemite, for I have provided for myself a king among his sons" (1 Sam. 16:1). It turns out that the young shepherd boy named David was the one God was calling to be the next king: "Arise, anoint him, for this is he" (16:12). God turned to the smallest of the clans of Judah, and from that clan he took the youngest, and he called him to be the king of Israel.

What is special about Bethlehem is that God chose that insignificant, little town from which to call the future king, David, the son of Jesse. That simple fact of God calling David completely turned around Bethlehem's fortunes. It flipped them 180 degrees. Think of the prophecy of Micah 5:2: "But you, O Bethlehem Ephrathah,

who are too little to be among the clans of Judah." Micah no doubt
remembers the story of Samuel anointing the shepherd boy from
nowhere, and he prophesies that from this hick town of Bethlehem
God will call his Messiah. Now turn to Matthew 2:6, for that's where
we find Herod's court theologians quoting Micah 5. But note that
something is off in the way they quote the passage. What do we read
in Matthew 2:6? "And you, O Bethlehem, in the land of Judah, are
by no means least among the rulers of Judah." "You, O Bethlehem,
are *by no means least*." This so-called quotation completely flips
around the meaning of Micah 5:2. Micah says, "You . . . are too little
to be among the clans of Judah." Matthew says, "You . . . are *by no
means least* among the rulers of Judah." Micah says Bethlehem is
the smallest; Matthew says it is the greatest. Why this turn of events?
It seems there's only one possible explanation: when God chooses a
place, when God calls a person, this changes everything. God's calling changes a town from being the backwoods into being the center
of the universe; God's calling turns a filthy, little shepherd boy into
the king of Israel.

Bethlehem, that little town in the boondocks of Judah, becomes a
royal city. For Matthew, geography is important. "Jesus was born in
Bethlehem of Judea," Matthew tells us emphatically in 2:1, "in the
days of Herod the king." When the magi arrive in Jerusalem, they
ask, "Where is he who has been born king of the Jews?" (Matt. 2:2).
Bethlehem had become a royal town. And as a royal town, Bethlehem upstages Jerusalem. Herod can do all the scheming he wants,
murdering all the young boys in the town of Bethlehem, but God is
true to his calling.

Perhaps you are thinking, "This may all be true, but how am I part
of this story? The travels of Matthew 2 are the travels of the magi
and the travels of the holy family. They are not *my* travels." God's
choice of Bethlehem and his calling of David as the king of Israel are
references to a very particular town and a very particular king—and if
we follow Matthew's reading of Micah, they are references to a very
particular *messianic* king, Jesus Christ, the Son of God. All of this
is true. This passage is about the birth of God's Son. It is about *his*
life being threatened by Herod. It is about *his* birth in Bethlehem. It
is about *his* escape to Egypt. And it is about *his* return to the land of

Israel. The events that Matthew describes in this chapter are events at a particular time in history, long ago.

True, but the incarnation is not just a long-ago event. The story of Jesus' birth in Bethlehem is also the story of *our* birth in Bethlehem. And it's the same with the rest of the events in the life of Christ. We too have our place in those events. This story in Matthew's Gospel is also about *us* being called. It is also about *our* flight to Egypt. And it is also about *our* return to the Promised Land. The reason is really quite simple. The Heidelberg Catechism, in Lord's Day 12, asks two questions. First it asks, "Why is he called 'Christ,' meaning 'anointed'?" It answers that Christ is anointed with the Holy Spirit as prophet, priest, and king. Much like Samuel with his horn of oil anointed David as king, so God has anointed Christ as the messianic king. Then the Catechism goes on and asks, "But why are *you* called a Christian?" The answer is, "Because by faith I am a member of Christ, and so I share in his anointing." I share in the anointing of Christ, the Catechism says. That means that I too am a prophet, a priest, and a king. Christ is anointed as Messiah-King, and because he is the Messiah-King—capital *M*, capital *K*—we too are messiah-kings and messiah-queens—small *m*, small *k*, small *q*. The reason this story in Matthew's Gospel is also about you and me is that we have been anointed along with Christ.

That's a close link between Christ and us. The Bible makes the same link. It tells us that we are God's children, his sons and daughters. When we pray to God, we say, "Our Father who art in heaven." God is our Father; we are his children. How come? Well, it has everything to do with the incarnation. It has everything to do with Bethlehem. St. Paul talks about this same event in Galatians 4: "When the fullness of time had come, God sent forth his Son, born of a woman, born under law" (4:4). The apostle then goes on to say that not only did God send his Son, born of Mary, but also he sent the Spirit of his Son into our hearts, so that we too can call out, "Abba, Father!" (Gal. 4:6). Paul's conclusion is we are no longer slaves, but children of God. Because Christ is the Son of God, we too are sons and daughters of God (Gal. 4:7). Christ has become our brother. He is the "firstborn," the eldest "among many brothers" (Rom. 8:29).

Along with Christ, we are sons and daughters of God. Bethlehem is our native town. The implication of this is astounding. You and

I, we are royalty. Let's pause here for a moment and reflect on it. As God's children, we are royalty. After all, the Bible often links the two: to be God's child is to be royalty, offspring of the great King. When God promised David that Solomon would rule over Israel, God said, "I will be to him [Solomon] a father, and he shall be to me a son" (2 Sam. 7:14). When God calls to mind how special his relationship with the king is, he says in Psalm 89, "He [the king] shall cry to me, 'You are my *Father*, my God, and the Rock of my salvation.' And I will make him the *firstborn*, the highest of the kings of the earth" (Ps. 89:26–27). God is David's Father; David is God's firstborn son. God is our Father; we are God's adopted sons and daughters. You and I, we are royalty. We are royalty because Bethlehem is our native town. We are royalty because we are kings and queens in Christ. With him, we have been anointed with the Spirit of God.

The second pit stop that our GPS points to is Egypt. "Out of Egypt I called my son" (Matt. 2:15). Son language in the Bible isn't just about the king. Son language is about the whole people of God; it's about all of us. Think back to the story of the exodus. When Moses stands face-to-face with Pharaoh in Exodus 4, what does God tell him to say to Pharaoh? "Then you shall say to Pharaoh, 'Thus says the LORD, Israel is my firstborn son.'" Notice that? It's not just the king who is God's firstborn. The whole people together, they too are God's firstborn son. "Thus says the LORD, Israel is my firstborn son, and I say to you, 'Let my son go that he may serve me.' If you refuse to let him go, behold, I will kill your firstborn son" (Exod. 4:22–23). Because Pharaoh imprisoned and enslaved God's firstborn son, God is going to kill Pharaoh's firstborn son. Israel is God's son; Israel is God's firstborn son; Israel is God's special son.

"Out of Egypt I called my son." That is the exodus story in a nutshell, isn't it? "Out of Egypt I called my son." God deeply loved that son. The prophecies of Hosea are all about God's love for his son—and, sadly enough, about his son's betrayal of that love. Hosea 11:1 says, "When Israel was a child, I loved him, and out of Egypt I called my son." But you and I know the rest of the story. Hosea knew it too: "The more they were called, the more they went away; they kept sacrificing to the Baals and burning offerings to idols" (Hosea 11:2). Hosea could not have pictured more poignantly the pain of

God's fatherly love: "Yet it was I who taught Ephraim to walk; I took them up by their arms, but they did not know that I healed them. I led them with cords of kindness, with the bands of love" (Hosea 11:3–4). Israel turned up its nose at God's calling. Israel acted like a rebellious teenager. "Will they not return to Egypt and will not Assyria rule over them because they refuse to repent?" (Hosea 11:5 NIV). Israel's heavenly Father was so frustrated with his children that he sent them back to where they came from.

When you and I think of the exile of Israel and Judah, we think of Assyria and of Babylon. And that's exactly right. Those are the two countries to which Israel and Judah were deported. But Matthew reminds us that the Jews were scattered not just in these countries, but all over the place. Many of them actually went back to Egypt! When the angel tells Joseph to go to Egypt, he doesn't tell him to go to some isolated desert place. At that time, probably about a million Jews lived in Egypt in the city of Alexandria. Egypt had turned into a major center of the Jewish Diaspora. All these Jews living in Egypt were a sad reminder that God's firstborn son had rebelled. So they had returned to the place they had come from. They had gone back to Egypt. That is the place the angel tells Joseph to take the child and his mother: Egypt, the place where the wicked king had brutally oppressed Israel and murdered so many of its innocent children. Egypt, the very personification of opposition and hatred of God. Egypt, the horrid house of slavery to which God's rebellious teenager returned because he rejected the love of the one who had graciously adopted him.

"Out of Egypt I called my son." Why does God tell Joseph to take the child and his mother into Egypt? Why does he tell Joseph to flee from Bethlehem? Why does he tell Joseph to stay in Egypt until Herod's death? Obviously, you say, to save the child! Sure, but why Egypt? Why not any other place? Isn't it because you and I so often return to the fleshpots of Egypt? Isn't it because you and I are just like the Israelites, and our misdirected desires often lead us back to Egypt? There "we sat by the meat pots and ate bread to the full," we say to ourselves, while here we are in the wilderness, starving to death (Exod. 16:3). The amazing grace of the gospel, the astounding love of God, is this: not only does the eternal Son of God take on human flesh, not only does he go to Bethlehem so that we can have a place alongside him in Bethlehem; no, he goes all the way to where we are. He goes all the way to Egypt. He goes all the way to the very place of slavery and oppression. He goes all the way to our country of exile. He goes all the way to the objects of our misdirected desires. He goes all the way to the center of our darkest labyrinths.

"Out of Egypt I called my son." That Jesus goes to Egypt is amazing grace. It means God identifies with you and me in the places of our disorientation and confusion. But the most astounding part of the message is not even this, for our GPS points beyond the pit stops of Bethlehem and Egypt. There is a third location on the map. And this one is more than a pit stop. "Out of Egypt I called my son." Where does God call us? Where does he tell us to go? Well, where does the angel tell Joseph to take the child? Matthew 2:20 says, "Rise, take the child and his mother and go *to the land of Israel*." Then again in the next verse: "And he rose and took the child and his mother and went *to the land of Israel*" (Matt. 2:21). Israel is the third place on our GPS. It is also our final destination. The land of Israel is the Promised Land.

This is the final great promise that Matthew's Gospel offers us here. With Christ we may go back to the Promised Land. Our future is the heavenly glory of Christ himself. He has already gone before us. He has ascended into heaven itself. The Promised Land is his. There he rules as King of Israel. He is, as the book of Revelation puts it, "the Lion of the tribe of Judah, the Root of David" (5:5). He is the "King of kings and Lord of lords" (19:16). Where he is—the Promised Land, his Father's throne—we will also be. Already he is calling us. Already he is inviting us to come back up, back into the Promised Land. So let's not linger. Let's not stay behind. Instead, let's hear him calling, and let's ascend along with him. He wants for you and me to rule with him (2 Tim. 2:12).

God often calls us precisely when we no longer see a way out of the darkness. He calls us just when we seem to have ended up in Egypt. But when bewilderment and disorientation threaten us, we need to remember these words: "Out of Egypt I called my son." These words remind us of a God whose GPS is reliable. They remind us of our calling. They remind us that our native town is Bethlehem, that we were born there, sons and daughters in Christ. And they remind us that Christ has entered Egypt, has entered our places of sickness, of suffering, of sin, and of death.

"Out of Egypt I called my son." Do these words not tell us of a return to the land of promise? Do they not hold out to us a resurrection from the dead? Do they not assure us of a calling to eternal life? Our God is telling us this morning, "Don't stare yourself blind looking at the corners of the labyrinth. Focus on the GPS that I have given you. It shows you Bethlehem. It shows you Egypt, and, above all, it shows you the end of your journey: the future of the Promised Land itself."

Preacher's Notes

With this sermon, we begin the second section of the book. We move from the happiness that the senses give us (Sensed Happiness) to the happiness that we experience as pilgrims on a journey (Pilgrim Happiness). We embark on this theme first by linking Matthew's interest in geography with the notion of calling, taken from the quotation of Hosea 11:1, "Out of Egypt I called my son." The result is that I center the sermon on the three places of the holy family's journey: Bethlehem as the place from which they start out, Egypt as the place to which they travel, and Israel as the final destiny, the place to which they return. As such, the pattern is that of exit (from Bethlehem to Egypt) and return (from Egypt back to Israel), and so of humiliation and exaltation.

As a result, I make the Matthew 2:15 quotation of Hosea 11:1 the focus of the sermon—a passage that the previous sermon touched on briefly. The preceding narrative is not irrelevant: the magi were also traveling, and their interactions with King Herod were important particularly since Matthew seems to treat Herod as a second Pharaoh, out to destroy the newborn king. I also pay some detailed attention to the earlier quotation in Matthew 2:6 of Micah 5:2, since Bethlehem as the starting point of the journey is a significant marker. Likewise of some importance (though, again, not central) is the middle paragraph, which relates Herod's slaughtering of the innocents—and as such brutally interrupts the flow of the narrative. While I include these contextual matters in the sermon, they are more or less tangential to the main point of the sermon.

This sermon is expository in the sense that exegesis informs every aspect of it. It will hopefully be clear that in preparing these sermons, I carefully analyzed the text. But it will also be evident that, for the most part, my preaching is not strictly expository. First, I do not sequentially follow the biblical account verse by verse or even word by word. Instead, I look for a theologically significant word, theme, or quotation that plays a prominent role in the biblical text. In this sermon, the theme is God calling his son from Egypt. I then link the theme—and other aspects related to it—to other parts of Scripture and to the way it speaks into our lives. Second, although I try to be careful not to impose a doctrinal or theological grid on to the text, I am very aware that Scripture is the church's book and that it speaks into our lives precisely as we come to it with theological questions and as it in turn matures us theologically. Avoiding a verse-by-verse exposition enables me to bring out the theological theme(s) more directly and emphatically.

Few things are as important to a sermon as a clear structure that the congregation can follow. This means that both the central message and the sermon's flow need to be clear. It doesn't necessarily mean that the central message or the sermon title needs to be spelled out explicitly. My central message in this particular sermon is that God gives us, his children in Christ, direction even in our darkest circumstances. Hence the title, "Out of Egypt." I unpack this central message in three steps by following a GPS: Bethlehem, Egypt, and Israel. I use the GPS metaphor as a mnemonic device to enable the congregation to keep track of where we are in the progression of the sermon. The GPS reference also helps the listeners identify with the narrative by reinforcing the sense of traveling along with Joseph, Mary, and the child.

Both Micah 5:2 and Hosea 11:1 function as part of the prophecy-fulfillment scheme that is prominent throughout Matthew's Gospel.[1] The fulfillment of Old Testament prophecies functions in Matthew,

---

1. See Jack D. Kingsbury, *Matthew as Story*, 2nd ed. (Philadelphia: Fortress, 1988), 28, 40–42.

at least in part, to underline that Jesus is the new Israel and the messianic Son of David.[2] Israel and her King are both personified by Jesus. Or as St. Irenaeus would have put it, Jesus recapitulates Israel and David—that is to say, Jesus is the head (*caput*) who retraces, without yielding to temptation, the chain of events that make up the story of Israel and of David.[3] Theologically, this means that we may view the biblical narrative like a set of Russian nesting dolls that we can open as we move from Israel and David, via Christ, to ourselves. In terms of traditional exegetical categories, we can map these three dolls on to the various levels of historical, allegorical, and tropological or moral interpretation. Significantly, these three do not simply follow one another sequentially but fit inside one another. The imagery of a set of Russian nesting dolls is particularly apt because it conveys the idea of sacramentality. The christological fulfillment is not arbitrarily imposed on to the historical narrative but is already present within it. Likewise, the congregation does not have to bridge a two-thousand-year gap to connect to the story: they already are present in the story as they are already in Christ.

In the sermon, I highlight God's love for us as a consequence of being included in the anointing of his sons and daughters with the following: "You and I, we are royalty. Let's pause here for a moment and reflect on it. As God's children, we are royalty." I expressly ask the congregation to pause at this point because the lack of direction that many experience (the sense of being stuck in a labyrinth) is often connected to the way we relate to God: as a distant king who issues commands and treats us according to the way we (hopefully) measure up. Not infrequently, loss of direction in life has to do with a sense of loneliness, a sense of abandonment.[4] The imagery of God as king may

2. See R. T. France, *The Gospel of Matthew*, New International Commentary on the New Testament (Grand Rapids: Eerdmans, 2007), 81, 124–36; Dale C. Allison Jr., *The New Moses: A Matthean Typology* (Minneapolis: Fortress, 1993), 140–65; Jack Dean Kingsbury, "The Title 'Son of David' in Matthew's Gospel," *Journal of Biblical Literature* 95 (1976): 591–602.

3. I discuss Irenaeus' notion of recapitulation in some detail in my book *Violence, Hospitality and the Cross: Reappropriating the Atonement Tradition* (Grand Rapids: Baker Academic, 2004).

4. For a solid pastoral guide to dealing with these issues, see Jean Vanier, *Becoming Human* (1998; repr. New York: Paulist Press, 2008).

well reinforce the notion that he is far removed from where we are, which in turn means we are left to figure out our calling on our own.

This idea of separation between God and the world has become culturally ingrained in us—both in Christian circles and outside them—because we have come to view the created order more as the result of God's command than as the outflow of his love. If creation is strictly the outcome of God's command—a royal edict leading to a self-contained result—then the implication is that God relates to us strictly from a distance as a lawgiver. But if creation is the outflow of his love, then in making the world God gives something of himself. It means that the world, and particularly human beings as his "first-born" children, in some way participates in the very love of God. In our contemporary culture, which has relegated God upstairs, we tend not to treat love as the common bond between God and ourselves. It is important, therefore, to highlight this notion in our preaching. To the extent that people in our churches suffer from lack of direction and loss of calling, preachers need to emphasize that the love of God gives us our identity, and therefore also our way out of the labyrinths of our lives. Scripture makes this task particularly easy since it regards God simultaneously as King and as Father, simultaneously as one who commands and as one who loves. God's calling is a calling in love: "When Israel was a child, I loved him, and out of Egypt I called my son. . . . I led them with cords of kindness, with the bands of love" (Hosea 11:1, 4). When God turns us into royalty, it means we become his sons and daughters: "He [the king] shall cry to me, 'You are my *Father*, my God, and the Rock of my salvation'" (Ps. 89:26).

7

Going Up the Hill

Psalm 24

Psalm 24

A Psalm of David.

¹ The earth is the Lᴏʀᴅ's and the fullness thereof,
   the world and those who dwell therein,
² for he has founded it upon the seas
   and established it upon the rivers.

³ Who shall ascend the hill of the Lᴏʀᴅ?
   And who shall stand in his holy place?
⁴ He who has clean hands and a pure heart,
   who does not lift up his soul to what is false
   and does not swear deceitfully.
⁵ He will receive blessing from the Lᴏʀᴅ
   and righteousness from the God of his salvation.
⁶ Such is the generation of those who seek him,
   who seek the face of the God of Jacob.

⁷ Lift up your heads, O gates!
   And be lifted up, O ancient doors,
   that the King of glory may come in.

[8] Who is this King of glory?
      The LORD, strong and mighty,
      the LORD, mighty in battle!
[9] Lift up your heads, O gates!
      And lift them up, O ancient doors,
      that the King of glory may come in.
[10] Who is this King of glory?
      The LORD of hosts,
      he is the King of glory!

Sunday, June 5, 2011

Ascension hardly seems like a feast to celebrate. Christmas? Yes, God takes on human flesh. Christmas means God with us, Immanuel. Easter? Yes, the crucified Lord has returned from the dead to be with us yet again. Easter means God with us, Immanuel. Pentecost? Yes again, the risen Lord pours out his Spirit on the church. Pentecost too means God with us, Immanuel. But Ascension Day is different. We can identify only too well with the disciples on that mountain, close to Bethany in Galilee. His hands stretched out in blessing, he is taken up into heaven before their very eyes. Before they realize what's going on, a cloud hides the Savior from their sight. "They were gazing into heaven as he went," St. Luke tells us in Acts 1:10. This is the part we identify with, for this is the moment of abandonment. This is the moment when the gains of Easter appear to become undone. How the disciples had rejoiced when their crucified Lord unexpectedly appeared in their midst! He was alive! He had risen from the dead! He was with them yet again. Immanuel, God with us. But now all that appears to have ended. The glorious forty days that Jesus spent in his disciples' midst, they seem like a dream. The hopes of Immanuel, God with us, are dashed yet again. The disciples are left alone, without their Lord.

You and I identify with the disciples in their lonely predicament. If only God were with us. If only the Lord had not ascended into heaven. We would come to Jesus with our questions. We would talk with Jesus about our troubles. We would rely on Jesus for our insecurities. The ascension is about the horrible absence of Jesus. He has left us; we're all alone—still gazing into heaven with the wistful desire that

Jesus would come back. Of course, we do believe that one day we will celebrate his great return, the second coming, the parousia. But for now, we're left alone—alone with our memories (written down for us in Scripture), alone with our hopes (that one day he will return).

And yet—for some strange reason we *celebrate* Ascension Day! Every year we come back to the *celebration* of Ascension Day. Why is it that we look at this day not as a day of mourning but as a day of celebration? Today we're going to turn to Psalm 24 to find an answer to this question. This psalm is the one to which we want to turn because from the very beginning of the church's history, people have looked at this psalm as speaking about the ascension. After all, just look at verse 3: "Who shall ascend the hill of the LORD?" This psalm is about ascension. And look at verse 7: "Lift up your heads, O gates! And be lifted up, O ancient doors, that the King of glory may come in." The gates are the gates of heaven; the doors are the doors of heaven. The King of glory—the risen Lord—enters into his heavenly home. It didn't take long for early Christians to recognize that this psalm is an ascension psalm that speaks of Christ's ascension into heaven.

But before we talk more about Christ's ascension, I would like us to look at the two questions the psalm puts before us. The first one is in verse 3: "Who shall ascend the hill of the LORD?" The second is in verse 8, and it's repeated in verse 10: "Who is this King of glory?" Let's focus first on the question in verse 3: "Who shall ascend the hill of the LORD?" This question is hugely important, for it deals with our deepest desire. We all want to ascend the hill of the Lord. The hill of the Lord is Mount Zion, the mountain on which Solomon built the temple. The hill of the Lord is the place where God lives. That's why the hill of the Lord is not just the temple that Solomon built, but is ultimately God's heavenly sanctuary, for that is where he really lives. The temple on Mount Zion is the place where God came down, the place where God graciously agreed to meet with Israel. That temple was simply a copy of the heavenly temple, the great and glorious sanctuary where God himself is seated on his throne. We all want to go there. We all want to ascend the hill of the Lord.

So, who *shall*, who *may*, ascend the hill of the Lord? Who may go into the temple? Who is going to make it into the heavenly presence of God? The psalmist's answer is crystal clear. He says in verse 4: "He who has clean hands and a pure heart, who does not lift up his soul to what is false and does not swear deceitfully." But the clarity of the answer is also disturbing, isn't it? Who has clean hands? Who has a pure heart? Who never lifts up his soul to what is false, to an idol? Who never swears deceitfully? The image of purity that the psalmist paints for us is a troubling one. At least the priests who served in the temple could become pure through ritual washings, through the sprinkling of blood—a few rituals, and they were clean again. But this psalm is much more rigorous. It doesn't talk about *ritual* cleansing; it speaks of *moral* cleansing—clean hands and a pure heart. All of a sudden we feel again like the disciples gazing into heaven, sensing our loneliness, our abandonment, our inability to ascend the hill of the Lord, our inability to gain our heavenly paradise. Really, it's like the strict teaching of Jesus in the Sermon on the Mount: "Blessed are the pure in heart, for they shall see God" (Matt. 5:8). How is that a Beatitude? It seems more like a curse than a blessing. Likewise this talk about ascension: it seems more like a reason for mourning than for celebrating. Heaven is out of reach if it is only for the pure of heart.

The one thing I cannot tell you this morning is that these clean hands, this pure heart, don't matter all that much. They do. This psalm is the last in a series of ten psalms. The series begins with Psalm 15. Psalms 15–24 are a unit; they belong together. Now, if we flip back to Psalm 15, what do we read there? "O Lord, who shall sojourn in your tent? Who shall dwell on your holy hill?" (15:1). It's the exact same question we have in Psalm 24, isn't it? And what is the answer in Psalm 15? "He who walks blamelessly and does what is right and speaks truth in his heart; who does not slander with his tongue and does no evil to his neighbor, nor takes up a reproach against his friend" (15:2–3). It's basically the same answer, isn't it? A blameless, righteous life is what God is after. Blessed are the pure in heart! They are the ones who may enter into the temple. They are the ones who reach their heavenly destiny. We cannot say that clean hands and pure hearts don't matter all that much. The very framework of this series of psalms tells us this is exactly what it's all about. The very Beatitudes of our Lord tell us this is exactly what it's all about. So there we stand, along with the disciples, gazing into heaven, wanting to go along with Jesus, but feeling left behind.

Yet we can hardly deny that a celebration is going on. Psalm 24 belongs in a victory parade. We don't know precisely how this song functioned in Israel's liturgy, but you probably recall that when the Israelites fought their wars, they would sometimes take the ark of the covenant with them into battle. That didn't always go well. On one occasion, the Philistines beat the Israelites and captured the ark. We read about that in 1 Samuel 4. The ark, the very throne of God, was gone. God's glory, his presence, had departed from Israel (1 Sam. 4:22). The Israelites stood there, mouths wide open, gazing—not up into heaven but toward the Philistine territory. God's presence had disappeared, had left them, and had gone into enemy territory. The sense of abandonment and of loneliness was palpable. How could God leave them so alone? That battle was certainly not followed by a victory parade.

But in this psalm the battle has been successful. There's every reason to sing a victory song. The soldiers are running up Jerusalem's hill victorious, the ark in their midst. They hear the welcoming party—quite possibly a choir of Levites—sing to them from the top of the hill: "Who is this King of glory?" And the warriors, surrounding the ark, respond, "The LORD, strong and mighty, the LORD, mighty in battle!" (Ps. 24:8). Perhaps together they sing, "Lift up your heads, O gates! And lift them up, O ancient doors, that the King of glory may come in" (24:9).

As I said, we don't know the exact liturgical use of this psalm back in the day. But that it was something along these lines is fair to assume. Now we recognize, no doubt, the New Testament message hidden in this text. Now we also know the true answer to that second question in verse 8: "Who is this King of glory?" The King is Jesus himself. After all, ascension is the return of the ark to the heart of the temple, the Most Holy Place. Ascension, therefore, is Jesus returning from battle, receiving an astounding reception in heaven. Ascension is the celebration of Jesus' victory over death. Ascension is King Jesus' victory parade.

Look at him, surrounded by angels—divine warriors—as he makes his way up! "Lift up your heads, O gates! And be lifted up, O ancient doors," the angels cry out (24:7). The heavenly gates swing open. But the doorframe isn't nearly tall enough: "Lift up your heads," the angels shout. The entrance is far too small, far too tiny, for the royal figure who is about to enter. No matter what the size, *any* frame needs readjustment for the King of glory to fit through. This King is beyond all measurement, beyond all size; he needs gates that reach up to infinity. Lift up your heads, O gates of heaven, for the King of glory is returning to his holy dwelling place! It's a remarkable celebration.

We can imagine the welcoming party of angels on the lookout by the heavenly entry asking, "Who is this King of glory?" And other angels, the warriors who are traveling with Jesus toward his heavenly paradise, shouting back: "The LORD, strong and mighty, the LORD, mighty in battle!" And this back and forth is repeated. We find it not just in verse 8, but it comes back again in verse 10. The heavenly celebration is in full swing. The Lord Jesus is returning from the battlefield. He has fought the devil; he has entered the domain of darkness; he has returned victorious! This is indeed a victory song.

But how, we may wonder, can this victory be ours? Victory for Jesus, yes! The angels rejoicing, yes! Christ returning to his paradisal home, yes! But aren't *we* still left gazing into heaven, abandoned and alone? I want us to look once more at the question of verse 3, "Who shall ascend the hill of the LORD?" The answer is, "He who has clean hands and a pure heart" (24:4). How, we wondered earlier, with *our* hands and *our* hearts, can we ascend to the heavenly temple?

But remember, there are two questions—not just the one of verse 3, but also that of verse 8: "Who is this King of glory?" The first question is about ordinary people: "Who shall ascend the hill of the LORD?" The second question is about Christ: "Who is this King of glory?" The two questions seem to be talking about two different individuals. First the psalm talks about us, about our moral character (or lack thereof), in verses 3 and 4. Then suddenly, without any warning, the psalm switches in verse 8 to talking about Christ, about his victory. Isn't this a rather strange turn in the psalm?

Or is it? Let's think this through. What does the first question ask: "Who shall ascend the hill of the LORD?" Who may ascend? Is that question really just about you and me and about our moral character? Or is that first question also about Jesus, our King? Isn't he the one who ascends? And, come to think about it, isn't he the one who has clean hands? Isn't he the one who has a pure heart? When we look for purity of heart, where do we look? Don't we look to Jesus? Isn't he the very definition of purity of heart? Aren't the Beatitudes also basically self-descriptions of Jesus? "Blessed are the pure in heart," he says, "for they shall see God" (Matt. 5:8). But isn't he the one who is pure in heart? Doesn't he always see God? And doesn't he certainly—now that he has ascended to God's right hand—see him face-to-face?

When we look at it this way, both questions—the one in verse 3 as well as the one in verse 8—have a double answer, don't they? Who shall ascend the hill of the Lord? Not just Christians, as long as they are pure of heart, but Jesus himself! And because Jesus gets to ascend the hill of the Lord, you and I, who belong to him, who through the Spirit are part of his body, we too get to ascend the hill of the Lord. It's the same with the second question, "Who is this King of glory?" Yes, of course, it is Jesus. But because the Spirit unites us to Jesus, we are kings and queens in him. We too are kings and queens of glory.

If indeed it were true that Christ had abandoned us, that we were just standing there, wistfully looking up into heaven, we would be in dire straits. It would mean Christ is in heaven and we are on earth. What then would happen to the clean hands and to the pure heart? How would we be clean? How would we be sanctified? But remember what Jesus says in John's Gospel: "It is to your advantage that I go away, for if I do not go away, the Helper will not come to you" (John 16:7). The Helper renews us and unites us with Christ. The Helper gives us clean hands and a pure heart. The Helper secures our ascent to the hill of the Lord. We're not alone; we are not abandoned. We're still united to Christ.

The well-known fourth-century theologian Athanasius beautifully depicts us entering heaven in the presence of Christ:

> As [Christ] himself, who sanctifies all, also says that he sanctifies himself to the Father *for our sakes*, not that the Word may become holy but that he himself may in himself sanctify all of *us*, in like manner we must take the present phrase, "He highly exalted him"—not that he himself needed to be exalted, for he is already the highest, but that he may become righteousness for *us*, and that *we* may be exalted in him and may enter the gates of heaven, which he has also opened for

us, the forerunners saying, "Lift up your gates, O you rulers, and be lifted up, you everlasting doors, and the King of glory shall come in."[1]

What Athanasius is saying is that Christ didn't ascend for his own sake. Everything he did, he did for us. That means his ascension was also for us. He is exalted to the highest place, opening the gates of heaven so we too may enter in.

The idea that on Ascension Day we are left to just stand there, gazing into heaven, turns out to be drastically wrong. Our sense of abandonment and of loneliness is entirely misplaced. We are not standing here on earth gazing into heaven. Because Christ is our head and we are his body, we are already in heaven along with Christ. Isn't that what St. Paul says, "[God] raised us up with him [Christ] and seated us with him in the heavenly places in Christ Jesus" (Eph. 2:6)? Today you and I are seated with Christ in the heavenly places. The ascension isn't just about the ascension of Jesus, of some other person, who sadly has left us behind gazing up into heaven. No, the ascension of Jesus is our ascension too. God has seated us with him in the heavenly places. We have been raised to new life. We too have gone up into heaven. We too have heard the angels welcome us with, "Who shall ascend the hill of the Lord?" and "Who is this King of glory?" For us too the ancient doors are forced to lift their gates—for it is along with our infinite Lord that we have entered into the heavenly places. There we too are already allowed to see the face of the God of Jacob.

The shift in perspective is profound. We used to think of ourselves as being here on earth, first and foremost. Sure, all along we knew that we are pilgrims on a journey to the heavenly places, a journey one day to see God face-to-face. And all of this is true. We are still looking forward to the return of Christ and to the resurrection of the dead. But now that we've read Psalm 24 and have seen how it speaks at its heart about us, along with Christ, entering into the heavenly places, now we know that with him we are already at God's right hand. There is a sense in which our pilgrimage has already reached

1. Quoted in Craig A. Blaising and Carmen S. Hardin, eds., *Psalms 1–50*, Ancient Christian Commentary on Scripture (Downers Grove, IL: InterVarsity, 2008), 189 (emphasis added).

its destination. What is more, if it is true that the earthly temple of Psalm 24 is just a copy of the heavenly one, then first and foremost we are in heaven, and our place here on earth is secondary. Faith says that who and where we are is not determined by what we see but by our identity in Christ. Already we belong to him. And in him we are already allowed to see the face of God. So we don't mourn Ascension Day. We celebrate it. The reason is as simple as it is astonishing. In and with Jesus, we have a new life, a heavenly life. Our life is the life of Christ. Ascension Day too means God with us, Immanuel.

Preacher's Notes

Throughout the centuries, Psalm 24 has been associated with the ascension of Christ. It is quite interesting to read patristic expositions on this text. In the fourth century, Gregory of Nyssa provides the first historical evidence of a distinct liturgical celebration of the ascension in a sermon dealing with Psalms 23 and 24.[2] He explains that God has come to earth in Christ, and he asks, "Why then his coming? To take you out of the depths of sin and to lead you onto the royal mountain, using the life of virtue as a chariot toward the impenetrable place."[3] Gregory describes with obvious delight the angelic dialogue that takes place when Christ ascends to heaven. The heavenly angels, St. Gregory explains, do not recognize the king at first, since he is clothed in the "dirty garment of our life," which has turned red with blood.[4] But

2. The sermon, *On the Ascension of Christ*, has not been translated into English. The Greek text can be found in *In ascensionem Christi oratio*, in *Gregorii Nysseni Opera*, vol. 9, ed. Ernestus Gebhardt (Leiden: Brill, 1992), 323–27. For a French translation, see *Homélie sur l'Ascension*, in *Grégoire de Nysse: Le Christ pascal: Cinq homélies pascales, homélie sur l'Ascension, traité "Quand le Fils aura tout soumis,"* trans. Christian Bouchet and Mariette Canévet, ed. A.-G. Hamman (Paris: Migne, 1994), 101–6.

For the assertion that this sermon is the first evidence of a distinct liturgical celebration of the ascension, see Jean Daniélou, "La Chronologie des sermons de Grégoire de Nysse," *Recherches de science religieuse* 29 (1955): 370–72; Daniélou, "Grégoire de Nysse et l'origine de la fête de l'Ascension," in *Kyriakon: Festschrift Johannes Quasten*, vol. 2, ed. Patrick Granfield and Josef A. Jungmann (Münster: Aschendorff, 1970), 663–66.

3. Gregory of Nyssa, *In ascensionem Christi*, 325.7–10.

4. Ibid., 326.22–23.

other angels accompany Jesus on his ascent, and they make clear to the heavenly angels that he is the "Lord of hosts" (Ps. 24:10), "who has recapitulated [*anakephalaiōsas*] all things in himself, who ranks first among all things, who has restored all things [*apokatastēsas ta panta*] to the first creation."[5]

Gregory has his own unique approach to this psalm, as he gives expression to his universalist notion that Christ restores all things to their initial paradisal state. But Gregory roots this belief in his rather traditional conviction, derived historically from Irenaeus in the late second century, that Christ recapitulates (or retraces) all things and so brings about redemption. Gregory's reflections on the angelic welcome, which Christ receives in heaven on his ascension, are also quite commonplace. To be sure, different interpreters have elaborated in a variety of ways on the details regarding the roles that the angels play in connection with Christ's ascension. This is hardly surprising, seeing that even in historical exegesis the question of the identity of the various characters in the liturgical dialogue allows for a variety of responses. One needs only to turn to a couple of historical commentaries on this psalm to recognize that a variety of approaches are possible.[6]

It is perhaps not so much that different preachers have reconstructed the dialogue in Psalm 24 in different ways that is curious to contemporary readers. Much more controversial is the identification of the King as Christ, of the King's entry into Jerusalem as Christ's ascension, and of some of the (originally Levitical?) speakers as angels. My approach to this psalm stands in obvious continuity with patristic and medieval readings. The basis for this approach lies in the assumption that the psalms must be read sacramentally, so that Christ is seen as present under the surface of the text. A sacramental reading allows us to see the real presence of Jesus' ascension in Psalm 24.

5. Ibid., 327.1–3. Gregory is echoing Eph. 1:10 and Acts 3:21.
6. Commentaries commonly refer to the difficulties and disagreements in trying to determine the original historical context of Ps. 24. See, e.g., Hans-Joachim Kraus, *Psalms 1–59: A Commentary*, trans. Hilton C. Oswald (Minneapolis: Augsburg, 1988), 312; A. A. Anderson, *The Book of Psalms*, vol. 1 (Greenwood, SC: Attic Press, 1972), 200–201; Peter C. Craigie, *Psalms 1–50*, Word Biblical Commentary 19 (Waco: Word, 1983), 211.

This christological reading in no way undermines historical investigation into how this psalm may have functioned in ancient Jewish liturgies. After all, in my sermon I also make historical assumptions about the use of the ark of the covenant in liturgical processions when the Israelites returned from the battlefield. To be sure, the caveat is that by delving into the history behind the text, or into the way the text functioned in Jewish liturgies, we end up with reconstructions of what *may* have been the case, with varying degrees of likelihood. Such reconstructions typically do not provide absolute certainty.[7] More important, they are but the first stage of the interpretive process. As an initial step, they help us to approximate what the text *meant*, but they don't tell us what the text *means*. That said, reconstructing the surface-level meaning of the psalm is profoundly helpful, not in the least because this activity also opens the way to the sacramental reality that the psalm makes present.

I make the exegetical move from history to spirit on a christological basis. Following the coming of Christ, we read the Old Testament, including Psalm 24, in the light of his coming. So, patristic exegesis of this psalm (as well as my sermon on it) proceeds on the basis of Philip's approach, which we looked at in the first sermon (cf. Acts 8:35). Beginning with Psalm 24, we preach the good news about Jesus. Once we identify, along with Hebrews 8:5 and 9:23–24, the heavenly temple as the original and the earthly as its copy, it becomes difficult not to read Psalm 24 in light of Christ's ascension into heaven. And once we have made this step, it hardly seems out of place to regard the soldiers and the welcoming Levites as copying the angelic hosts.

As we have noted before, a key question is how we bring this sacramental exegesis into the sermon. Answering this question requires careful reflection, since many of today's listeners may not be used to this kind of exegesis. In this sermon I do this by raising the question of how we can treat Ascension Day as a day of celebration rather than a day of mourning, which means I do not start with an explanation of Psalm 24. Instead, I first ask the congregation to think of Ascension Day, and only when the key question regarding

---

7. It is commonly accepted, however, that in the postexilic period Levites would have sung Ps. 24 on Sundays to accompany the daily temple sacrifices. See J. A. Smith, "Which Psalms Were Sung in the Temple?," *Music & Letters* 71 (1990): 167–86, at 169.

Christ's ascension has been placed at the center, do I then take the congregation to a couple of key moments in the psalm (particularly vv. 3 and 8), so that they can see the topic of the sermon reflected in it. In the next paragraph I then draw attention to how the earthly temple always functioned as a mirror of the larger cosmos, with God's throne in heaven having a counterpart in the ark in the Most Holy Place.[8] My experience in preaching is that once some of these basic cosmological identification markers are in place, most people in the pew will no longer experience the corresponding sacramental exegesis as a stretch.

While my sermon focuses on the ascension, it is hardly the only point of theological significance in the psalm. The psalmist begins in the first two verses with the basic affirmation that God is the Creator and the earth belongs to him. He deals with ascension in the context of the doctrine of creation. It is quite possible to preach a sermon on Psalm 24 that focuses on the relationship between creation and redemption. It is important, however, that a sermon be focused, and in this instance I choose to zero in on the believer's identification with Christ in his ascension. It is this key christological event, after all, that allows me to dwell on some of the hermeneutical issues that I want to bring to the fore, and it is our union with Christ that allows me to reflect on the question of how we can enter into God's presence without being perfect in and of ourselves.

Without using doctrinal theological categories, I also call attention to atonement theology, in particular to the *Christus Victor* theme. As Paul states in Colossians 2:15, Christ has done battle with the powers of darkness, and in that light, this sermon follows Psalm 24 in depicting his ascension as a victory march. However, it is not my intention in the sermon to limit the atonement to the *Christus Victor* model. On my understanding, a full-orbed picture of Christ's work of redemption emerges only when we combine the warfare model of atonement with the other two main traditional models, that of

---

8. For a wonderful explanation of the functioning of temple imagery, as well as ancient biblical cosmology more broadly, see Robin A. Parry, *The Biblical Cosmos: A Pilgrim's Guide to the Weird and Wonderful World of the Bible* (Eugene, OR: Cascade, 2014).

satisfaction and moral influence.[9] In my sermon I indirectly allude to these models through the quotation from Athanasius focusing on our purity and exaltation in Christ. This quotation makes clear that it is precisely *by identifying with us* that Christ gains the victory and that he also enables our ascension or exaltation with him to heavenly glory. The theme of *Christus Victor*, while certainly important and clearly a central focus in this psalm, does not on its own explain our redemption from sin. Redemption is anchored in our ascent with Christ into the heavenly places.

9. See Hans Boersma, *Violence, Hospitality, and the Cross: Reappropriating the Atonement Tradition* (Grand Rapids: Baker Academic, 2004).

8

God's Own Rest

Hebrews 3:7–4:13

Hebrews 3:7–4:13

> [7] Therefore, as the Holy Spirit says,
> "Today, if you hear his voice,
> [8] do not harden your hearts as in the rebellion,
>   on the day of testing in the wilderness,
> [9] where your fathers put me to the test
>   and saw my works for forty years.
> [10] Therefore I was provoked with that generation,
>   and said, 'They always go astray in their heart;
> they have not known my ways.'
> [11] As I swore in my wrath,
>   'They shall not enter my rest.'"

[12] Take care, brothers, lest there be in any of you an evil, unbelieving heart, leading you to fall away from the living God. [13] But exhort one another every day, as long as it is called "today," that none of you may be hardened by the deceitfulness of sin. [14] For we have come to share in Christ, if indeed we hold our original confidence firm to the end. [15] As it is said,

> "Today, if you hear his voice,
> do not harden your hearts as in the rebellion."

16 For who were those who heard and yet rebelled? Was it not all those who left Egypt led by Moses? **17** And with whom was he provoked for forty years? Was it not with those who sinned, whose bodies fell in the wilderness? **18** And to whom did he swear that they would not enter his rest, but to those who were disobedient? **19** So we see that they were unable to enter because of unbelief.

4:1 Therefore, while the promise of entering his rest still stands, let us fear lest any of you should seem to have failed to reach it. **2** For good news came to us just as to them, but the message they heard did not benefit them, because they were not united by faith with those who listened. **3** For we who have believed enter that rest, as he has said,

> "As I swore in my wrath,
> 'They shall not enter my rest,'"

although his works were finished from the foundation of the world. **4** For he has somewhere spoken of the seventh day in this way: "And God rested on the seventh day from all his works." **5** And again in this passage he said,

> "They shall not enter my rest."

6 Since therefore it remains for some to enter it, and those who formerly received the good news failed to enter because of disobedience, **7** again he appoints a certain day, "Today," saying through David so long afterward, in the words already quoted,

> "Today, if you hear his voice,
> do not harden your hearts."

8 For if Joshua had given them rest, God would not have spoken of another day later on. **9** So then, there remains a Sabbath rest for the people of God, **10** for whoever has entered God's rest has also rested from his works as God did from his.
11 Let us therefore strive to enter that rest, so that no one may fall by the same sort of disobedience. **12** For the word of God is living and active, sharper than any two-edged sword, piercing to the division of soul and of spirit, of joints and of marrow, and discerning the thoughts and intentions of the heart. **13** And no creature is hidden from his sight, but all are naked and exposed to the eyes of him to whom we must give account.

Sunday, August 3, 2014

The stakes couldn't be higher. We either cross into the Promised Land, entering everlasting rest, or we turn back, ending up dead in the wilderness. The Israelites were hoping for rest, but they ended up dead in the wilderness. This morning, therefore, we have no time for niceties. We need to perk up our ears and listen right from the start. Eternity is at stake in this passage—as it is elsewhere in the Letter to the Hebrews. This passage makes us sit up and take note.

Our passage is not the easiest one. It is a complicated account, with many layers, numerous allusions to Old Testament stories, and many quotations from Old Testament texts. So we have some hard work to do. But with so much at stake, we dare not be careless; the stakes are worth every bit of our effort in scrutinizing this difficult text. We want to make sure we actually enter the land of rest to which we've been traveling.

Though it's true that these are difficult chapters, in an important sense our passage is actually quite straightforward. It simply tells us this: the one thing that counts is rest. It always was about rest. It is still about rest, and it always will be about rest. The gospel message, the good news, is about rest. It's as simple as Jesus saying in Matthew 11: "Come to me, all who labor and are heavy laden, and I will give you rest. Take my yoke upon you, and learn from me, for I am gentle and lowly in heart, and you will find rest for your souls. For my yoke is easy, and my burden is light" (vv. 28–30).

This morning, then, I want us to *hear* the good news of Jesus in Hebrews 3 and 4. I want us to *see* the rest that he offers. Both senses are involved—hearing and seeing, ears and eyes. So, let's do what this passage in Hebrews asks us to do: imagine ourselves among the Israelites in the wilderness of Paran, south of the Promised Land, craning our necks as we see the twelve spies return. With our own ears we hear them reporting good news: "We came to the land to which you sent us. It flows with milk and honey, and this is its fruit" (Num. 13:27). And with our own eyes we see the cluster of grapes as well as the pomegranates and figs that the spies carry back (13:23).

But then the whole thing unravels. Ten of the spies are afraid of the strong giants in the land. They bring a bad report of the land (13:32).

Joshua and Caleb give good news—the other ten, bad news. No one around us dares to take a cue from the wonderful things they've just heard and seen. Only Joshua and Caleb are willing to go up, into the hill country, into the land of rest. The people begin to grumble; they rebel. They have heard the good news; they have seen the fruit of the land of rest. But they refuse to enter; they dare not move into enemy territory. It is at this point that God swears an oath (14:21): only Joshua and Caleb will be allowed to enter the Promised Land. All those who grumbled will wander in the desert for an additional forty years, and the entire generation will die in the wilderness (14:29–30).

That is the story we're supposed to call to mind when we read Hebrews 3 and 4. It's a story that made a huge impact on the collective mind-set of the people of Israel. After all, they had arrived—almost. They stood at the edge of the Promised Land. They heard the good news, saw the beautiful fruit of the land of rest. And then they backed down . . . with disastrous results. This event carved itself into the psyche of God's people. Israel's poets wrote about this momentous event, and they treated it as a lesson never to forget. That's what the songwriter of Psalm 95 does, the psalm that is quoted in our passage:

> Today, if you hear his voice,
> do not harden your hearts as in the rebellion,
>   on the day of testing in the wilderness,
> where your fathers put me to the test
>   and saw my works for forty years.
> Therefore I was provoked with that generation,
> and said, "They always go astray in their heart;
>   they have not known my ways."
> As I swore in my wrath,
>   "They shall not enter my rest."
>   (Psalm 95:7–11 as quoted in Hebrews 3:7–11)

Notice that one little word plunked in the middle of this psalm—the word "therefore." "*Therefore* I was provoked with that generation" (Heb. 3:10). The reason for failing to enter the rest was lack of trust. The reason people died in the wilderness rather than enter the rest was that they hardened their hearts. They refused to follow up on the promise of God.

It's not that God is not willing to take us. It's not that we don't know whether the land of rest is actually there, also for us, beyond the wilderness. There's no way God is two-faced in his promise to us. No, God led the Israelites all the way to the Promised Land, all the way to the land of rest. And he was ready to take them in. But *the people* put God to the test. *They* hardened their hearts. Hebrews 4 is explicit: they heard the gospel, the good news. They weren't able to enter because they didn't believe, because they disobeyed (Heb. 4:2, 6).

I'm not suggesting to you that the message this morning isn't a pointed one. These two chapters certainly make us take note. They won't let us sit back and relax. Obviously, the story of Numbers 13 and 14, the song of Psalm 95, and the warnings of Hebrews 3 and 4 are meant to pry open the deepest intentions of our hearts. But what they don't do is present a God who is arbitrary in character, a God we can't count on, a God who might strike anyone at any time. It is not *God's* faithfulness that's in question in this story; it is *our* faithfulness that's in question. We are so easily tempted to put God in the dock, questioning his faithfulness, disputing his goodness, doubting his peaceful intentions. But when we really look at what took place on the outer edge of the Promised Land, we soon realize: *we* sit in the dock, not God. *Our* faithfulness, not God's, is in doubt. It is we, not God, who are two-faced about entering his rest.

Let's zero in a little more closely on that promise of rest. Several times now, I've talked both about the Promised Land and about the land of rest as if they were one and the same. And in a real sense, they are. Both Psalm 95 and Hebrews talk about the land of Canaan as the land that the Israelites should have entered but didn't. As God said, "I swore in my wrath, 'They shall not enter my rest'" (Ps. 95:11; Heb. 3:11). That's the same as saying, "They shall not enter the Promised Land." Still, the word "rest" says more than the word "Canaan." Rest isn't *just* another name for the country that God promised to give to the Israelites. To be sure, that's one meaning of the word "rest." But rest is more than just Canaan.

All along, as the Israelites have been making their journey to Canaan, we've heard about rest. When God revealed himself to Moses in that famous story, causing his face to shine, he promised Moses that his very own presence would accompany the Israelites on their wilderness journey. He said, "My presence will go with you, and I will give you *rest*" (Exod. 33:14). God promised to give Moses rest. And Moses, in turn, held out that same promise to the Israelites just before they finally entered the land: "You have not as yet come to the *rest* and to the inheritance that the LORD your God is giving you," he said to the people. And then he went on, "But when you go over the Jordan and live in the land that the LORD your God is giving you to inherit, [he will give] you *rest* from all your enemies around, so that you live in safety" (Deut. 12:9–10). Here, rest indeed means Canaan. But "rest" is not *just* a word to identify a country on the map. "Rest" means that God will protect his people. "Rest" means that enemies won't be able to harass them. "Rest" means they'll live in a situation of genuine happiness.

Joshua was supposed to lead his people into this rest, into this situation of happiness. But there's a problem when we compare what the Old Testament says Joshua did and what Hebrews says Joshua did. After Moses dies, Joshua explicitly reminds the people of the promise of rest that Moses has made. He does that right off the bat in Joshua 1:13: "Remember the word that Moses the servant of the LORD commanded you, saying, 'The LORD your God is providing you a place of *rest* and will give you this land.'" When we get toward the end of the book in Joshua 21:44, we see that Moses' words have come true. "And the LORD gave them *rest* on every side just as he had sworn to their fathers. Not one of all their enemies had withstood them, for the LORD had given all their enemies into their hands." The enemies are defeated; God has given rest to his people. What is so strange about this is that the book of Hebrews says the exact opposite. It says that Joshua did *not* give rest to the Israelites. "For," it says in Hebrews 4:8, "if Joshua *had* given them rest, God would not have spoken of another day later on." What is going on here? Which book has it right—Joshua or Hebrews? Did Joshua give the people rest or did he not?

Actually, both are true. It all depends on what we mean by "rest." Hebrews 3 and 4 speaks of rest not just in one way but in no fewer than three ways, though all three are connected. Now, this is going to be a bit of work, looking at these three meanings of rest. But the payoff will be substantial. By going through this we'll come to realize how

Joshua can say that the Lord gave the Israelites rest, while Hebrews says he did not. But we'll find out something even more important: the God we meet in Numbers 13 and 14, in Psalm 95, and in Hebrews 3 and 4 is a God we can count on. Looking at the three meanings of the word "rest," we'll see how thoroughly gracious, how completely dependable, how deeply loving God truly is.

Perhaps I can best explain by quoting one of the great preachers of the early church, John Chrysostom, also known as John Golden Mouth, so-called because of the amazing sermons he preached to his fourth-century congregation. Here is what Chrysostom says:

> [Hebrews] says that there are "three" rests: one, that of the sabbath, in which God rested from works; the second, that of Palestine, in which, when the Jews had entered, they would be at rest from their hardships and labors; the third, that which is rest indeed, the kingdom of heaven, where those who obtain it do indeed rest from their labors and troubles.[1]

There are three rests in this passage, Chrysostom says: Sabbath, Palestine, and heaven. He is exactly right. Leaving the Sabbath rest aside for a moment, so far we have mostly talked about the second rest, that of Palestine. And although an entire generation missed out on it, Joshua did give his people rest if by "rest" we mean that second rest, Palestine. But he did not give them rest if by "rest" we mean the third rest that Hebrews mentions. Joshua did not give the people the rest of heaven itself.

Now, there is one more step we need to take—and then we'll get a glimpse of how gracious God's plans for his people really are. We all know that the three rests follow one another, one after the other, on a historical time line. First we have God's rest, when he rests on the Sabbath. That's at the very beginning of the biblical story, in Genesis 2:2. Hebrews talks about this rest in 4:4, "For [God] has somewhere spoken of the seventh day in this way: 'And God rested on the seventh day from all his works.'" This is God's very own rest,

1. John Chrysostom, *On the Epistle to the Hebrews* 6.1, as quoted in Erik M. Heen and Philip D. W. Krey, eds., *Hebrews*, Ancient Christian Commentary on Scripture (Downers Grove, IL: InterVarsity, 2005), 60.

the Sabbath rest, at the very beginning of the Bible. Next we have the rest of the Promised Land. Even though it was postponed for forty years, eventually Joshua led the Israelites to rest in the land of Canaan. Much of Hebrews 3 and 4 is about this second rest. Lastly, the third rest is the rest of the eternal kingdom, of heaven. That's the "rest" of 4:9: "So then, there remains a Sabbath rest for the people of God." It's the "rest" we find again two verses down: "Let us therefore strive to enter that rest, so that no one may fall by the same sort of disobedience" (4:11). You and I, Hebrews is saying, should do everything we can to enter the third rest, the rest of the kingdom of heaven.

Our passage links these three rests on a historical time line. But what Hebrews says is this: there is another, even more important way that these three rests are connected—not horizontally, as three points on a time line, but vertically, linking up to heaven, to Jesus himself. Note this small but important detail, the word "my." "They shall not enter *my* rest" (3:11). It speaks of *God's own rest*, which he took after his work of creation back in Genesis 2. "*My* rest," God says. But how does it make sense to say that the Israelites listening to the twelve spies weren't allowed to enter *God's* rest, the rest of Genesis 2? It almost seems like Hebrews is mixing up the second rest (that of Palestine) with the first (that of Sabbath in Genesis). And not only that, but Hebrews seems also to mix up heaven's rest with the rest in Genesis. Just look at Hebrews 4:6: "It remains for some to enter it." Here, "it" is *God's* rest! The Israelites in Joshua's day, and you and I today, are we supposed to enter God's own rest that he enjoyed back in Genesis 2?

That's exactly right! What God wants for us—for Joshua and the Israelites, for you and me—is to enter into *his own* rest. He wants us to join the rest of Genesis 2. Each one of the six creation days concludes with the words, "And there was evening and there was morning," such-and-such a day. We read that refrain six times. But we don't read it after day seven, after the Sabbath day. All we read is this: "So God blessed the seventh day and made it holy, because on it God rested from all his work that he had done in creation" (Gen. 2:3). What Hebrews seems to be saying is that unlike the other six days, God's Sabbath rest never came to an end; it's still there. God's

Sabbath rest is like a picture of heaven with an open door: it is always there for people to join.

In some ways, the Israelites joined the rest of God whenever they stopped work on Friday evening and took a day off. Their day off allowed them to share in God's own rest. It was much the same when Joshua brought the people to the Promised Land, to the land of rest. That Promised Land was a way of sharing in God's own rest. And guess what happens when we enter the kingdom of heaven? We'll come to share in God's own rest like never before!

That's how utterly gracious and kind our God is. He is like the father of the prodigal son, opening wide his arms, and saying to us: "I want you in my house. We'll kill the fattened calf. We'll put on the tunes and start dancing. All that is mine is yours." God shares with us everything that is his. He even shares with us his very own rest, his very own happiness. The happiness of God's rest is not only waiting for us at the end of the story—horizontally. God's rest is always there—vertically—up above. God's rest is heaven itself. And heaven is open to us. It's been open ever since Genesis 2. Throughout the story, God's arms are outstretched. God wants to share with us nothing less than the infinite happiness of his very own life.

Sometimes I think we need to look up much more than we do. Much of the time we're looking ahead of ourselves. We've got plans to make. We've got projects to map out. We've got programs to finish. There's nothing wrong with any of that. But this passage is quite clear. We need to "strive to enter" God's rest (Heb. 4:11). And that means faith not only looks forward; it also looks up—for it's by looking up that we see Jesus. He is the one who has gone ahead of us. He has already passed through the heavens (4:14). It is when we look up that we see Jesus. And it is when we share in him (3:14) that we share in God's very own rest—"Come to me, all who labor and are heavy laden, and I will give you rest" (Matt. 11:28).

Yes, it is true, this is a sharp passage. It tells us that when we stand in front of the Promised Land, we will either be bold and enter the rest, or we'll turn back and die in the wilderness. Eternity itself is at stake in this passage. But the two possible outcomes do not mean that God is two-faced. You and I, *we* are often two-faced. *We* often draw back. *We* often don't follow. *We* often rebel. God is the opposite.

He is a dependable God. He is a God of grace. He is a God who preaches good news. He is a God who reaches down to us with a cluster of grapes in his hand, hoping we'll take it and enter his rest. From that first Sabbath in Genesis, God has opened his life to us that we may enter his heavenly rest. So let's look up. Let's look "to Jesus, the founder and perfecter of our faith" (Heb. 12:2), for he is God's rest, and God has no deeper desire than to share him forever with us.

Preacher's Notes

This sermon is one in which I do not explicitly address the hermeneutical question of how we should read the Old Testament. I do, however, closely follow Hebrews 3 and 4 as an interpretive model, and outline for the congregation how Hebrews reads the Old Testament. The basic hermeneutical lesson that I convey is that biblical interpretation is participatory in character, though I avoid participation language. To show this, I mention the Christian Platonist expression "sharing in Christ" (*metochoi tou Christou*, Heb. 3:14). This language of participation or sharing reminds us that in this letter, not only horizontal, historical categories matter (though they certainly do!) but also vertical, participatory notions. The rest is waiting for us both at the end of history—the eschatological new covenant of Hebrews 8—and in the heavenly reality of the eternal tabernacle of chapter 9. Hebrews uses historical and participatory categories for the same purpose. The happiness of our eternal rest, Christ himself, is found both by looking ahead and by looking up. These two ways of speaking are combined in Hebrews 10:1, which states that "the law has but a shadow [*skian*] of the good things to come instead of the true form [*eikona*] of these [heavenly] realities." The eternal rest, the "true form" of the Old Testament "shadows," is Christ himself.

Hermeneutically, this means the true form of Christ was sacramentally present in the shadow of the Old Testament. God's own rest of Genesis 2:2 turns out to be identical to that of Christ (Matt. 11:28–30) and identical also to the eschatological Sabbath rest that still remains (Heb. 4:9). What is more, the rest of Canaan, as well as the weekly Jewish Sabbath celebration, were a sharing or participating in the eternal Sabbath rest of God. The doctrine of divine simplicity says that the being of God is identical to each of the characteristics or attributes we may predicate of him. This would appear to entail that God's Sabbath rest is God himself. When God in Christ offers us his rest, he gives himself to us. We are allowed to join the divine life, to participate in God's rest.

This doctrine of participation implies nothing less than the deification or *theosis* that theologians throughout the tradition have affirmed.[2] In line with my reticence to turn sermons into doctrinal treatises, I steer clear not just of the term *deification* but also of the theological issues that it entails. Let me simply comment here that the doctrine of deification is important in that it allows us to avoid a one-sided emphasis on juridical and forensic categories in speaking about our relationship with God. Much as in the previous sermon, so in this one I focus on the love of God who in Christ shares his very own life with us. While God is transcendent and reaches infinitely beyond his creatures, at the same time he is "actually not far from each one of us" since "in him we live and move and have our being" (Acts 17:27–28). Seeing that in contemporary Western society we have increasingly removed God from our day-to-day lives, recent retrievals of the theologies of participation and deification are particularly noteworthy and encouraging.[3]

The preacher faces a difficult task in connection with this passage. It is important that the congregation be addressed not just intellectually so that they follow what goes on in the text, but also affectively. If the Letter to the Hebrews invites and encourages us to enter into the rest of the heavenly tabernacle—displaying for us the immense grace and goodness of God—the preacher has the corresponding

2. For helpful introductions, see Norman Russell, *Fellow Workers with God: Orthodox Thinking on Theosis* (New York: St Vladimir's Seminary Press, 2009); Michael J. Christensen and Jeffery A. Wittung, eds., *Partakers of the Divine Nature: The History and Development of Deification in the Christian Traditions* (Grand Rapids: Baker Academic, 2007).

3. See J. Todd Billings, *Union with Christ: Reframing Theology and Ministry for the Church* (Grand Rapids: Baker Academic, 2011); Billings, *Calvin, Participation, and the Gift: The Activity of Believers in Union with Christ* (Oxford: Oxford University Press, 2007); Robert Letham, *Union with Christ: In Scripture, History, and Theology* (Phillipsburg, NJ: P&R, 2011).

task of conveying a sense of the desirability of entering into this rest. Doing so is not easy in light of the complexity of the passage. The many allusions to and quotations from the Old Testament, the intricate theological argumentation, and the underlying participatory framework at play in this epistle render the preacher's task particularly challenging.

I try to deal with this challenge in several ways. First, I do not try to explain everything in the passage. I omit any mention of the Israelites' grumbling at Massah and Meribah, which Psalm 95:8 (and Heb. 3:8, 15; 4:7) takes from Exodus 17:1–7. I also leave out the theologically significant language of "today" (*sēmeron*), which this passage borrows from Psalm 95:7. And I ignore the relationship between grace and works. While my sermon highlights the theme of divine grace, the passage is primarily exhortatory, and the relationship between work and rest (both God's and ours) is a fruitful theme for additional reflection.

Second, more than in most sermons, I try to reassure my audience by explaining that the Hebrews passage is actually quite straightforward since it's all about rest. I also hold out a payoff for our effort in listening as we figure out how the three "rests" relate to one another, and hint that the intellectual work is almost done (saying "there is one more step we need to take"). While eschewing any and all patronizing attitudes, it is nonetheless important for the preacher to convey an awareness of and sympathy with the difficult task that the listeners have as they try to follow along.

Finally, I try to build the structure of the sermon as clearly as possible—always an important thing to do but particularly when dealing with a passage like this. My sermon is bracketed by the issue of the high stakes at play in this passage. I approach this issue by taking three steps in the course of the sermon, pointing out that (1) God's punishment of his people comes only in reaction to their rejection of his gracious offer of rest; (2) God's Sabbath rest is always open for us to enter; and (3) God offers us his life through our sharing it in Jesus.

I also try to take one step at a time in dealing with the complexity of the meaning of "rest." I first explain that "rest" refers to the land of Canaan and involves a situation of genuine happiness. Next, I touch on the apparent contradiction between Joshua 21:44 and Hebrews 4:8:

Did Joshua lead the people into the rest or did he not? This problem functions as a bridge to the explanation of three distinct (though related) rests in Hebrews. As the final step, I explain that the three rests relate not only horizontally (as historically distinct moments) but also vertically (by way of participation).

While I try to achieve structural transparency, such clarity always carries the danger that the sermon may sound like a mechanical listing of various items to which the congregation does not feel connected. There is no magical solution to this difficulty, though it helps to locate the reader in the events that the text describes. For example, we imagined ourselves among the Israelites in the wilderness. "What God wants for us—for Joshua and the Israelites, for you and me—is for us to enter into *his own* rest." The repeated references to the abundance of divine grace are important in this regard: they help God's people to find their way through the various textual layers this passage uses to deliver the offer of rest.

Heavenly Happiness

*U*p to this point, we have found ourselves surrounded by the realities of time and place. We asked questions such as, "How do we deal with the objects that we access through the senses?" (part 1, "Sensed Happiness"), and, "What does it mean to embark on a pilgrimage that takes us from where we are to where we want be?" (part 2, "Pilgrim Happiness"). We noted that happiness can be found throughout. From beginning to end, Christians find joy in the life God gives them. At the same time, the notion of pilgrimage implies that the end determines the character of the journey, a journey that takes us out of Egypt, leads us up the hill, and brings us into rest.

In part 3, we arrive at our destination. We come to heaven itself. To be sure, Scripture speaks of our future destiny as a "new heaven and a new earth" (Rev. 21:1), not just as heaven. Nonetheless, all our speech of the hereafter, including Revelation 21, is metaphorical because the reality far outweighs our earthly imagination. Thus to say that our destiny is heavenly happiness is not literally to indicate a place we can find on a map. Instead, the phrase's two words form a tautology: both speak of the reality of Christ in whom we find the final purpose of life. As we will see in these sermons, heavenly happiness comes to us in the blessed figure of the man (Ps. 1). It is beyond our earthly imagining (Luke 20). And it comes with the fitting attire of white wedding garments (Rev. 22).

9

Happiness in Christ

Psalm 1

Psalm 1

¹Blessed is the man
  who walks not in the counsel of the wicked,
nor stands in the way of sinners,
  nor sits in the seat of scoffers;
²but his delight is in the law of the Lᴏʀᴅ,
  and on his law he meditates day and night.

³He is like a tree
  planted by streams of water
that yields its fruit in its season,
  and its leaf does not wither.
In all that he does, he prospers.
⁴The wicked are not so,
  but are like chaff that the wind drives away.

⁵Therefore the wicked will not stand in the judgment,
  nor sinners in the congregation of the righteous;
⁶for the Lᴏʀᴅ knows the way of the righteous,
  but the way of the wicked will perish.

Sunday, November 2, 2008

Happiness is the one thing in life that everyone is after. Whether
you're a Christian, a Muslim, or a Hindu; a believer, or an unbeliever,
it doesn't matter. Happiness is the one thing in life that everyone
hopes for. One of the interesting things we find when we read the
great Christian theologians over the centuries is that they're pretty
much unanimous on this. Throughout the Christian tradition, people
agree that our one purpose in life, the one desire for which we all
aim, is happiness. "The goal of a life in accord with virtue," insists
a fourth-century theologian by the name of Gregory of Nyssa, "is
happiness."[1] "Is not the happy life that which all desire, which indeed
no one fails to desire?" St. Augustine asks in the *Confessions*.[2] Happiness, Thomas Aquinas says, "is called man's supreme good, because
it is the attainment or enjoyment of the supreme good."[3] John Calvin
agrees. The enjoyment of God's benefits, "clear and pure from every
vice . . . is the [pinnacle] of happiness," explains the reformer from
Geneva.[4] Each of these theologians unabashedly affirms that what
we seek is happiness.

We all recognize that the word "happiness" is open to misunderstanding. The reason is that people understand it in all sorts of
different ways. When we look at the *contents* of happiness, we find
all kinds of things that people figure will give them happiness: riches,
honors, glory, power, bodily health, and pleasure. And each of these
does give us a kind of satisfaction. But none of them gives what
we're *really* after. We find out as soon as we try them. When you set
your heart on a fancy car, and when you somehow scrape the money
together and get it, before long the car loses much of its appeal. It
turns out there are other, nicer vehicles that soon tickle your fancy.

1. Gregory of Nyssa, "The Beatitudes," in *The Lord's Prayer, The Beatitudes*,
trans. and ed. Hilda C. Graef, Ancient Christian Writers 18 (New York: Paulist Press,
1954), 87.

2. Augustine, *Confessions*, trans. and ed. Henry Chadwick (Oxford: Oxford University Press, 1998), X.xx (29), 196. See also Augustine, *De civitate dei* VI.12.

3. Thomas Aquinas, *Summa Theologica*, trans. Fathers of the English Dominican
Province (1948; repr. Notre Dame, IN: Ave Maria Press, 1981), I/II, q.3, a.1.

4. John Calvin, *Institutes of the Christian Religion*, trans. Ford Lewis Battles, ed.
John T. McNeill (Philadelphia: Westminster, 1960), III.xxv.11.

Material wealth does not give true happiness. If it did, North Americans would be the happiest people in the world. But we struggle with *un*happiness more than many people elsewhere. Or take bodily health. Of course, bodily health has certain benefits. But does it really give us what we aim for in life? Does it give us ultimate happiness? Let's think outside the box for a minute. If bodily health gave happiness, then many of the animals would be happier than we are: elephants can live longer, lions are far more muscular, and cougars run much faster than human beings.

Or take something else that is supposed to give happiness: an exotic vacation to Hawaii. Yes, we can get a certain degree of pleasure out of lounging on the beach. But it's one of the most fleeting pleasures in the world. After a couple of weeks at most, you're back on the plane, and before you know it you're in your own kitchen again, doing the dishes. There are lots of earthly things that you and I set our hearts on, things that we aim for, things we desire in life. All too often we desire them so much that we make the mistake of thinking they will give us the happiness we're really after. If we're honest with ourselves, we recognize that none of these things that we desire and pursue fulfills our deepest desire. The reason is simple: ultimate happiness is found in God alone. He alone is true happiness. Happiness is a heavenly thing.[5]

So, happiness and heaven are tied together. But Psalm 1 doesn't seem to make this connection. It talks about happiness, but it doesn't mention heaven, does it? Actually, I would like us to pause there for just a moment. Do we or do we not find heaven in this psalm? As we scan the text for the word "heaven," fair enough, it doesn't show on the radar. But let me repeat the question: Do we or do we not find heaven in this psalm? Actually, there are reasons to think that we find heaven in *several* places in this psalm. For now, I want to focus on just one of the places that speaks to us about heaven, and that is the very first word: "blessed," or, as we could also translate, "happy." When the psalmist pronounces us blessed or happy, isn't he simply using another way to say we find ourselves in heaven? If we don't find heaven in the very first word of this psalm, where *else* could

5. Thomas Aquinas, *Summa Theologica*, I/II, q.2, a.8.

we possibly find it? Isn't heaven all about happiness? Isn't heaven all about the great fulfillment of our deepest desire? Didn't we just see that only the reality of God himself gives us happiness? And if happiness means being with the Triune God in heaven, then where else except in heaven could you and I possibly be happy or blessed?

There's something really beautiful about the book of Psalms beginning with a beatitude, with a blessing, with a word about happiness. What that does is to tell us right from the start that we need to look to the one reality that really counts. And that reality is heaven. The first two psalms really belong together, because together they form the opening to the rest of the book. And where Psalm 1 *begins* with a beatitude—"Blessed is the man who walks not in the counsel of the wicked" (1:1)—Psalm 2 *ends* with one, "Blessed are all who take refuge in him" (2:12). The first two psalms, we could say, are held up on both ends by beatitudes. From both ends, heavenly happiness shines in on these two psalms. From these first two psalms, heavenly happiness rolls down into the rest of the book. As you may be aware, our one book of 150 psalms is actually made up of five distinct books. The first of these five books ends at Psalm 41. Beautifully structured, the first book concludes much like the way it started. "Blessed is the man who makes the LORD his trust," says Psalm 40:4, and, "Blessed is the one who considers the poor," says Psalm 41:1. The entire first book of Psalms, we could say, is about happiness. The first two psalms and the last two psalms tell us that life is all about looking for happiness. And together with these first and last two psalms, the whole first book—all the way from Psalm 1 through Psalm 41—draws us into heaven. It pulls us toward the happiness we find there.

"Blessed is the man who walks not in the counsel of the wicked, nor stands in the way of sinners, nor sits in the seat of scoffers" (Ps. 1:1). Who is this man the psalmist is talking about? Who are these words pointing to? Yes, I recognize they are about you and me. But they are not about you and me *first* of all. The very first comment St. Augustine makes in his commentary on the Psalms is this: "This statement," about blessed is the man, "should be understood as referring to our Lord Jesus Christ." The blessed man is Jesus Christ. Augustine then contrasts this heavenly man, Christ, with what he calls "the earthly man who conspired with his wife, already beguiled by the serpent, to disregard God's commandments. . . . Christ certainly came in the way of sinners by being born as sinners are; but he did not stand in it, for worldly allurement did not hold him."[6] Isn't this a beautiful opening line to a commentary on the book of Psalms? And isn't it a statement not just on the first words of the psalm but also about whatever God calls us to do? "Blessed are you," the psalmist says to you and me, "if in everything you do, you aim at Christ, the Word incarnate. Only in Christ can we find true happiness. Indeed, the very definition of happiness is a person. Happiness is Christ."

To be sure, we don't always look to Christ. We often look elsewhere for happiness. But even when we look in all the wrong places, it is still happiness that we are looking for. When we clutch at food or money or possessions, it is really happiness we're looking for. When we are distracted by sexually suggestive images, it is really happiness we are looking for. When we set our hearts on those things, it is not as if we do not aim for happiness; it is just that we define happiness in the wrong way. Happiness doesn't lie in food, in possessions, in sexual gratification. Happiness is Christ. To be sure, food, possessions, sexuality—all these are God's good gifts, and they have their own proper place in relation to Christ. But so often we stare ourselves blind at them because we think happiness depends on them. But our happiness is Christ. The fact that our generation struggles so tremendously with addictions of various sorts is, therefore, really a spiritual problem. It's a problem that is the result of misidentifying happiness. No matter how much stuff we own, no matter how much glory and praise we get coming our way, no matter how much sexual stimulus we find, none of it gives us lasting happiness. Again, the reason is simple: happiness is a heavenly, not an earthly, reality.

Where do we find happiness? So far, I have suggested to you two answers: we find it in Christ, and we find it in heaven. But really, these are not two different answers. They are one and the same. Think about it: space travel, no matter how technically advanced, cannot bring us all the way to heaven. Heaven is not a place far beyond the stars that

6. Augustine, "Exposition of Psalm 1," in *Expositions of the Psalms 1–32*, trans. and ed. Maria Boulding, vol. III/15 of *The Works of Saint Augustine: A Translation for the 21st Century*, ed. John Rotelle (Hyde Park, NY: New City, 2000), 67.

we could reach if only we had a faster or more advanced space shuttle. Really, heaven is Christ himself. Heaven is the eternal Son of God who took on human flesh. I once read a quote that says, "We draw near to heaven, indeed, we enter into heaven, to the extent that we draw near to Jesus and enter into communion with him."[7] How true. "We draw near to heaven, indeed, we enter into heaven, to the extent that we draw near to Jesus and enter into communion with him." Happiness is found in Christ. Happiness is found in heaven. These are two different ways of saying the same thing. What this means, of course, is that the heavenly happiness of which Psalm 1 speaks isn't just something for later. It exists already today. Already we are seated "in the heavenly places in Christ Jesus," St. Paul says (Eph. 2:6; cf. 1:3). We are in heaven *already* because we are in Christ *already*.

"Blessed is the man," our psalm says, "who *walks* not in the counsel of the wicked, nor *stands* in the way of sinners, nor *sits* in the seat of scoffers" (Ps. 1:1). Walk, stand, sit. These are action words; they are verbs. To be sure, the word "sit" is rather an *in*active action word—there's not much movement there. But even when the psalmist talks about sitting, it is clear that he has in mind the lived reality of a life of sin. He is talking about the life of the wicked, of sinners, of scoffers. Many Christian families used to have a picture hanging in their hallways with a title on top, "The Broad and the Narrow Way." The broad way depicted a life of fun and merriment, ending in the destruction of eternal fire. The narrow way showed a life of holiness and piety, leading to the joy of the heavenly city. That picture goes back, of course, to Jesus' words in the Sermon on the Mount: "Enter by the narrow gate. For the gate is wide and the way is easy that leads to destruction, and those who enter by it are many. For the gate is narrow and the way is hard that leads to life, and those who find it are few" (Matt. 7:13–14). Why did these words become so popular? Why did people turn them into a picture and hang it in their hallways? The reason, it seems to me, is that Christians throughout the centuries have recognized that both Jesus' words about the broad and the narrow way, and the psalmist's depiction of the way

7. Pope Benedict XVI, "The Ascension Invites Us to a Profound Communion with Jesus," https://zenit.org/articles/benedict-xvi-s-homily-at-miranda-plaza-in-cassino/.

of the righteous compared to the way of the wicked, teach us that we cannot, at least not without consequences, walk along our self-determined paths in life. Some ways of life lead to destruction; other ways of life lead to happiness.

C. S. Lewis raises the question of how it is possible for us to delight in the law, as Psalm 1:2 says. That word "delight" is, of course, an echo of the exuberant praise of the law that we find especially in Psalm 119. "In the way of your testimonies I delight as much as in all riches," says the psalmist (119:14). "Open my eyes, that I may behold wondrous things out of your law" (v. 18). "Your statutes have been my songs in the house of my sojourning" (v. 54). "The law of your mouth is better to me than thousands of gold and silver pieces" (v. 72). "How sweet are your words to my taste, sweeter than honey to my mouth!" (v. 103). How is it possible to talk this way about commandments? Lewis says this:

> A man held back by his unfortunate previous marriage to some lunatic or criminal who never dies from some woman whom he faithfully loves, or a hungry man left alone, without money, in a shop filled with the smell and sight of new bread, roasting coffee, or fresh strawberries—can these find the prohibition of adultery or of theft at all like honey? They may obey, they may still respect the "statute." But surely it could be more aptly compared to the dentist's [pliers] or the front line than to anything enjoyable and sweet.[8]

I suspect all of us feel that way at times about the Christian life. And like the people in Lewis's two examples, we find it difficult to remain faithful to God's will. Lewis suggests, however, that there is a way to look at the law that makes it feel different from the dentist's pliers. The law is not an imposition of arbitrary, tyrannical commandments. The laws that God gives are good not simply because God commands them. Instead, God commands them because they are good, because they are in line with his good character.[9] There's a subtle difference there, isn't there? Nothing is more precious than being in line with the good character of God.

8. C. S. Lewis, *Reflections on the Psalms* (London: Bles, 1958), 55.
9. Ibid., 61.

And if this is true of the Old Testament law, how much more is it true of Christ, the fulfillment of the law, who in his very person is "the way, and the truth, and the life" (John 14:6)? How could we *not* say with the psalmist, "In the way of Christ I delight as much as in all riches"; and "Open my eyes that I may behold wondrous things out of your Son"; and "My Savior has been my song in the house of my sojourning"; and "The eternal Word of your mouth is better to me than thousands of gold and silver pieces"; and "How sweet is my Lord Jesus to my taste, sweeter than honey to my mouth"? Jesus is good not simply because the Father gives him to us. Rather, the Father gives him to us because Jesus is good, because he is in line with the good character of the Father (Heb. 1:3).

There are no dentist's pliers here. What we have instead is heaven itself cascading down to earth! Think about the implications of this. It is one thing to say that Christ is the blessed man, the heavenly happiness, of Psalm 1:1. But it's quite something else to say the Christ is also the law of verse 2, for that means Christ is also the way to get to heavenly happiness. Talk about the means fitting the end! Christ is the way, and Christ is the end. Happiness is not just a future ideal, but it is something we already enjoy today as we travel along the way. For the Christian, Christ is everything from beginning to end.

So, why is it that we look for happiness in all the wrong places? Why is it that we imagine we can find it in riches, honors, glory, power, bodily health, and pleasure? Isn't the bottom line quite simply this: that it's easier to believe in all of these things than it is to believe in Christ? We can hear, see, touch, smell, and taste the goods of this earth. God, Christ, heaven, these are realities we cannot access with the senses. They are spiritual realities. To live like there really are two ways—to act like the life of virtue really is linked with eternal consequences—requires faith. Could it be that the reason you and I find it so difficult to give up some of our habits, habits that we know chain us down to earthly goods, is that we have a hard time believing in heavenly realities?

So, this morning, let us go in faith. Let's go to heaven. Let's delight in our Lord. Let's sing of Jesus on the road. Let's trust the sweetness of our Savior. Remember, "we enter into heaven, to the extent that we draw near to Jesus and enter into communion with him." We could also say: whenever Jesus gives himself to us, heaven itself comes down to us. God knows our weaknesses. He knows our difficulty in keeping our eyes on heaven. He knows how tempting it is for you and me to look for happiness in all the wrong places. So, what he does is this: he brings heaven down to earth. He gives us his good Spirit, and he makes us hear, see, touch, smell, and even taste heaven itself. As he fills us with his Spirit, Christ gives us his heavenly body to eat; he gives us his heavenly blood to drink. Thanks be to God for the heavenly happiness he gives us in Christ!

Preacher's Notes

I base this sermon on two key assumptions. The first is a theological one not directly derived from Psalm 1: Christ is the proper definition of happiness or blessedness. The second is an exegetical choice, namely, seeing Christ as the man mentioned in verse 1.[10] As a result, my sermon moves seamlessly from the man to Christ to happiness. I assumed that as readers we find ourselves in this psalm through seeking to identify with each of these three.

The theological identification of God or of Christ as happiness is common in the Christian tradition. This identification goes back to passages such as 1 Timothy 6:15, which speaks of God as the one "who is the blessed and only Sovereign, the King of kings and Lord of lords." Our blessedness or happiness, on this understanding, depends on the degree to which we share in God's own blessedness or happiness. Gregory of Nyssa was keenly aware that our happiness is derived happiness.[11] Because he regarded the heavenly future of God in Christ as our aim, he took the Psalter as a whole to be a means of attaining this eschatological blessedness of the divine life. The book

10. The inclusive use of the term "man" may be troubling to some readers. I have retained the ESV translation in part because it facilitates the christological reading. Needless to say, both the term "man" (*ish*) and the New Testament understanding of Christ as the second Adam are inclusive of male and female.

11. Gregory comments, e.g., "Among humans . . . that beatitude, which is the nature of the one participated in [*tou metechomenou*], occurs to a certain extent, and is specified by participation [*tē methexei*] in true being. Likeness to God, therefore, is a definition of human blessedness." *Gregory of Nyssa's Treatise on the Inscriptions of the Psalms*, trans. and ed. Ronald E. Heine (Oxford: Clarendon, 1995), 84.

of Psalms leads one to the blessedness that is first mentioned in Psalm 1 and is finally victoriously celebrated in Psalm 150. Each of the five sections of the Psalter, according to St. Gregory, functions as a stage in our ascent (*anabasis*) to this blessedness of heaven.[12] From beginning to end, the Psalter points the way to blessedness.

The participatory view of reality undergirding Gregory's view of happiness is much debated today, particularly because theologians from the Radical Orthodoxy movement have been advocating it.[13] Whatever we may think of this recent theological movement, participatory ontology—and certainly the notion that our happiness is a participation in the perfection of happiness in God—is not a recent invention. It is part of the common stock of historic Christianity, and the fact that it may strike us at first as novel—and perhaps in some ways unnerving—has to do with the loss of traditional understandings of reality in the modern period. In light of Scripture, a participatory ontology has a great deal to commend itself: the biblical teaching that our happiness can be found only in God means we cannot find it in any earthly goods, and we can obtain it only by sharing in the happiness of God himself.

Gregory's theological exegesis of Psalm 1 understands the happiness of salvation as participation in Christ—or, to use the common Pauline phrase, as being in Christ. In this, St. Gregory was hardly alone. Many, motivated by the fact that our salvation lies anchored in Christ, have looked for the christological reality (*res*) underneath the surface of the text (*sacramentum*) of the psalms. After all, not just we, but also the texts and melodies of the psalms, make present in some way the happy or blessed reality of Christ. This is why we need personal transformation—a deepening participation in Christ—to be able to discern the sacramental meaning of the text. As we grow more deeply in our union with Christ, we are continuously better equipped to perceive this same happiness in the *sacramentum* of the psalm.

The question of *where* we can find Christ in Psalm 1 has been answered in different ways. In this sermon, I focus on the man (1:1) and

12. Ibid., 95–96.
13. See John Milbank, Catherine Pickstock, and Graham Ward, eds., *Radical Orthodoxy: A New Theology* (London: Routledge, 1999). For a helpful introduction to Radical Orthodoxy, see James K. A. Smith, *Introducing Radical Orthodoxy: Mapping a Post-secular Theology* (Grand Rapids: Baker Academic, 2005).

on "the law of the LORD" (1:2) as references to Christ. The exegetical choice of identifying the man as Christ is no doubt controversial, and I suspect that some will regard this christological reading as alien to a proper exegetical analysis of the text. It is important to recall, however, that exegesis is not a scientific endeavor, at least not in our common understanding of the term "scientific." Exegesis is much more interested in what is fitting than in what is indubitable scientific truth. Earlier generations of theologians spoke of fittingness or *convenientia*, a Latin term quite different in meaning from our contemporary word "convenience." In exegesis we look not for the reading we find most convenient. Instead, we aim for an understanding that is fitting with the spiritual reality to which the text points. The bane of much modern theology is taking the methodologies of the hard sciences as models for exegesis.[14] It seems to me that exegesis has much more in common with the arts and the humanities than it does with the sciences.

Premodern exegetes were much more aware than we are that biblical exegesis requires its own distinct approach. As a result, they were much more open to multiple readings of the text than we tend to be in the modern period. Having identified the man of Psalm 1:1, and hence also the tree of verse 3, with Christ, Augustine proceeds to explain how we might identify the streams of water beside which the tree is planted, and he gives no fewer than three exegetical options.[15] The phrase may refer to our common humanity, which Christ assumed, since "what is said in another psalm, *the river of God is brimming with water* (Ps. 64:10 [65:9]), can also be taken in this sense."[16] Or the streams of water may refer to the Holy Spirit, since Jesus repeatedly associates the Spirit with water (Matt. 3:11; John 4:10, 13–14; 7:37). Then again, "by streams of water" may mean "because of the sins of the peoples," both because Revelation 17:15 speaks of peoples as waters and because a running stream may be understood as falling, "something which is applicable to wrongdoing."[17]

14. See the penetrating analysis by Andrew Louth, *Discerning the Mystery: An Essay on the Nature of Theology* (1983; repr., Oxford: Clarendon, 2003).
15. See Augustine, "Exposition of Psalm 1," 68.
16. Ibid.
17. Ibid.

It is not my purpose to defend any of these options Augustine gives. My sermon doesn't deal with the streams of water, and I am simply mentioning Augustine's three options to draw attention to how the bishop of Hippo appears singularly unconcerned about making a choice between them. Presumably, he feels that each of them is in line with the church's faith and has the potential to build up the congregation's faith. This is just one example of Augustine presenting the possibility of multiple meanings in a text. In his exegetical work he frequently mentions two or more possible interpretations. Sometimes he appears uncertain which option to choose. Other times he seems to suggest that various interpretations each yield spiritual benefit. Multiplicity of meaning clearly did not present the kind of existential angst among premodern exegetes that it often produces in us.[18]

This is not to say that a rational discussion about which interpretation to choose is impossible. Some interpretations may well be more fitting than others. Thus while Augustine follows a line of interpretation that sees Christ in the man in Psalm 1:1, the earlier bishop of Poitiers, St. Hilary, opposed such an interpretation as "wrong both in method and reasoning."[19] He believed the psalmist would never have seen Christ as delighting in the law if Christ is its author, nor would the psalmist have likened Christ to a mere tree, as if a tree could be happier than the Son of God.[20] I come down on Augustine's side in this disagreement. The Pauline notion of the faithfulness of Christ implies that the Son, in his humiliation, does submit himself in obedience to the Father's will and so to the law. It hardly seems to me that when the psalmist compares the man to a tree, he means to imply that the latter is happier than the former. If the tree is indeed the standard of happiness in the text, then this is a problem not just for a *christological* reading of the man but for any identification of this person.

Hilary's rejection of Christ as the man does not mean, however, that he was opposed to a christological reading of Psalm 1 in general.

---

18. See Henri de Lubac, *Medieval Exegesis: The Four Senses of Scripture*, trans. Marc Sebanc (Grand Rapids: Eerdmans, 1998), 1:82–89.

19. Hilary of Poitiers, "Psalm I," in *Homilies on the Psalms, Nicene and Post-Nicene Fathers*, Second Series, trans. E. W. Watson, L. Pullan, et al., ed. W. Sanday (1899; repr., Peabody, MA: Hendrickson, 1994), 9:236.

20. Ibid., 236–37.

"The whole of the Psalter is to be referred to Him [Christ]," Hilary comments.[21] Regardless of differences of opinion as to the fittingness of particular interpretations, the church fathers largely agreed that Christ is the mystery present in the text of the Psalter and that it is the task of the theologian to find him there.[22] The basic framework of patristic exegesis is sacramental in character: Christ is the mystical reality (*res*) present in the sacrament (*sacramentum*) of the text. It is a sacramentality grounded in the recognition that earthly happiness participates in heavenly happiness.

21. Ibid., 236.
22. I hope to argue this in more detail in a forthcoming book with Baker Academic on patristic exegesis.

10

Resurrection Faithfulness

Luke 20:27–40

Luke 20:27–40

²⁷ There came to him some Sadducees, those who deny that there is a resurrection, ²⁸ and they asked him a question, saying, "Teacher, Moses wrote for us that if a man's brother dies, having a wife but no children, the man must take the widow and raise up offspring for his brother. ²⁹ Now there were seven brothers. The first took a wife, and died without children. ³⁰ And the second ³¹ and the third took her, and likewise all seven left no children and died. ³² Afterward the woman also died. ³³ In the resurrection, therefore, whose wife will the woman be? For the seven had her as wife."

³⁴ And Jesus said to them, "The sons of this age marry and are given in marriage, ³⁵ but those who are considered worthy to attain to that age and to the resurrection from the dead neither marry nor are given in marriage, ³⁶ for they cannot die anymore, because they are equal to angels and are sons of God, being sons of the resurrection. ³⁷ But that the dead are raised, even Moses showed, in the passage about the bush, where he calls the Lord the God of Abraham and the God of Isaac and the God of Jacob. ³⁸ Now he is not God of the dead, but of the living, for all live to him." ³⁹ Then

some of the scribes answered, "Teacher, you have spoken well."
[40] For they no longer dared to ask him any question.

Sunday, August 10, 2014

Today's passage is most remarkable, both for the ingenuity of the Sadducees and for the defense of the resurrection that Jesus offers in response. His rejoinder is what we are really interested in, but to understand it, we have to see how it is that the Sadducees are trying to stump Jesus. They present us with this strange story—a story about seven brothers, no less, each of whom married the same woman in turn, in hopes of somehow producing a child for their brother. But each of them died before they were able to do so, and in the end, the woman also passed away.

To understand why the Sadducees tell this story, we need to know two things. First, for the Sadducees, only the five Books of Moses are authoritative. The other Old Testament books may be of interest, but you don't go there to see what you should and should not believe. Much less are you going to turn to later tradition for that. For the Sadducees, it's a radical sort of *sola Scriptura* that's in play: only the five Books of Moses—Genesis through Deuteronomy—are the basis of what we ought to believe and how we ought to live. Second, this means that the Sadducees are minimalists in terms of the doctrines they do and do not hold. Since life after death doesn't really seem to show up in the Books of Moses, they don't believe either in an immortal soul that lives on after death or in a resurrection of the body at the end of time. Both ideas are out for the Sadducees.

So they try to show Jesus the foolishness of his and the Pharisees' belief in resurrection from the dead. Their masterstroke is this concoction of a story—just a few verses in our Bibles, but in real life taking many, many years to play itself out. The Sadducees play their game on home turf; they're basing their story on the law of Moses, Deuteronomy 25:5: "If brothers dwell together, and one of them dies and has no son, the wife of the dead man shall not be married outside the family to a stranger. Her husband's brother shall go in to her and take her as his wife and perform the duty of a husband's brother to her." We know the kind of marriage Deuteronomy 25 is talking about as levirate marriage, the Latin word *levir* meaning a husband's brother. If a husband died childless, his brother, the *levir*, would have the duty of marrying the widow. That way, the widow might still bear a child, perhaps a firstborn son, and the little boy would then continue the dead brother's name and lineage (25:6).

Clearly, the Sadducees' story is absurd. It would never actually happen that seven brothers would each marry the same woman and each of them leave her childless. Still, even absurd examples can be instructive. On some occasions, *especially* absurd examples are enlightening. And that would seem to be the case here. The obvious purpose of the story is to show that the whole idea of resurrection is nonsensical. If we're going accept resurrection, we'll have to explain what it will look like for someone who has had more than one spouse in his or her life—all the more if not just two but seven spouses were in play during the course of one's life. Imagine the weird situation of this woman looking her seven husbands in the eye in the hereafter and wondering whose wife she might be! Deuteronomy 25 clearly holds open the possible scenario of a woman legitimately having more than one husband during her lifetime. The conclusion seems evident enough: the five Books of Moses don't just *ignore* the topic of resurrection; they positively *exclude* such a teaching. It's an open-and-shut case. If we just think through the consequences of the belief in resurrection, we quickly come to see how ludicrous the idea really is.

Before we turn to Jesus' response, we might just let the weight of the Sadducees' dilemma sink in for a moment. The difficulty they present is one that we face too. We no longer have levirate marriage, but we do have people remarrying after the death of their spouse, and we have situations of divorce and remarriage. Either way, how do we rhyme these situations with belief in resurrection? Remember, just because the Sadducees' story is an outlandish one doesn't make it any less compelling. It is so compelling that we would do well to spend some time thinking about how we can square belief in resurrection with the reality of multiple marriage partners.

Both in Matthew 22 and in Mark 12, where we find the same confrontation between Jesus and the Sadducees, our Lord responds with words we don't find in Luke's Gospel. His initial reply in both of the other Gospels is that the Sadducees are wrong because they "know neither the Scriptures nor the power of God" (Matt. 22:29; Mark 12:24). In the rest of today's sermon I want to focus on each of these points that Jesus makes: the Sadducees' ignorance of the Scriptures and their ignorance of God's power. But we'll take them in reverse order. We'll first look at what Jesus says about God's power, and then we'll see what he says about the Scriptures.

If there is one thing that stands out in the story the Sadducees are peddling, it is that in their depiction of it, the resurrection life looks remarkably like the life we live here on earth. The Sadducees simply assume that if resurrection were possible—something they strenuously reject—it would lead to a situation much like what we have today. We would not only recognize people we had known during our earthly lives, but we would also continue to live with them much like we used to live with them before we died. Only if there's marriage in the hereafter does the story of the Sadducees make any sense at all. To be sure, the Sadducees realize there'd be some new variables in play in a possible resurrection: with people going back all the way to Adam and Eve returning to life, we'd have to reckon with the fact that suddenly many more people would be populating the globe. But mostly, resurrection life wouldn't look much different from the life we live today.

Jesus immediately zeroes in on the key issue. His words point out that the Sadducees' imagination is severely hampered, limited to categories taken from the things we meet around us in our lives today. In line with this, the Sadducees also see the power of God as limited to this-worldly categories. They have no clue what God's power can and will do in the resurrection. Jesus' very first words blow up the limited horizons of the Sadducees. What he says is that their very question—"In the resurrection, therefore, whose wife will the woman be?" (Luke 20:33)—is based on a wrong assumption. The entire story loses its punch once that assumption no longer holds. The assumption is this: there will be marriage in the resurrection much like we have marriage today. It is that assumption, Jesus says, that shows the limited character of the Sadducees' imagination. "In the resurrection," Jesus answers flatly, "they neither marry nor are given in marriage, but are like angels in heaven" (Matt. 22:30; Mark 12:15).

Now, let's pause here for a moment. Isn't there a problem with Jesus' comment? In fact, aren't there two problems? Maybe out of reverence we might want to keep quiet. But if we dared raise our hand, wouldn't we have asked, "Where, Jesus, do you get the idea that there will be no marriage in the resurrection? Where in the Old Testament does it say that? And didn't God himself start the idea of marriage at the beginning of creation? In doing so, didn't God make something good? Isn't it true that God will not abandon the work of his hands? So, wouldn't there be marriage also in the hereafter? Aren't we going to be drinking our favorite beers in the hereafter? Won't we be looking at the *Mona Lisa* and reading Shakespeare? Don't both Micah and Zechariah have very this-worldly pictures of the eschaton that suggest that we will sit under our own vine and our own fig tree (Mic. 4:4; Zech. 3:10), each on the little plot of ground that will be ours in the renewed world?"

But Jesus chides this response for its lack of imagination. I don't mean lack of imagination in a general sense, but lack of imagination in regard to who God is, his power. "You know neither the Scriptures nor the power of God." Jesus doesn't fall in line with our logic that all that is good here today must go on forever. In dramatic fashion, he simply states that there will be no marriage in the hereafter. True, what Jesus says here about marriage isn't all there is to say about it. Marriage is a good thing. Jesus would agree. But the goodness of the institution of marriage is not the topic of debate. The topic of debate is whether there is such a thing as resurrection. Making the case that there is *not*, the Sadducees go on the assumption that any notion of resurrection would imply a continuation of the same kind of life—or almost the same kind of life—that we lead here today, including marital relationships. It is this assumption that Jesus exposes and discounts. He wants to expand our imaginative horizons. He wants us to think of resurrection in a way that leads us beyond the categories and the realities of our life here today.

He then adds—and this must really have boggled the Sadducees' minds—that we will be "equal to angels" (Luke 20:36) or "like angels in heaven," as the other Gospels put it (Matt. 22:30; Mark 12:25). Jesus doesn't explain in detail what he means. But clearly for the Sadducees who likely didn't believe in angels at all (Acts 23:8), and for Christians today who don't reckon much with angels in their day-to-day lives either, the notion that in the resurrection we'll be like the angels carries implications we may never have thought of before. Think it through for a moment. First, it means we'll become immortal. Jesus says that in the resurrection we cannot die anymore because we'll be equal to angels, children of God, children of the resurrection (Luke 20:36). That we'll be like angels means we will live forever. Second, being like angels means that marriage and having children are a thing of the past. Right? Jesus directly links death along with marriage to the "sons of this age" (Luke 20:34), and he links eternal life along with angels to the "sons of the resurrection" (20:36). Birth-and-death patterns go with marriage; eternal life is typical of angels. Angels don't marry; angels don't have sexual relations; and angels don't have children.

Jesus doesn't need a text from the Bible that says there will be no marriage in the resurrection. The very notion of resurrection implies there can be no marriage. Marriage, Jesus says, makes sense only as part of the life-and-death cycle we know here today. Once that cycle is gone, we'll have a new, eternal, angelic kind of life, which implies that marriage will have outlived its usefulness. The wife of seven husbands won't have any of the seven as her husband anymore.

My hunch is that Christians of earlier centuries sometimes had a better grasp of these things than we do. They knew that there's a sharp difference between the life we live here today and the future resurrection life. They also knew that marriage and sexuality do not define who we are: one day, they will both disappear. And these earlier Christians knew from Jesus' words that marriage is part of the life-and-death cycle that we have today. Without marriage—or without sexual activity, we should perhaps say—there'd be neither birth nor death. Marriage, or sexual activity, cannot but result in death: that's simply the pattern of life and death. But the power of God is such that he can overcome the life-and-death cycle in which we are caught up today. The power of God is such that he can turn mortal people into immortal people. The power of God is such that when he raises people from the dead, he gives them a heavenly, angel-like dimension that is beyond anything we have ever dared to ask or imagine.

For the Sadducees, Moses' talk of levirate marriage makes any belief in resurrection simply impossible. Having had two, or maybe even seven, spouses means that in the hereafter you'd face an impossible dilemma: Whose spouse would you be? Not so, Jesus says. You don't know the power of God. And he unmasks their limited imagination. They shouldn't think of resurrection in terms taken simply and directly from the here and now. So, what Jesus does in Luke 20:34–36 is to show that resurrection does make sense—that the regulation of Deuteronomy 25 does not make it impossible. God is the God of life; with him nothing is impossible.

But up till now, we have really just seen the negative side. Jesus has simply shown that Moses' regulation doesn't mean a *rejection* of resurrection. Now Jesus goes on to show also the positive. Moses' law doesn't just leave open the possibility of resurrection; it positively teaches it. Now this is an eyepopper. I want us to get a sense of just how revolutionary Jesus must have sounded to the Sadducees at this point. Remember, for them resurrection is out of the question in part just because it's not there, anywhere, in the law of Moses. They were on solid ground, so they thought. They knew the Scriptures. If the Pharisees wanted to argue for the resurrection, well, they would have to go to some of the later books of the Old Testament, or to later tradition. But Moses' law clearly didn't teach resurrection from the dead. With that, the Pharisees would simply be forced to agree.

So what does Jesus do? He moves from the one passage of Moses' law (Deuteronomy 25) to another (Exodus 3), the passage of the burning bush. There God says to Moses, "I am the God of Abraham and the God of Isaac and the God of Jacob" (Exod. 3:6). Jesus says this passage shows that the law of Moses actually teaches positively that the dead will rise—what is more, that they're alive right now with God.

Again, our first inclination may be to protest. How is this passage even remotely relevant to the debate? Jesus' evidence simply seems to miss the point. Still, his words make a powerful impact. Some of the scribes—and we know from earlier in the chapter that they weren't particularly favorable toward Jesus—are forced to admit, "Teacher, you have spoken well" (Luke 20:39). What is it that makes them recognize the force of Jesus' words? Let's turn for a moment to the passage of the burning bush. Here God calls Moses to become the leader of his people. When Moses sees the bush on fire without it burning up, God calls to him from the bush, "Do not come near; take your sandals off your feet, for the place on which you are standing is holy ground" (Exod. 3:5). Throughout the passage that follows, one issue is front and center: the question of who God is, the character of his identity. God explains to Moses that he is the faithful God, the God who rescues his people from death and brings them back to life. Just as he was the faithful God of life for Abraham, Isaac, and Jacob, so he will be the faithful God of life for the Israelites escaping Egypt. That's who God is; that's his identity. He is the God who rescues people from the dead. That's why God immediately adds to Moses, in Exodus 3:6, the words that Jesus quotes: "I am the God of your father, the God of Abraham, the God of Isaac, and the God of Jacob." At this, Moses hides his face, afraid to look at God.

And Moses seems equally afraid to go to Pharaoh, or even to talk to his own fellow Israelites. Will they accept him as their leader? "If I come to the people of Israel and say to them, 'The God of your fathers has sent me to you,' and they ask me, 'What is his name?' what shall I say to them?" (Exod. 3:13). The Lord then reveals his identity to Moses in 3:14: "I AM WHO I AM." And he adds, "Say this to the people of Israel, 'I AM has sent me to you.'" God reiterates his link with the Israelites' ancestors: "Say this to the people of Israel, 'The Lord, the God of your fathers, the God of Abraham, the God of Isaac, and the God of Jacob, has sent me to you'" (3:15). The very next verse, we read the same thing once again as God tells Moses to say to the Israelite elders, "The Lord, the God of your fathers, the God of Abraham, of Isaac, and of Jacob, has appeared to me" (3:16).

Three times in verses 6, 15, and 16, God links his name, Yahweh—the Lord in capital letters, or I AM WHO I AM—to the fact that he is the God of Abraham, Isaac, and Jacob. The point is: just as God was faithful long ago to *them*, so he will be faithful also to the *Israelites* today. God saw the affliction of his people, he heard their cry, he knows their suffering, and now he has come down (3:6–8). This God is a faithful God. He is a God you can count on. He is a God of new life. God's self-identification—"I am the God of your father, the God of Abraham, the God of Isaac, and the God of Jacob"—is a confidence booster, both for Moses and for the oppressed Israelites. God is not just a God of power; he is also a God of faithfulness.

All good and well, you say. But we don't read anywhere here that the dead will rise. That God is a faithful God, yes. But a resurrection God? We don't read in God's words to Moses anything about resurrection. Certainly, nothing in Exodus 3 states what Jesus says in Luke 20:38, that Abraham, Isaac, and Jacob are alive right now and that they "live to him." How does Jesus arrive at this conclusion? To answer this question, I briefly want to take you to Romans 6. There St. Paul uses the imagery of water to speak of us being baptized into the death of Christ and of us being united to Christ in his resurrection (Rom. 6:3–5). There is a reason why, throughout the tradition, the story of the exodus from Egypt—the Israelites passing through the waters of the Red Sea—has served as an image of resurrection, of entry into a new kind of life. This story of Moses leading the people out of Egypt has functioned all through history as the paradigm of what redemption means, what liberation means, what freedom means, and therefore also what resurrection means. The exodus story is a story that speaks to us of people being raised from the dead. The exodus story is a story about resurrection.

God not only has the *power* to raise people from the dead—remember Jesus' warning to the Sadducees, "You don't know the power of God"—but he also has the *faithfulness* to raise them from the dead. To show us his faithfulness—and to show us why the faithfulness of God's character means that Abraham, Isaac, and Jacob are alive with God even *today*—Jesus teaches us to read Exodus 3 in ways we may not have read it before. Jesus' point is this: if God was truly faithful to Abraham, Isaac, and Jacob, if God in Exodus 3 mentions them no fewer than three times to show Moses that he can and will raise the Israelites out of slavery, then these three patriarchs had better be alive. Only if they have passed from death to life, only if they have escaped their suffering and have truly arrived at the Promised Land— eternal life—does it make sense to hold them up to the Israelites as an example of the faithfulness of God in bringing his people through the exodus into eternal life.

The Sadducees suffer from a stifled imagination. All they go by is what the words on the page literally say. All they have is the surface meaning of the text. But Jesus takes us beyond the surface level to a deeper, spiritual meaning of the passage. It's not that with a sleight of hand Jesus changes the meaning of the text. It's not that he puts into the passage of the burning bush something that wasn't already there. No, the imagination Jesus puts to work is an imagination that lies deeply anchored in the text, in the very words on the page. And more important, perhaps, it is an imagination directly based on the faithful character of God.

Remember Jesus' words: "You know neither the Scriptures nor the power of God." What's at stake is the Sadducees' ignorance of the Scriptures. They claim the law of Moses as their own; they're radical *sola Scriptura* people. But they really don't know the Scriptures. Of course, in some ways they do. No doubt, they know the story of the burning bush. No doubt, they know it says there, "I am the God of Abraham, the God of Isaac, and the God of Jacob." But in a deeper sense, they really don't know the story of the burning bush. They don't know what God says with these words, "I am the God of your father, the God of Abraham, the God of Isaac, and the God of Jacob."

What God says is this: Abraham, Isaac, and Jacob are alive in the presence of God. They may still be waiting for the resurrection, but already they live in the presence of God. With that conclusion, Jesus opens up our imagination. He opens it up to the power of God—a power that brings a kind of life so different from our existence here today that only by comparing it to the life of angels do we even come close to understanding. Resurrection glory will shatter our wildest of dreams. And Jesus also opens up our imagination beyond the story line we find in the Scriptures. The Sadducees cannot see beyond the basics of the story of the burning bush. But Jesus looks for the love of God revealed in the depths of the text, and he says to you and me: "God's faithfulness will shatter your wildest of dreams."

Preacher's Notes

I was first seriously confronted by this passage when studying Gregory of Nyssa's views on embodiment.[1] The fourth-century Cappadocian, I found, was enamored with Luke 20:35–36. These verses seemed to

---

1. See Hans Boersma, *Embodiment and Virtue in Gregory of Nyssa: An Anagogical Approach* (Oxford: Oxford University Press, 2013).

him to imply that our aim in life should be the genderless existence of the angels, that marriage and sexuality are therefore not integral to our identity as human beings, that these aspects of life are the outcome of the fall, and that virginity is something to be prized as an anticipation of our angelic future state. In this sermon, I do not refer to Gregory or reiterate each of his convictions; nor am I convinced of every aspect of them. But I have become convinced that Gregory's otherworldliness has something to teach us, and that he can alert us to aspects of biblical teaching that we easily overlook as a result of our cultural constraints.

These constraints are not all that different from those of the Sadducees. Though our historical knowledge of the Sadducees is relatively limited, they appear to have belonged to a priestly caste, were part of the elite of Jewish society, and were well connected with the Roman oppressors.[2] If all this is true, then their social position fit their theological convictions, which tended to affirm the status quo, rejecting the immortality of the soul and barring undue theological speculation, particularly in the areas of angelology and the afterlife. Many of these convictions appear to have been linked to their strict insistence on the primacy of the law of Moses. Contemporary Christians, at least in the West, tend likewise to be socially at home in the world. And as I will discuss below, it seems clear to me that our general stance of social accommodation is reflected in our approaches to marriage and sexuality, our understanding of the hereafter, and our literalist approaches to biblical interpretation.

I bring each of these three topics to the fore in this sermon on Luke 20, which places me as a preacher in a somewhat difficult predicament. Both biblically and rhetorically, I needed to make a convincing case for a fairly significant shift in direction in the way we engage with marriage and sexuality, eschatology, and biblical interpretation. Two considerations may be of help. First, I tried not to place on myself the burden of the illusion that, with one sermon, I was going to resolve these issues or affect a major change in my listeners' perspective. Preachers do well to remember that they are just one voice among the people of

2. N. T. Wright, *The New Testament and the People of God*, vol. 1 of *Christian Origins and the Question of God* (Minneapolis: Fortress, 1996), 209–13.

God, and they may be encouraged by the knowledge that their Sunday morning sermon will be followed by another one next week. Second, since all theology is supposed to be biblical, it is always good just to let the text speak for itself. I don't mean to suggest that theological considerations should not enter into our exegesis of the text. Most of this book is devoted to arguing the opposite. But preachers should never preach their own hobbyhorse; they are to open up the Scriptures. My experience has been that when we rely on the Scriptures themselves in our exposition of the biblical text, the people of God are usually open to what we may have to say. To be sure, this is no absolute rule, as Paul's comment about itching ears in 2 Timothy 4:3 makes clear.

I do not have the space to elaborate in detail on each of the three areas in the sermon that present challenges in our cultural context: marriage and sexuality, continuity versus discontinuity in the eschaton, and spiritual interpretation. But it may be helpful at least to observe that the approach we take in any one of these areas is closely linked to the way we treat the other two. That today we have difficulty putting limits on sexual expression goes hand in hand with the recent proclivity among theologians to see the resurrection life primarily in terms of continuity rather than discontinuity with this life. And both approaches fit with our modern rejection of multiple levels of interpretation and our focus on the literal meaning of the text. In each of these areas, modernity has taught us to focus on sensible realities. Patristic and medieval readers of Scripture would have been much less inclined to try to find in this-worldly realities the ultimate meaning of life.

In this sermon, I purposely focus on the Sadducees' lack of imagination. It seems to me that the narrow horizons of modernity make it difficult for us to look beyond the immediate in each of the three areas just mentioned. A materialist or scientist mind-set limits us in many ways. Sexuality gets reduced to *just* a physical, bodily act. The result is that almost any sexual activity becomes acceptable as long as it gives pleasure and doesn't harm anyone else. But if it is true that life in Christ, not sexuality, defines our identity, then virginity, and singleness more broadly speaking, can be a signpost of the resurrection life. Likewise, a materialist mind-set leads to eschatological convictions that are often out of step with the focus on heaven and on the beatific vision of God in the hereafter that characterized much of the earlier tradition. The eschaton tends to become a continuation of all the good things we enjoy here today, only on a grander, more elaborate scale. Such a Sadducean view of the eschaton implies a reduction of our horizons to the goods of this world and is ignorant of the fact that the enjoyment of God himself is infinitely better than the enjoyment of any created goods. Finally, exegesis has also suffered from the materialist and scientist mind-sets of modernity. The reduction of meaning to the literal sense of the text or to a reconstructed history behind it makes it impossible to let theological considerations—such as the faithfulness of God in raising people from the dead—impact the exegetical choices we make. The result is a drastic narrowing of imaginative horizons. In each of these areas, I attempt in this sermon to show a biblically faithful way forward.

One comment may be in order regarding my interpretation of Jesus' reading of the comment from Exodus 3 that God is the God of Abraham, the God of Isaac, and the God of Jacob. Matthew and Mark quote the verse directly from Exodus 3:6, as they include the "I am" part of the quotation: "I am the God of Abraham, and the God of Isaac, and the God of Jacob" (Matt. 22:32; Mark 12:26). Luke's Gospel refers to the comment indirectly by stating that Moses "calls the Lord the God of Abraham and the God of Isaac and the God of Jacob" (Luke 20:37). Along with other interpreters, we might focus on the "I am" segment of the quotation, and hence regard it as implicit also in Luke 20. If we did, the fact that God at the time of the exodus claimed to be the God of Abraham, Isaac, and Jacob would prove that the three ancestors were alive in God's presence when the exodus took place.

This is a plausible reading, though I don't take this approach in the sermon. The emphasis on God's faithfulness in Exodus 3, the thrice-repeated highlighting of God's faithfulness to Israel's patriarchs, and the death-resurrection pattern implied in the larger exodus narrative all hint that more is going on. I suspect that Jesus deliberately made the point that God's faithfulness brought Israel's patriarchs through death to life, so that the Israelites could count on God doing the same thing for the entire nation through the exodus. I doubt this theological reading of Exodus 3 is exactly what the human author of the exodus narrative had in mind. But Jesus nonetheless appears to use this reading to oppose the Sadducees' narrow literalism, which isn't able to spot the doctrine of the resurrection in the law of Moses.[3] Of course, authorial intent is also left behind in the more cautious interpretation that focuses on the "I am" part of Jesus' quotation of Exodus 3 and hence on the fact that the patriarchs live in God's presence at the time of the exodus. On either reading, Jesus opens up horizons of meaning that can be found only by reaching beyond the letter of the text to its deeper, sacramental reality.

3. As an aside, some interpreters see in the Sadducees' question an allusion to the deuterocanonical story of Tobit, in which Sarah, daughter of Raguel, survives seven husbands, all of whom are killed by the evil demon Asmodeus. Sarah then ends up marrying Tobias, Tobit's son, as her eighth husband. For an extended argument that the book of Tobit lies behind the Sadducees' question, see Peter G. Bolt, "What Were the Sadducees Reading? An Enquiry into the Literary Background of Mark 12:18–23," *Tyndale Bulletin* 45 (1994): 369–94.

11

Perfect Blessing

Revelation 22:14

Revelation 22:12–15

¹² "Behold, I am coming soon, bringing my recompense with me, to repay each one for what he has done. ¹³ I am the Alpha and the Omega, the first and the last, the beginning and the end."

¹⁴ Blessed are those who wash their robes, so that they may have the right to the tree of life and that they may enter the city by the gates. ¹⁵ Outside are the dogs and sorcerers and the sexually immoral and murderers and idolaters, and everyone who loves and practices falsehood.

Sunday, November 9, 2014

The final chapter of the last book of the Bible tells us what everything has been all about. Everything—from alpha to omega (A to Z, that is), from beginning to end, from first to last—has been about Jesus. The entire story of the Bible, beginning with the creation of the world in Genesis all the way to the unveiling of our destiny in Revelation, is about Jesus. Because he is the one who both *writes* the story and

forms the *contents* of the story, we may trust that the *ending* is going
to be all about him as well—that the ending is going to be true to
the blessing of the very last verse of the Bible: "The grace of the
Lord Jesus be with all" (Rev. 22:21). That's exactly the point of this
morning's passage. It gives us a word of blessing: "Blessed are those
who wash their robes, so that they may have the right to the tree of
life and that they may enter the city by the gates" (Rev. 22:14). Our
text is a word of blessing, an encouragement as we look forward to
the climax of the story, to the end of history.

Blessedness is the salvation Jesus offers us. We could also call it "happiness." Jesus has come to make us happy. The word "blessed" simply
means happy. Not that I want to cheapen the word "blessedness." I
don't want us to think of the smiley faces we litter our text messages
with. No, the happiness we find in our passage reaches infinitely beyond
such cheapening of happiness. The blessedness or the happiness that
our text talks about is ultimate happiness; it is perfect happiness. The
happiness that our text talks about is the happiness that the psalmist
describes in Psalm 1: "Blessed [or, happy] is the man who walks not
in the counsel of the wicked, nor stands in the way of sinners, nor sits
in the seat of scoffers; but his delight is in the law of the LORD, and
on his law he meditates day and night" (vv. 1–2). This happiness is the
delight we experience when meditating on God's Word—on our Lord
Jesus himself. The happiness that our text talks about is the happiness
we encounter in the Beatitudes of Matthew 5: "Blessed are the poor
in spirit, for theirs is the kingdom of heaven. Blessed are those who
mourn, for they shall be comforted" (5:3–4), and so on. This is the
happiness of eternal life—nothing less than perfect happiness.

That the happiness of Revelation 22:14 is perfect happiness is going
to be the focus of today's sermon. We see the perfection of happiness both in the rewards and in the robes our passage talks about.
Both speak to the perfect happiness that God gives to us: both the
rewards and the robes are perfect. Together, the perfect rewards and
the perfect robes make up our perfect happiness. The text speaks
first of perfect robes, then of perfect rewards. We're first going to
deal with perfect rewards, and we'll deal with the perfect robes later.

Perfect happiness. It seems too good to be true. Yet that is exactly
what Jesus promises us here: perfect happiness. The word "blessed"

is a term we find not just in this verse in Revelation; it's sprinkled throughout the book. And it's been sprinkled rather deliberately: exactly seven times. The book of Revelation is almost like an expanded version of the Beatitudes in Jesus' Sermon on the Mount. There we find not seven but eight blessings in a row—although, as St. Augustine notes, the reward of the first and of the last are identical.[1] Both hold out the promise of the kingdom of heaven. So, perhaps we could say that in the Beatitudes Jesus also gives us seven, not eight, blessings. In any case, as we well know, the number seven speaks to us of perfection. Seven creation days, seven gifts of the Spirit, feasts that last seven days—the Bible is replete with the number seven. But nowhere do we see the number seven as much as in the book of Revelation. Here we have seven churches, seven letters, seven seals, seven horns, seven trumpets, seven crowns, and on and on. Likewise, we have seven beatitudes, seven words of blessing. This blessing, this happiness that Jesus wants to give to us, is nothing less than perfect blessing.

The string of seven blessings begins right in the first chapter, Revelation 1:3: "*Blessed* is the one who reads aloud the words of this prophecy, and blessed are those who hear, and who keep what is written in it." Next we hear a voice from heaven in 14:13: "*Blessed* are the dead who die in the Lord from now on." Then two chapters later in 16:15: "Behold, I am coming like a thief! *Blessed* is the one who stays awake, keeping his garments on, that he may not go about naked and be seen exposed!" Again, we read in 19:9: "*Blessed* are those who are invited to the marriage supper of the Lamb." And in 20:6: "*Blessed* and holy is the one who shares in the first resurrection!" Then we move on to our chapter, first to 22:7: "*Blessed* is the one who keeps the words of the prophecy of this book," which finally brings us to the verse of our text, 22:14: "*Blessed* are those who wash their robes." The blessings keep cascading into our lives, one after the next. It's the fullness of perfect blessing that Jesus offers in the book of Revelation. It's like we're back on the mountain, sitting at Jesus' feet all over again, waiting for the perfect blessing he holds out to us.

1. Augustine makes this point in *Our Lord's Sermon on the Mount* I.iii.10, trans. William Findlay, rev. D. S. Schaff, in *Nicene and Post-Nicene Fathers*, First Series, ed. Philip Schaff (1888; repr., Peabody, MA: Hendrickson, 1994), 6:6.

I'm not going through all seven of these beatitudes to see exactly
what type of happiness Jesus gives to us. Let's just say they have
everything to do with the perfect happiness of heaven. But I do want
to make an exception with our text. Here we do need to ask: What
is the reward Jesus holds out to us? In some ways, the description
is rather straightforward: "Blessed are those who wash their robes,
so that they may have the right to the tree of life and that they may
enter the city by the gates" (22:14). The reward Jesus promises here
is twofold: it's the tree of life and it's the New Jerusalem. We get to
eat of the one, and we get to enter into the other.

These images should not be unfamiliar to us. They've both been
mentioned before. The city is already there back in chapter 21: "I saw
the holy city, new Jerusalem, coming down out of heaven from God,
prepared as a bride adorned for her husband" (v. 2). And the tree of
life came up at the beginning of chapter 22, which talks about the
river of life streaming through the city with, "on either side of the
river, the tree of life with its twelve kinds of fruit, yielding its fruit
each month" (v. 2). These two chapters give us two pictures: the one
of a city, the other of a garden; the one the New Jerusalem, the other
paradise restored.

The two images stand side by side. They fit together. The city
comes "out of heaven from God" (21:2, 10); it comes from above,
not from below. If perhaps we had the illusion that we could bring
about our own perfection, the sight of this city coming down "out
of heaven from God" would quickly bring us to our senses. This
city—its radiance, its jewels, its perfect size—is a blessing. And a
blessing is always a gift. Likewise the tree: it's the paradisal tree of
life, the tree by the river in the garden of Eden, which the Lord God
planted in the east (Gen. 2:8). A tree of life, with "twelve kinds of
fruit" every month of the year, good for "the healing of the nations"
(Rev. 22:2)—it's hardly the kind of tree *we* have planted, is it? This
tree, this Edenic fruitfulness, is a blessing. And a blessing is always
a gift.

This garden city is a blessing. But as we have already seen, it is
not just any blessing; it is a perfect blessing. This reward is a perfect
reward. That's why we need both the city and the tree; that's why
we need two lengthy chapters; that's why we need such elaborate

descriptions. Jesus wants to give us not just any kind of happiness. He wants to give us perfect happiness.

For the most part, cities and gardens exclude each other. If we want to build a city, we first have to remove the greenery. To be sure, some cities leave more space for gardens and parks than others. Teaching in Vancouver, I am always enthralled by the beauty of Stanley Park, right by the city's downtown core. When I visit my home country and go to Amsterdam, I cannot but be impressed with the Amsterdamse Bos and the Vondelpark. And when we go to visit our kids in New York City, they love to take us to the magnificent Central Park in Manhattan. Many cities try to carve out some little paradise in the midst of the urban space. But even the most wonderful parks cannot obscure how, at a basic level, city and garden don't go together. Where we have buildings, greenery gets pushed out of the way. Where there are parks, we don't construct high-rise apartments.

It's different with the garden city of the last two chapters of the Bible. True, the river of life runs *through* the city, and the tree of life straddles both sides of the river *in* the city. But these two pictures—a city and a tree—don't really represent two different things. They're not two different blessings. They both refer to the same thing. In John's vision, the reality far outshines the picture he sees. It's not like a literal city is going to come from the sky one day. It's not like there are literally walls with twelve foundations, each made of a special kind of jewel, each gate made of a single pearl, and streets of pure gold. It's not like we should think of a literal river flowing through the city, with a tree straddling both sides of the river, blossoming like no tree ever blossomed before, yielding quantities of fruit like no tree ever before. We all recognize that Jesus gives us mere pictures. The reality far outshines the images of the city and the tree. We cannot do without the pictures. They're essential. But pictures are limited; they're never quite perfect.

What Jesus wants to give us in this beatitude is not just *a* blessing—say, a city or a tree. Jesus wants to give us *perfect* blessing, *perfect* reward. Jesus wants to give us himself. In some way, that should not surprise us. To enter the city is to see the Lamb. According to Revelation 21, somehow the Lamb is both the temple and the lamp that gives light for the city (vv. 22–24). Jesus' presence suffuses the city. Likewise, to eat from the tree of life is to taste the goodness of Jesus. Wisdom, Proverbs 3:18 says, "is a tree of life to those who lay hold of her; those who hold her fast are called blessed." Why does Proverbs call wisdom a tree of life? Because it is only the wisdom of God that gives us perfect happiness. Why does Revelation give us the image of a tree of life? Because it is only Christ as the eternal Wisdom of God who gives us perfect happiness. Both of the images—city and tree—give us perfect happiness; both speak of Jesus.

When Jesus speaks beatitudes to us, when he offers us his sevenfold, perfect blessedness, what else would he offer us but himself? When he says to us in the verse immediately before our text, "I am the Alpha and the Omega, the first and the last, the beginning and the end" (Rev. 22:13), are these not descriptions of perfection? Come to think of it, these are descriptions not just of Jesus, but also of God. "'I am the Alpha and the Omega,' says the Lord God, 'who is and who was and who is to come, the Almighty'" (1:8). That's a description of the Lord God himself. But here, in chapter 22, the Alpha and the Omega speaks of Jesus. Jesus could hardly have put it more clearly: he is God himself. If you're looking for perfection, you need to come to him. True blessedness, genuine happiness, is found only in Jesus' perfect, self-giving love.

So far, we've looked at the perfect rewards—the city and the tree—and we saw that, really, they're actually one reward: Jesus himself. Now we need to look at the robes. After all, perfect happiness, I said, is made up of perfect rewards and of perfect robes. Jesus says in our text, "Blessed are those who wash their robes" (22:14). Then he proceeds to tell us what the reward is: the tree of life and the New Jerusalem. "Blessed are those who wash their robes." That's not only a blessing; it's also a condition, isn't it? It's like saying, "If you want to eat from the tree of life, and if you want to enter the city by the gates, then you need to wash your robes."

We all have some inkling as to why we need to wash our robes. Washing makes them white. For you and me, white clothes contrast with colored clothes. When we go out in the street, we see all kinds of colors: blue, red, green, yellow, and so forth. A guy wearing a white suit definitely sticks out. But that's not what John has in mind. Most people in biblical times didn't wear all kinds of differently colored clothes. They wore something bland, like grayish, brownish, off-white. Take into account that people didn't have washing machines like you and I do, and you can imagine it was generally kind of a dirty, bland world. In *that* world, if people showed up in dazzlingly white robes, they stood out—not because they didn't wear red or blue or yellow, but because their white robes—washed, clean and white—provided a sharp contrast with the dirty and dusty attire of the other people around them. In John's vision, the world has become dirty, filthy, brown, but the people in white stand out. Those who have conquered and "have not soiled their garments" will be clothed in white robes (3:4–5), as will those who've been martyred for their faith (6:11) and who come out of the great tribulation (7:14).

White robes. When we let the implications sink in, this may be a dispiriting picture. If we get to enter the city and eat of the tree only if we've first made sure that our robes are perfectly white, then what we have here is a curse, not a blessing. And if we take the context of our verse seriously, we have to admit that there's not just blessing, but also curse: "Let the evildoer still do evil, and the filthy still be filthy" (22:11). "Outside are the dogs and sorcerers and the sexually immoral and murderers and idolaters, and everyone who loves and practices falsehood" (v. 15). We can't get around those words, and if we're honest, we realize they may well apply to us. How, in this light, does the beatitude of verse 14 still hold out perfect blessing? If for the perfect reward we're in need of perfect robes, how is there any encouragement in this blessing at all?

What we cannot do is solve the difficulty by saying that perfect robes don't matter. They do! Remember the letters to the seven churches in Revelation 2 and 3? Some of them are pretty sharp. What does the church in Sardis get to hear? "I know your works. You have the reputation of being alive, but you are dead" (3:1). Then we read in 3:4, "Yet you have still a few names in Sardis, people who have not soiled their garments, and they will walk with me in white, for they are worthy." Remarkable language, isn't it? And this is not the only time we find this kind of talk. The people of Laodicea say in the final section of chapter 3, "I am rich, I have prospered, and I need nothing." They don't realize they're poor. They don't realize they're "wretched, pitiable, poor, blind, and naked" (3:17). So what they need to do is buy white garments so at least they can cover their nakedness (3:18). They're naked, and they need to buy white clothes! Perfect, white robes are an absolute must!

But there is one word in our text we haven't looked at carefully yet. It's the word "wash": "Blessed are those who *wash* their robes" (22:14). How do we wash our robes so that they become white? One answer John gives us is that we need to *live* a certain way: "the fine linen is the righteous deeds of the saints" (19:8). The white robes have everything to do with how we live. But there's also a second answer. We find that in 7:14, which says that the martyrs "have washed their robes and made them white in the blood of the Lamb." Here it is the blood of the Lamb—red blood, amazingly—that turns our robes white. We often find it hard to keep those two answers together: our righteous deeds and the blood of the Lamb. For us, it's often the one or the other. As a result, we either end up trying to save ourselves, or we start preaching cheap grace.

Jesus really does give us white robes, perfect robes. Or we could say he gives us just *one* robe, his own seamless robe. Just like the two rewards—city and tree—are really just one reward, so too our many white robes are really just one robe. Jesus gives us not just the reward; he also gives us the robe. That is to say, he gives us himself. And when he does that, when he drenches us in his blood, he washes us perfectly clean. It is *in his blood* that he changes us. It is *in his blood* that we become clean. It is *in his blood* that our robes turn white. You see, when it's *in his blood* that we do what we do, then it's not *either* us *or* Jesus, *either* our deeds *or* his blood. Instead, we say with Paul, "I have been crucified with Christ. It is no longer I who live, but Christ who lives in me" (Gal. 2:20). United to Jesus, *my* robe turns white, drenched in the blood that's dripping from *his*.

Jesus' blessing really is perfect. We already saw that the reward is perfect: the perfect tree, the perfect city. With these images Jesus offers us himself as our reward. Now we come to realize that also the robe is perfect. Our robes get washed perfectly white in his blood. Jesus—he is our reward and our robe. Jesus—he defines our perfect happiness. It's all about Jesus, from A to Z, from first to last, from beginning to end.

Preacher's Notes

In this sermon I intend to make clear that our heavenly happiness is Christ-centered. Christ is the reality of every sacrament, which means that he is also the reality of Jerusalem and of the tree of life. The two rewards of which Revelation 22:14 speaks—the city and the tree—function as sacraments that point to and make present Jesus as the reality of the blessing God gives to us. With regard to the first of the two rewards, I recognize that Revelation 21 presents the New Jerusalem as the bride (21:2, 9–10), and hence as a picture of the people of God, while my sermon focuses on Jesus as the contents of our reward. But the metaphor of the city speaks also of Jesus. It is in him that the bride finds her perfection. It is Jesus' perfect humanity that perfects the church. Thus the glorious descriptions of the church apply to Jesus and vice versa. The church, as St. Augustine was wont to say, is the *totus Christus*, the whole Christ.

As to the second reward, the suggestion that the tree of life is Christ himself is not original to me. Interpreters throughout the tradition have made this allegorical identification.[2] The reasons are mainly theological: since Christ is the Wisdom of God who gives us eternal life, we may see this wisdom foreshadowed in the paradisal tree of life. After all, eating from the original tree would have given eternal life (Gen. 3:22). Hence, when Proverbs 3:18 identifies wisdom as the tree of life that blesses those who hold fast to her, the christological link should jump off the page: partaking of Christ—the Wisdom of God—gives the blessing of eternal life. None of this is particularly revolutionary; certainly it isn't arbitrary. Rather, it is the kind of allegorizing to which a serious theological reading of the text almost inevitably leads.

This rationale for identifying Christ as the tree of life helps us respond to the charge of arbitrariness, commonly made in the direction of spiritual exegesis.[3] The accusation usually ignores the remarkable

2. See Menahem Kister, "The Tree of Life and the Turning Sword," in *Paradise in Antiquity: Jewish and Christian Views*, ed. Markus Bockmuehl and Guy G. Stroumsa (Cambridge: Cambridge University Press, 2010), 140n8.

3. See, e.g., G. W. H. Lampe's accusations of arbitrariness, as discussed by Peter Bouteneff, *Beginnings: Ancient Christian Readings of Biblical Creation Narratives* (Grand Rapids: Baker Academic, 2008), 177.

similarities in the exegesis of premodern theologians. The notion of
Christ as tree of life runs like a thread throughout the tradition. This
is something we would hardly expect if allegorizing were mostly an
arbitrary exercise. Indeed, I am convinced that most Christian use
of allegory is anything but arbitrary. It is typically christologically
grounded, and theological considerations—such as the ones described
above—determine the appropriateness of its use.[4] As a result, there
tends to be a great deal more similarity in exegetical outcome among
advocates of spiritual interpretation than among those who restrict
themselves to literal or historical exegetical methods. Once a common
theological starting point no longer enters into the exegetical practice,
exegesis inevitably becomes dependent on the insights of individual
historians. And experience teaches that these insights tend to vary
more than the interpretations of those who consciously stand in line
with the christological exegesis of the great tradition of the church.

The Christocentricity of my sermon is in some way to be expected
because Jesus is speaking in the text. At least that's how I read the
passage. Some translations see Revelation 22:14–15 as Johannine
commentary sandwiched between Jesus' words in 22:12–13 and 16.
Certainty is impossible on this score, but the unity of the passage is
more obvious if we take the entire section (22:12–16) as spoken by
Jesus. The beauty of such a reading is that Jesus holds himself out
to us as the blessing of eternal life, much as he does in the Beatitudes
of the Sermon on the Mount.

Of still greater christological significance is the underlying doctrine
of participation, which says that our works are good simply because
their identity lies in our connection with Christ. Without a doctrine
of participation, the emphasis on works in the book of Revelation
would seem to be seriously problematic. First, it would lead to an
irreconcilable tension within the book: How does one accept both
that we will be judged according to our works (Rev. 2:23; 20:12–13)

4. One might argue that similarities in premodern exegesis are simply the result
of various interpreters slavishly following one another and that the initial interpretive
choices may have been arbitrary. Such exegetical imitation undoubtedly happened a
great deal. But the centrality of Christology nonetheless provides the overall sense
of continuity within much premodern exegesis, and this Christ-centeredness pleads
against the notion that patristic allegory is arbitrary in character.

and that we are saved by the blood of the Lamb? Furthermore, if works are indeed a prior condition that we are to fulfill before we can participate in the blessing, then avoiding Pelagian implications becomes almost impossible because we are then faced with the arduous task of conjuring up our own virtuous lives. The right approach is to say that God in Christ is himself our perfect happiness, and that by faith in Christ we come to participate in this happiness. This implies that the righteous deeds of the saints and the washing of our robes in the blood of the Lamb are simply two different angles from which to look at the same thing, namely, our participation in Christ. Union with Christ—participation in him—is thus the theologically proper response to the otherwise interminable quandary of grace versus works.[5] Salvation is indeed *sola gratia*. One aspect of this grace is that God generously forgives us our many remaining sins and weaknesses in and through Christ. But salvation is not *sola gratia* in the sense that our works don't matter in bringing us to perfect happiness; the book of Revelation is unambiguous on that score. Rather, it is *sola gratia* in the sense that our works are also the result of Christ graciously enabling us to share or participate in the blessing of his life.

I bring out the participatory aspect of salvation in two places in the sermon. The first occurrence is when, twice in a row, I make the point that "a blessing is always a gift." That is to say, both the city and the tree are God's gifts to us. We don't create the conditions for the arrival of the kingdom of God. Only when we construe human activity as something separate from what God does in history can we arrive at the notion that we ourselves bring about the kingdom of God. I emphasize this point because some see in the city metaphor of Revelation 21 an emphasis on the continuity between our cultural endeavors today and the future resurrection life. Such a reading fails to recognize that the city comes "out of heaven from God" (21:2), and it ignores the fact that paradisal imagery (lacking any sort of human accomplishment) accompanies that of the city. Also here, participation theology would seem eminently helpful. The second occurrence

5. See the excellent book by Charles Raith, *Aquinas and Calvin on Romans: God's Justification and Our Participation* (Oxford: Oxford University Press, 2014).

is when I more explicitly address the question of how we can obtain white garments, through the blood of Christ or through our works. Again, we should avoid any false dichotomy. For St. John, it appears that both are the case. It is by the doctrine of participation that one avoids any sense of Pelagian works righteousness.

Part 4

Unveiled Happiness

*C*learly, the happiness for which we aim is an ineffable reality; words simply don't match up to it. This happiness reaches far beyond any satisfaction we gain from this-worldly goods (part 1, "Sensed Happiness"). Therefore, this happiness makes our pilgrimage eminently worthwhile (part 2, "Pilgrim Happiness"). Only the endpoint of the journey, heaven, satisfies our desires and gives us Christ as happiness (part 3, "Heavenly Happiness").

At this point, we come to the most significant aspect of heavenly happiness: God's promise that we will see him face-to-face. Thus much of the discussion in part 4 is centered on the topic of the beatific vision. As we will see, this contemplation of God is what Jacob experiences in his dream at Bethel (Gen. 28). It is also the vision of the divine chariot, symbolizing God's glory and power, which startles Ezekiel (Ezek. 1). And it is the transforming vision that St. Paul speaks of when he insists that, with unveiled faces, we can behold the glory of God in Christ (2 Cor. 3). We've reached the summit of happiness when, at the top of the ladder, God gives us a glimpse of his face.

12

The Gate of Heaven

Genesis 28:10–22

Genesis 28:10–22

¹⁰ Jacob left Beersheba and went toward Haran. ¹¹ And he came to a certain place and stayed there that night, because the sun had set. Taking one of the stones of the place, he put it under his head and lay down in that place to sleep. ¹² And he dreamed, and behold, there was a ladder set up on the earth, and the top of it reached to heaven. And behold, the angels of God were ascending and descending on it! ¹³ And behold, the Lord stood above it and said, "I am the Lord, the God of Abraham your father and the God of Isaac. The land on which you lie I will give to you and to your offspring. ¹⁴ Your offspring shall be like the dust of the earth, and you shall spread abroad to the west and to the east and to the north and to the south, and in you and your offspring shall all the families of the earth be blessed. ¹⁵ Behold, I am with you and will keep you wherever you go, and will bring you back to this land. For I will not leave you until I have done what I have promised you." ¹⁶ Then Jacob awoke from his sleep and said, "Surely the Lord is in this place, and I did not know it." ¹⁷ And he was afraid and said, "How awesome is this place! This is none other than the house of God, and this is the gate of heaven."

¹⁸ So early in the morning Jacob took the stone that he had put under his head and set it up for a pillar and poured oil on the top of it. ¹⁹ He called the name of that place Bethel, but the name of the city was Luz at the first. ²⁰ Then Jacob made a vow, saying, "If God will be with me and will keep me in this way that I go, and will give me bread to eat and clothing to wear, ²¹ so that I come again to my father's house in peace, then the Lᴏʀᴅ shall be my God, ²² and this stone, which I have set up for a pillar, shall be God's house. And of all that you give me I will give a full tenth to you."

John 1:43–51

⁴³ The next day Jesus decided to go to Galilee. He found Philip and said to him, "Follow me." ⁴⁴ Now Philip was from Bethsaida, the city of Andrew and Peter. ⁴⁵ Philip found Nathanael and said to him, "We have found him of whom Moses in the Law and also the prophets wrote, Jesus of Nazareth, the son of Joseph." ⁴⁶ Nathanael said to him, "Can anything good come out of Nazareth?" Philip said to him, "Come and see." ⁴⁷ Jesus saw Nathanael coming toward him and said of him, "Behold, an Israelite indeed, in whom there is no deceit!" ⁴⁸ Nathanael said to him, "How do you know me?" Jesus answered him, "Before Philip called you, when you were under the fig tree, I saw you." ⁴⁹ Nathanael answered him, "Rabbi, you are the Son of God! You are the King of Israel!" ⁵⁰ Jesus answered him, "Because I said to you, 'I saw you under the fig tree,' do you believe? You will see greater things than these." ⁵¹ And he said to him, "Truly, truly, I say to you, you will see heaven opened, and the angels of God ascending and descending on the Son of Man."

Sunday, August 18, 2013

In today's passage, Jacob is traveling, and he spends the night, as we read in Genesis 28:11, at "a certain place." This morning we are going to travel with Jacob, and I want to explore with you what it means for us to spend the night with Jacob at "a certain place." We find the word "place" six times in this story, so it's not a bad thing for us to spend some time thinking about it. You and I are modern-day nomads. Cars and airplanes have made it easy for us to travel. Many of us, I'm sure, have gone through several moves in our lifetime. I have relocated numerous times over the years. Most of my students at Regent College have uprooted and planted themselves for a couple of years in a completely new environment in Vancouver. At some level, this is just the way things are. Today's world makes it *possible* for us, and often simply *requires* us, to move around from place to place. Perhaps our many travels make us more aware than preceding generations of the deep significance of the particularity of "a certain place."

We have here the story of someone who is uprooted, who has no place to call his own. You remember what has led up to this. With the help of his mother, Rebekah, Jacob deceived his father. Pretending to be his elder brother Esau, Jacob entered his father Isaac's tent with meat that he claimed to have hunted in the field. Although Isaac, pretty much blind, was suspicious about the identity of the son he had in front of him, he ended up giving Jacob the blessing of the firstborn. Esau cried out with "an exceedingly great and bitter cry," we read (Gen. 27:34): "Bless me, even me also, O my father!" But Isaac responded, "Your brother came deceitfully, and he has taken away your blessing" (27:35). With Esau seething with anger, Jacob was forced to flee. So he has become a nomad and has set out on a long trek—about 550 miles in all—from Beersheba in the south to Haran in the north, in Syria where Rebekah's brother Laban lives with his family.

With nothing but a staff in his hand (32:10) and the blessing of the firstborn in his mind, Jacob sets out from home to a country about which he has only ever heard stories that his mother told him as a child. It is evening, and as the sun goes down, Jacob looks for a place to spend the night. All the fugitive has is a stone to use as a pillow to lay down his head. We don't read what Jacob is thinking or how he is feeling as he spends this first night out in the open near the town of Luz. Whatever may be going through his head, clearly the misery he is experiencing is the sad consequence of his and his mother's selfish, foolish duplicity. Yet God decides to work in the midst of this web of deception. Jacob has a dream. "*Behold*, there was a ladder" (28:12). "And *behold*, the angels of God were ascending and descending on it!" (v. 12). "And *behold*, the LORD stood above it" (v. 13). Finally, in verse 15 we read, "*Behold*, I am with you." God clearly wants us to sit up and listen. There's something important going on here. And as we'll soon find out, something startling is indeed about to take place.

Jacob sees this ladder that reaches from earth to heaven. Now, I don't want us to think of the kind of ladder that we use to clean out the gutters in the spring. Most Bible scholars agree that what Jacob sees is called a ziggurat. I want to show you one on the picture here.

Figure 2. Ziggurat

At the time of Abraham, Isaac, and Jacob, these huge structures were common in the areas of modern-day Iraq and Iran. No doubt Grandfather Abraham had seen them around Ur of the Chaldeans before God told him, "Go from your country and your kindred and your father's house to the land that I will show you" (12:1). As a little child, Jacob had heard stories about ziggurats. They were impressive structures with huge staircases leading to the top. Ziggurats were giant temples. At the very top lived the gods themselves. In other words, the very way ziggurats were built said something about what they were meant to do: they were meant to link heaven and earth. The huge staircase running to the top of the ziggurat conveyed to the worshipers: the gods may live up there in heaven at the top of the structure, and we may live down here, but the staircase is a link. We're not alone in the world. This is a place that links heaven and earth, that connects us to the gods above.

In his dream, Jacob sees angels ascending and descending on the staircase. And then we get the astonishing comment: "And behold, the LORD stood above it" (28:13). Jacob sees the Lord himself. To be sure, it's in a dream. Nonetheless, this dream is a God-induced dream, and the one standing in heaven at the top of the ziggurat genuinely relates something to Jacob in the dream. "I am the LORD, the God of Abraham your father and the God of Isaac. The land on which you lie I will give to you and to your offspring. Your offspring shall be like the dust of the earth, and you shall spread abroad to the west and to the east and to the north and to the south, and in you and your offspring shall all the families of the earth be blessed" (28:13–14). The words sound familiar to Jacob. These words, these promises—the promise of land, the promise of offspring "like the dust of the earth," the promise that through him God's blessing will extend to "all the families of the earth"—God had made them before. The words of God's promises, spoken to Abraham (12:2–3; 13:14–16), had no doubt been kept in the family, carefully guarded and passed down from generation to generation. And now, at the point where Jacob has failed morally, and where he is suffering the harshest consequences as a homeless fugitive, God appears to Jacob at the top of the staircase and reiterates the very words he spoke earlier to Abraham. For good measure, God adds the promises to protect Jacob and to bring him back home one day, and that he will definitely not leave him (28:15). God's promises will stand.

These promises come as a sudden thunderbolt. They are astounding. No doubt in part because they are so obviously undeserved, Jacob's reaction is fear. He is afraid, we read. "How awesome is this place!" he exclaims (28:17). As a bit of an aside, the word "awesome" must be one of the most misused words on the planet. We talk about successful school trips being awesome, and we call movies awesome when we like them. We've hollowed out the word "awesome." It's not just the *word* "awesome" that has lost its gravity; we have largely forgotten the *reality* of it too. When we say "awesome" we should get connotations of fearful, terrible, and dreadful, as in awe-inspiring.

What Jacob is experiencing—what anyone experiences in the presence of God and his holy angels, let alone someone as morally and spiritually bankrupt as Jacob—is dread, fear, and awe before God who appears to him here, at a certain place. And appearing not in order to condemn, not to tell Jacob, "You should've known better." Not to launch a blistering attack on this good-for-nothing failure of a man. No, appearing in order to say, "I'm still continuing with you. After all this deception, I'm still going to be your God, and the promises I have made are still going to come true. I will not let even your moral failure stand in the way."

Well, we know the rest of Jacob's reaction. He first recognizes that place matters. He recognizes the meaning of the staircase or the ziggurat. This is the "house of God," he says, "the gate of heaven" (28:17). And what do you do in the house of God? You offer worship. That's what Jacob does. He upends the stone pillow and anoints it with oil, so that it turns into a pillar of worship. He changes the name of the place from Luz to Bethel—Bethel means "house of God," after all. And Jacob responds to God's promises by saying that if God is really going to be true to what he has just said, and if God will allow him to come back home one day, then he will worship the Lord, Yahweh, as his God (28:20–21). Bethel is going to be a place of worship. It is going to be what its name indicates: the house of God.

This is not part of today's story, but twenty years later Jacob indeed comes back, and this is exactly what happens. We read about it in Genesis 35. God again appears to Jacob at the same place. God again gives him the same promise of offspring and of land. And then we read in 35:14: "And Jacob set up a pillar in the place where he had spoken with him, a pillar of stone. He poured out a drink offering on it and poured oil on it. So Jacob called the name of the place where God had spoken with him Bethel."

This is a beautiful story. It draws us in. We identify with Jacob—with his failures, with his sense of being uprooted, with his trust in the God of second chances. And we're right to do so. Even at a very basic, surface level, this story already allows our lives to enter into it. And so perhaps we're tempted to say, "Let's just leave it there." Surely, the text doesn't say anything more than this. Perhaps we should leave well enough alone, and take from the text what we can just by reading it in its own narrative context. But let me be blunt: I am convinced we should never do that. We can never *just* read it as a historical narrative.

Reading the Old Testament is kind of like celebrating the Lord's Supper. On the surface, when we celebrate the Eucharist, all we do is eat bread and drink wine. But, of course, as Christians we know better. So, when we pass the bread and the wine, we say to one another, "This is the body of Christ. This is the blood of Christ." In faith, we know there's more than just the earthly realities of bread and wine; there's the heavenly, sacramental reality of Jesus Christ himself. In partaking of the sacrament, we on earth partake of the heavenly Christ. Much the same happens when we read the Old Testament. On the surface when we read this Scripture, what we get is the story of Jacob's dream, of the stone becoming a pillar of worship, and of a city renamed Bethel. But also here, as Christians we know better: God wants us to share in a greater, sacramental reality.

How do we know this? And how do we know what sacramental reality the story is describing? The most basic indication that we should read this story like a sacrament is that Jesus reads it this way. We can see his reading of it at two points in John 1. The first is when Jesus says to Nathanael, "Behold, an Israelite indeed, in whom there is no deceit!" (John 1:47). Now this may seem like a strange comment. And even stranger—quite humorous, really, at some level—is Nathanael's innocent response: "How do you know me?" (1:48). Somehow I suspect if Jesus confronted you and me with that same comment, "Behold, an Israelite indeed, in whom there is no deceit," we wouldn't quite dare own that comment. We'd say instead, "Well, I think you *don't* actually quite know who I am. If you really knew me, you'd know that I am often quite deceitful." Not Nathanael. "How do you know me?" he responds, and we can imagine John winking at us who are listening in.

But what does Jesus mean when he calls Nathanael an Israelite in whom there is no deceit? Well, think back to Genesis. Who is deceitful all the way through? Exactly: Jacob! Jacob is a deceiver. He is a moral failure. He is not a true Israelite. We're only in Genesis 28, after all. It's not until chapter 32, when Jacob comes back from Haran and wrestles with God at the Jabbok River, that God changes his name

from Jacob to Israel. In our story, Jacob isn't a true Israelite quite yet.
He comes laden with the guilt of being a deceiver. But in John 1, as
soon as Jesus sees Nathanael, he says, "Behold, an Israelite indeed,
in whom there is no deceit!" Jesus points out that Nathanael already
has the moral character appropriate for a mature disciple of Christ.

But there's a second thing we should note in John 1. Nathanael is
dumbfounded that Jesus knows he had been sitting under a fig tree
when Philip asked him to come along to Jesus. In amazement, Nathanael calls out, "Rabbi, you are the Son of God! You are the King
of Israel!" (John 1:49). Then what does Jesus say? He makes clear
that his ability to spot Nathanael without being physically present
with him is really just a minor miracle: "You will see greater things
than these. . . . Truly, truly, I say to you, you will see heaven opened,
and the angels of God ascending and descending on the Son of Man"
(1:50–51). Aren't these the very words from Genesis 28? Didn't Jacob
see the angels of God ascending and descending on the ladder? Nathanael is the true Israelite. He is like Jacob, in a way, but he is Jacob
transformed, Jacob changed, Jacob renamed. He is going to see the
same thing Jacob saw, but with one difference. Jesus doesn't say, "You
will see the angels of God ascending and descending on the ladder."
He says, "You will see the angels of God ascending and descending
on the Son of Man."

Now this is really *awesome*—fearful, terrible, dreadful. Jesus
speaks to Nathanael of the true ziggurat. Not the type of ziggurat
you see in dreams; no, the real thing. Jesus speaks to him of the true
Bethel. Not the house of God that Jacob notices after a long day's
traveling; no, the real thing. Jesus speaks to him of a place anointed
with oil. Not a stone upended as a pillar and anointed with oil; no,
the real thing. Jesus speaks to him of the gate of heaven. Not the
kind of gate that allows for a vision of God at the end of the ladder;
no, the real thing. Jesus is pointing Nathanael to himself. Jesus says,
"In me, you find the real ziggurat, the real house of God (Bethel),
the one really anointed with oil, the real gate of heaven. In me, you
find the reality of the sacrament." In Jesus, then, we find the ladder
between heaven and earth. Heaven and earth are united in him. The
heavenly Word of God takes on earthly human flesh. The story of
Jacob's ladder gives us a glimpse into the mystery of the incarnation.

In Christ, God sets up a ladder so he can be present with us and we can belong to him.

A moment ago, I said that reading the Old Testament is kind of like celebrating the Lord's Supper. Why is that? In the Eucharist earthly objects (bread and wine) make present to us heavenly realities (the body and blood of Christ). The story of Jacob's ladder does much the same thing. This isn't just the story of Jacob the deceiver being encouraged despite his moral failure. That's just the surface level. This story says to you and me that there is a certain place you can identify as the house of God, as the gate of heaven. Jesus Christ is that place. When you stay at that place, you will be changed, you will be transformed. Instead of Jacob, you will be called "an Israelite indeed, in whom there is no deceit."

This is really an awesome story. It tells us there's a certain place, a place where we see heaven open and the angels of God ascending and descending. Perhaps sometimes our nights stay dark and heaven remains closed to us. If so, perhaps we need to ask ourselves: Do we actually spend the night at Bethel? Obviously, I am not talking at the superficial, bread-and-wine level of the story of Genesis 28. I am speaking about the deeper reality of it, about Christ himself. Do we spend the night in his presence? God reminds us today that heaven is always open, that the angels always ascend and descend, that he always welcomes us into his presence. The question is not, why is God not present with me? The question is, am I in the kind of place where God can be found? God's love for us is constant, his goodness always real. But his love and goodness are given to us at "a certain place." So often we try to travel alone. But Jesus says to us, "You need to be where I am. If you stay with me, you will certainly see heaven open." And he will address us as if we were Jacob, as if we were Nathanael: "Behold," he will say to you and to me, "an Israelite indeed, in whom there is no deceit!"

Preacher's Notes

By drawing a parallel in this sermon between our reading of Genesis 28 and our eating of bread and wine in the Lord's Supper, I made explicit what is merely implicit in most of the other sermons in this book: that biblical exegesis is a sacramental practice. When we see Christ in the Old Testament, it is not because we've put him there but because we find him there. Christ is really present in the text, whether we see him there or not. The deepest and truest meaning of Genesis 28 is the one we read in the Gospel of John. We haven't really understood the ladder of Genesis 28 until we see the angels ascending and descending on the Son of Man.

It is important to understand the exact nature of this claim. Many contemporary readers recognize the link between Genesis 28 and John 1. Many exegetes agree that Jesus views himself against the backdrop of the earlier Jacob narrative. That Jesus is the antitype of earlier biblical types that foreshadow him is also commonly acknowledged. Typology is a widely accepted interpretive strategy also advocated by well-known biblical scholars.[1] Before I continue, we need to pause and duly note this fairly broad acceptance of typological exegesis. It is something to be celebrated since it treats the canon as a unity and understands Christ against the Old Testament background, which sheds genuine light on who he is and what he does.

But let's raise a follow-up question. Is Jesus' use of Genesis 28 proper exegesis? I wouldn't be surprised if many of those who recognize the typological similarities between the two chapters would balk at this. Yes, Jesus understands himself as the link between heaven and earth, and as such he is the true ziggurat. He understands himself in the light of the narrative of Genesis 28. But many contemporary readers will shy away from the additional claim that by pointing to himself as the reality of the Genesis story, Jesus is actually opening up the *meaning* of this Old Testament chapter. Not that this is seen as a shortcoming in Jesus. Rather, it is simply

1. Much of N. T. Wright's exegesis, e.g., is typological. Wright develops a sevenfold typology of the exodus in relationship to Jesus in *Simply Jesus: A New Vision of Who He Was, What He Did, and Why It Matters* (New York: HarperOne, 2011), 63–66, 174–76. Wright also recognizes the typological correspondence between the story of Elizabeth and Zechariah in Luke 1 and Hannah and Elkanah in 1 Samuel 1:1–2:11 in *The New Testament and the People of God*, vol. 1 of *Christian Origins and the Question of God* (Minneapolis: Fortress, 1992), 379–81, though he immediately adds that "this is neither random nor arbitrary: it is held firmly *within a historical scheme*" (381, emphasis original).

not his intention to interpret Genesis 28. He merely wishes to point out certain similarities between Nathanael and Jacob and between himself and the ziggurat. At most, perhaps, the coming of Jesus is regarded as adding a dimension to our understanding of Genesis 28 that previously wasn't there, so that when we see Christ in the Old Testament, we arrive at a fuller meaning (*sensus plenior*) than we had before.[2]

My claim in this book goes beyond acknowledging that there are similarities between Genesis 28 and John 1. I am convinced that what Jesus is doing in John 1 is bringing out the actual meaning of Genesis 28. That is to say, he interprets this chapter and claims that, at its deepest level, it is about him. He is not merely pointing to typological similarities between Old and New. Rather, he is saying that the New was always already present in the Old. He himself is the reality (*res*) of the sacrament (*sacramentum*) of the text. The biblical text is a sacrament, and Christ is really present in it. We don't put him there; we find him there.

Back in the late 1940s, a brief but important public debate took place between two Jesuit patristic scholars and friends—Henri de Lubac and Jean Daniélou—on precisely this issue.[3] Daniélou took the stance that proper, typological exegesis should look for both similarities and dissimilarities between the Old and the New Testaments. Such typological exegesis, he insisted, does justice to the author's intent and genuinely takes into account Scripture's historical

2. For further discussion on the topic of *sensus plenior*, see Raymond Edward Brown, *The* Sensus Plenior *of Sacred Scripture* (Baltimore: St. Mary's University Press, 1955); Douglas J. Moo, "The Problem of *Sensus Plenior*," in *Hermeneutics, Authority, and Canon*, ed. D. A. Carson and John D. Woodbridge (Grand Rapids: Academie Books, 1986), 179–211.

3. Setting off the public discussion between de Lubac and Daniélou was the latter's essay, "Traversée de la Mer Rouge et baptême aux premiers siècles," *Recherches de science religieuse* 33 (1946): 402–30. De Lubac reacted in "'Typologie' et 'allégorisme,'" *Recherches de science religieuse* 34 (1947): 180–226; English translation: de Lubac, "Typology and Allegorization," in *Theological Fragments*, trans. Rebecca Howell Balinski (San Francisco: Ignatius, 1989), 129–64. Without mentioning de Lubac by name, Daniélou responded the next year with "Les divers sens de l'Écriture dans la tradition chrétienne primitive," *Ephemerides theologicae lovanienses* 24 (1948): 119–26. For detailed discussion of the debate, see Hans Boersma, *Nouvelle Théologie and Sacramental Ontology: A Return to Mystery* (Oxford: Oxford University Press, 2009), 180–90.

progression as it moves from type to antitype.[4] Daniélou believed that by contrast, the allegorical tradition of exegesis—found among many of the patristic and medieval followers of the third-century biblical interpreter Origen—does not take history seriously and ends up arbitrarily imposing alien meanings onto the biblical text. De Lubac strongly disagreed. He argued that Daniélou's contrast between typology and allegory was merely artificial, alien to the biblical scholarship in which the early church's preachers actually engaged. Moreover, de Lubac was also skeptical of Daniélou's criticisms of Origenist allegorizing, maintaining instead that allegorizing is the proper outcome of a sacramental hermeneutic. Allegory, de Lubac argued, is the result of identifying Christ as the mystery of the sacrament within the Old Testament.

For the most part, de Lubac had the better part of this debate. Patristic scholars today commonly acknowledge that the difference between typology and allegory doesn't do justice to the complexity of patristic approaches to the biblical text.[5] Also, de Lubac's in-depth work on patristic and medieval exegesis shows that Christology drives the sacramental exegesis of the premodern period. Although de Lubac may have been overly generous in his insistence that Origen always upheld the literal, historical character of events described in the Old Testament, he was right to claim that what motivates allegorical exegesis is the sacramental conviction that Christ is already present in the Old Testament narrative and that properly to interpret the Old Testament is to find him there, not to put him there.

In this sermon, I purposely recount the actual story of Jacob's journey to Haran and his vision of the ladder. Doing so enables the listeners to identify with what is going on in the sermon. Storytelling is an underrated but important homiletical approach. By telling the story, I also rhetorically set up the hearers for the unexpected moment when I ask whether perhaps we should limit ourselves to the surface level of the story. After all, doesn't narrative have its own attractive

4. It is important to note, however, that unlike exegetes who restrict themselves to only one meaning found in the intent of the author, Daniélou was willing to speak of two meanings: one literal and the other typological (or christological).

5. See the helpful discussion in Daniel J. Treier, *Introducing Theological Interpretation of Scripture* (Grand Rapids: Baker Academic, 2008), 45–51.

power? My response to this question is unequivocal: we should *never* restrict ourselves to just the story inasmuch as we *always* have to turn to Christ. The Old Testament's meaning and truth lie in its sacramental reality, which I am convinced drove the allegorizing approaches of earlier generations of Bible readers, and should continue to give shape to our preaching today.

13

When the Heavens Open Up

Ezekiel 1

Ezekiel 1

¹In the thirtieth year, in the fourth month, on the fifth day of the month, as I was among the exiles by the Chebar canal, the heavens were opened, and I saw visions of God. ²On the fifth day of the month (it was the fifth year of the exile of King Jehoiachin), ³the word of the Lord came to Ezekiel the priest, the son of Buzi, in the land of the Chaldeans by the Chebar canal, and the hand of the Lord was upon him there.

⁴As I looked, behold, a stormy wind came out of the north, and a great cloud, with brightness around it, and fire flashing forth continually, and in the midst of the fire, as it were gleaming metal. ⁵And from the midst of it came the likeness of four living creatures. And this was their appearance: they had a human likeness, ⁶but each had four faces, and each of them had four wings. ⁷Their legs were straight, and the soles of their feet were like the sole of a calf's foot. And they sparkled like burnished bronze. ⁸Under their wings on their four sides they had human hands. And the four had their faces and their wings thus: ⁹their wings touched one another. Each one of

them went straight forward, without turning as they went. [10] As for the likeness of their faces, each had a human face. The four had the face of a lion on the right side, the four had the face of an ox on the left side, and the four had the face of an eagle. [11] Such were their faces. And their wings were spread out above. Each creature had two wings, each of which touched the wing of another, while two covered their bodies. [12] And each went straight forward. Wherever the spirit would go, they went, without turning as they went. [13] As for the likeness of the living creatures, their appearance was like burning coals of fire, like the appearance of torches moving to and fro among the living creatures. And the fire was bright, and out of the fire went forth lightning. [14] And the living creatures darted to and fro, like the appearance of a flash of lightning.

[15] Now as I looked at the living creatures, I saw a wheel on the earth beside the living creatures, one for each of the four of them. [16] As for the appearance of the wheels and their construction: their appearance was like the gleaming of beryl. And the four had the same likeness, their appearance and construction being as it were a wheel within a wheel. [17] When they went, they went in any of their four directions without turning as they went. [18] And their rims were tall and awesome, and the rims of all four were full of eyes all around. [19] And when the living creatures went, the wheels went beside them; and when the living creatures rose from the earth, the wheels rose. [20] Wherever the spirit wanted to go, they went, and the wheels rose along with them, for the spirit of the living creatures was in the wheels. [21] When those went, these went; and when those stood, these stood; and when those rose from the earth, the wheels rose along with them, for the spirit of the living creatures was in the wheels.

[22] Over the heads of the living creatures there was the likeness of an expanse, shining like awe-inspiring crystal, spread out above their heads. [23] And under the expanse their wings were stretched out straight, one toward another. And each creature had two wings covering its body. [24] And when they went, I heard the sound of their wings like the sound of many waters, like the sound of the Almighty, a sound of tumult like the sound of an army. When they stood still, they let down their wings. [25] And there came a voice from above the expanse over their heads. When they stood still, they let down their wings.

[26] And above the expanse over their heads there was the likeness of a throne, in appearance like sapphire; and seated above the likeness of a throne was a likeness with a human appearance. [27] And upward from what had the appearance of his waist I saw as it were gleaming metal, like the appearance of fire enclosed all around. And

downward from what had the appearance of his waist I saw as it
were the appearance of fire, and there was brightness around him.
²⁸ Like the appearance of the bow that is in the cloud on the day of
rain, so was the appearance of the brightness all around.
Such was the appearance of the likeness of the glory of the Lᴏʀᴅ. And
when I saw it, I fell on my face, and I heard the voice of one speaking.

Sunday, December 16, 2007

What an assault on the senses, this vision of Ezekiel. It is like a 3-D
movie flashing in front of him. God grabs ahold of his senses: his *eyes*
as the brilliant fire flashes like lightning in front of him; his *ears* as the
wings of the four creatures roar like rushing waters and the wheels
rumble like an earthquake; his *touch* as, in chapter 3, the Spirit lifts
Ezekiel up from the ground and carries him to the exiles by the Chebar
canal; even his *taste*, as—again in chapter 3—the Lord hands Ezekiel a
scroll, which tastes as sweet as honey in his mouth. His eyes, his ears,
his touch, and his taste—Ezekiel's senses are inundated by the vision.
He is left speechless, flat on his face, stopped in his tracks for a week
(Ezek. 3:15), completely overwhelmed by the breathtaking experience.
This is what happens when the heavens open up. When the heavens
open up and God shows up, we are thrown off-kilter, our routines are
upset, our systems are shocked, we are knocked off our feet.

I should probably warn you right at the outset: the message of this
sermon follows Ezekiel's vision. It may upset our routines, shock our
systems, maybe even knock us off our feet. Sometimes we are perhaps
secretly jealous of Ezekiel and other biblical figures, wishing that God
would open up the heavens and show himself to us. All our questions
and fears would disappear. We would no longer have to *believe*. Instead, we would *know* God is real—we would *know* he loves us. Why,
he might even give us a special job to do, much like he gave Ezekiel
a job in these first couple of chapters, calling him to be his prophet.
But before we jump to conclusions, I need to put in a word of caution:
this sermon, much like Ezekiel's vision, comes with a sharp message.

The reason for this sharp message has to do with a basic question:
When is it that the heavens open up? In terms of simple chronology,
the answer is straightforward enough: "the thirtieth year, the fourth

month, the fifth day" (1:1). Translated, that means July 31, 593 BC. But the deeper, theological answer is: when it's time to go to war. God opens up the heavens when it's time to go to war! Ezekiel undoubtedly knew this, and we too had better realize what's going on. Let's look at just one example in Scripture: Psalm 18. This psalm presents a dramatic picture of God opening up the heavens and coming down as a warrior. In 18:9 we read, "He bowed the heavens and came down." That's quite similar to what we find in Ezekiel. What does the psalmist say God came down *for*? Well, look at the verses right before, verses 7–8: "The earth reeled and rocked; the foundations also of the mountains trembled and quaked, because he was angry. Smoke went up from his nostrils, and devouring fire from his mouth; glowing coals flamed forth from him." This is an intimidating picture of a furious God in whose angry presence even the foundations of the mountains shake. Then look at verses 13–14: "The LORD also thundered in the heavens, and the Most High uttered his voice, hailstones and coals of fire. And he sent out his arrows and scattered them; he flashed forth lightnings and routed them." This is a picture of God on the warpath. When God opens up the heavens, apparently, he goes to war.

Today's passage may not seem like much of an Advent text. True, here, just as at Christmas time, the heavens open up. But in the vision of Ezekiel, there's no baby in the manger. Instead, God is on the warpath. He is sitting on top of a state-of-the-art tank, the kind of chariot the Babylonians had used a couple of years earlier to conquer Israel, only much more powerful. Let me try to picture for you, as best I can, the way this war machine functions. Four living creatures—cherubim is what chapter 10 calls them—hold up the chariot. They are angelic creatures. Now, imagine a square. In each corner of the square, there's an angel. Each of the angels has four faces—so an angel with four faces on every corner. The human face of each angel is looking outward, away from the square, away from the chariot. The eagle face looks inward toward the center of the square, toward the middle of the chariot. The ox face looks toward the left, and the lion face toward the right. Now, each of the angels also has four wings. With their top wings spread out, they touch each other's wings. In this way, these top wings serve as the platform for the divine warrior to sit on. And with their bottom two wings, the angels cover their bodies.

There's a wheel beside each of the four cherubim. So, we have four wheels under the chariot. But now look at 1:16. It says the four wheels "had the same likeness, their appearance and construction being as it were a wheel within a wheel." In other words, each wheel seems to have another wheel stuck straight into it, the two intercrossing each other. So, we really don't have just four but eight wheels in total. The direct reason each of the cherubim has a double wheel seems to be that they allow the chariot to move in any direction: not just forward and backward but also left and right. As the angels move, we read in verse 17, "they went in any of their four directions without turning as they went." The intercrossing wheels allow the creatures to turn left and right without the wheels having to actually turn.

This war machine has amazing capacities. The wings allow it to move vertically, while the wheels enable it to move horizontally in any direction. It's small wonder that this chariot looks to Ezekiel like flashing lightning. Then look at the reach this thing has. Not only do the four living creatures each have four faces—and therefore eight eyes—but also the rims of the wheels are "full of eyes all around" (1:18; cf. 10:12). This is like a tank with Google Earth installed: it's able to see and reach wherever it wants. Compared to this thing, a regular Babylonian chariot is a countryside horse and buggy. Beside it, an M1 Abrams tank is nothing but a kid's toy.

How do you react when the heavens open up and you find out that God's throne is also his tank? It really depends, doesn't it? In Psalm 18, David is thrilled when the heavens open up. God's chariot isn't there to shoot him down; it's there to deliver him from his enemies. In the right situation, knowing about God's chariot is a marvelous thing. His almighty power can reach down and save us. Isaiah even *asks* God to open up the heavens. Chapter 64: "Oh that you would rend the heavens and come down, that the mountains might quake at your presence . . . to make your name known to your adversaries, and that the nations might tremble at your presence!" (vv. 1–2). David and Isaiah are absolutely overjoyed with the prospect of God opening up the heavens. This is when their *enemies* will be defeated and the divine warrior will set *them* free!

Sounds like the thing to wish for, doesn't it—for God to rend the heavens and come down? Indeed, it is. There's nothing more glorious than the sky splitting open because God comes down. And really, Ezekiel's vision isn't the polar opposite of the incarnation. Whether he comes in a divine chariot or in a manger, either way God comes as a warrior to do battle with his enemies and to bring salvation for his people. But the question is this: When God rends the heavens to come down, will he find us as his people or will we turn out to be his enemies? Remember John's Gospel: "The light has come into the world, and people loved the darkness rather than the light because their works were evil" (John 3:19). That was true not only at the time of Jesus' birth; it was also true in Ezekiel's day. The people of Israel loved the darkness. They rejected God, and they rebelled against him. It's good news when the heavens open up, but it's good news only if we love the light.

Let's ask the question again: *When* is it that the heavens open up? It is July 31, 593 BC. Five years ago, the Babylonian king Nebuchadnezzar had laid siege to Jerusalem. He had forced the upper crust of society to move to Babylon, to the area of the Chebar canal. As a twenty-five-year-old, Ezekiel had been one of those exiles. For the past five years, life back in Judah had gone on much like before. True, Judah is merely a pawn in the hand of the great Babylonian Empire. But its residents are still their own country. They still have their own king, Zedekiah, on the throne. The temple service still goes on as it always had.

But in another seven years, Nebuchadnezzar will be back in Jerusalem. He will destroy the temple and raze the city to the ground. No one knows this disaster is just around the corner. Both the people of Judah and the exiles in Babylon are pretty sure that Jerusalem and the temple will never be destroyed. Despite their rebellious attitude, they somehow have convinced themselves that Jerusalem remains God's chosen city, that the temple is still the place of his presence. Right between the cherubim on top of the ark, that is where God's glory dwells and will remain forever. Surely, before long, life will get back to normal. The exiles will return, and God will restore his people. As long as the temple is still standing, as long as God is between the cherubim, there is every reason for confidence.

So here is Ezekiel, sitting among the exiles by the Chebar canal. He looks up. Something appears on the horizon in the north. Verse 4: "A stormy wind came out of the north, and a great cloud, with brightness around it, and fire flashing forth continually, and in the midst of the fire, as it were gleaming metal." As the storm draws closer, Ezekiel soon realizes the heavens have opened up, and what he sees is God, the great warrior, riding on the clouds. We should let this sink in for a moment. God and his cherubim are on the move. They're coming from the north. Judging by the layout of the roads, they must have traveled from Jerusalem.

Only one conclusion is possible, and it must have registered with Ezekiel like a bombshell: God is still between the cherubim, but the cherubim are no longer in the temple. They look like they've flown straight off the ark. God has left his city, and he is on the warpath. This means he is no longer protecting Jerusalem and its temple. The unimaginable is happening: God is abandoning his people. Ezekiel 10 describes in detail what's happening in Jerusalem at this time: God is getting ready to leave the city, abandon the temple, and desert his people.

To be sure, God is still a warrior. Ezekiel's vision leaves no doubt about that. But the shocking conclusion we have to draw is that his enemy is no longer Babylon. God is turning in wrath and anger against his own people! "Oh that you would rend the heavens and come down," Isaiah cries out (Isa. 64:1). Perhaps—but be careful what you wish for. God might rend the heavens, get onto his chariot, and ride out in fury against his own people! You see, this is the one thing that sets Ezekiel apart from David and Isaiah. David and Isaiah thought of the heavens opening up as good news: God, the great warrior, was on his way! But when Ezekiel saw the exact same thing, it was reason for abject fear: God, the great warrior, was on his way! Yes, Christmas is a wonderful time of the year. But sometimes I wonder whether we have lost a sense of what we're dealing with when God comes down to us. We should not be fooled. We may think that Christmas is the most wonderful time of the year. It *can* be, if we're like David or Isaiah. But if we're like the people of Judah in Ezekiel's day—if we're smug, confident that, no matter what, in the end things will be just fine—then Christmas may just be the most dangerous time of the year. When God rends the heavens, in a chariot or a manger, it's good news—but only if we love the light.

So far, Ezekiel has seen God come riding on his cherubim—and we've concluded that we don't want to be among the enemies facing the force of this divine war machine. But Ezekiel sees more than just cherubim. He sees God himself. The last part of chapter 1 talks

about this astounding reality of Ezekiel seeing God. How is this
even possible: a mere creature looking at the living God? This event
is indescribable—perhaps even impossible! Certainly, words fail us.
Words fail Ezekiel. They cannot adequately capture what he sees.
Ezekiel keeps using words such as "like," "likeness," and "appearance"
to explain what he sees. I'll give you just a couple of examples, but
really, this is all over the place. Let's read just Ezekiel 1:26–28 together:

> Above the expanse over their [the cherubim's] heads there was the
> *likeness* of a throne, in *appearance like* sapphire; and seated above
> the *likeness* of a throne was a *likeness* with a human *appearance*. And
> upward from what had the *appearance* of his waist I saw *as it were*
> gleaming metal, *like* the *appearance* of fire enclosed all around. And
> downward from what had the *appearance* of his waist I saw as it were
> the *appearance* of fire, and there was brightness around him. *Like* the
> *appearance* of the bow that is in the cloud on the day of rain, so was
> the *appearance* of the brightness all around.

Words fail Ezekiel. The vision is indescribable.

God gives Ezekiel a glimpse into his throne room. Even that glimpse
Ezekiel cannot put into words. It's much like St. Paul, who, caught up
into the third heaven, hears "things that cannot be told, which man
may not utter" (2 Cor. 12:4). It's not surprising that at the end of the
vision, Ezekiel doesn't just say, "That's what my vision of God was
like." Instead, he says in the middle of 1:28, "Such was the *appearance*
of the *likeness* of the *glory* of the Lord." Even though Ezekiel gets
to see God's throne—his chariot-throne—Ezekiel remains a creature,
and his eyes do not grasp the infinite glory of God.

Some Bible readers have been so impressed with the glory of God
that they believe Ezekiel didn't actually see God himself. I don't think
such a reading is right. Still, the way Ezekiel talks about seeing God
reminds us of an important truth. Scripture says that "no one has ever
seen God" (John 1:18), and God "dwells in unapproachable light" so
that "no one has ever seen or can see" him (1 Tim. 6:16). We'd better
take these passages seriously. Whenever the Bible talks about seeing
God—or about not being able to see him—one thing stands out: God
is awe-inspiring. If there's one thing we should take from these passages, it is that we should completely rid ourselves of the familiarity

with which so many contemporary Christians treat the infinite God and Creator of the universe. Still, the question remains: How come Ezekiel sees God, yet the Bible insists that no one can see God and live?

Let's once more ask ourselves the question: When is it that the heavens open up? We know the most important answer to that question: "When the fullness of time had come, God sent forth his Son, born of woman, born under the law" (Gal. 4:4). "The Word became flesh and dwelt among us, and we have seen his glory" (John 1:14). The heavens open up in the incarnation. God stoops down to our level and shows us the Word become flesh. Isn't this the great mystery John writes about at the beginning of his first epistle? "That which was from the beginning, which we have heard, which we have seen with our eyes, which we looked upon and have touched with our hands, concerning the word of life . . . we proclaim to you" (1 John 1:1–2). That which we have heard, seen, and touched—these words bespeak the eternal Word of life. It is through the senses that God comes to us. Even in the incarnation—especially in the incarnation—he comes to us through the senses. That makes the incarnation the greatest sacrament ever. It is through our ears, through our eyes, and through our taste that God unveils himself to us. God always comes to us in sacraments. Ezekiel sees God in a sacrament: his vision at the Chebar canal. John sees God in a sacrament: he sees and touches the Word of life itself. We too see God in sacraments: he gives himself to us in human words, in bread and wine.

When Ezekiel comes face-to-face with the glory of God, we cannot but think of the glory of God in Jesus Christ. After all, Ezekiel's sacrament—the chariot of the presence of God—makes present to us the great sacrament of Christ himself. When a well-known medieval theologian, Gregory the Great, read in this chapter that the heavens opened up for Ezekiel, he too wondered how it could be that a human being could see the eternal, invisible God.[1] St. Gregory realized one thing: Ezekiel's vision is a sacrament that makes present the great sacrament of Christ. Gregory went so far as to suggest that even the wheels tell us something about the gospel of Christ. Gregory pictured

---

1. For Gregory's two homilies on the wheels in Ezekiel 1, see Gregory the Great, *Homilies on the Book of the Prophet Ezekiel*, 2nd ed. (Etna, CA: Center for Traditionalist Orthodox Studies, 2008), I.6 and I.7, pp. 95–132.

the wheels somewhat differently from the way I explained them earlier. When he read about the intercrossing wheels, he saw that 1:16 refers to "a wheel within a wheel." Gregory couldn't help but think of the inside wheel as the gospel hiding, as it were, within the outside wheel of the Old Testament. Hidden inside the Old Testament stories, he was convinced, are little gems, glittering like gospel gold. Just like the sacrament of baptism is more than just a sprinkling with water, so the wheel is more than just an axle with spokes and a rim. Just like the sacrament of Communion is, deep-down, participation in the body of Christ, so the Old Testament is a sacrament of the presence of Christ.

Gregory, in his wonderful sixth-century sermon, looked at the wheels just like the image in figure 1 (located at the front of this book), which is a wonderful painting by Fra Angelico from about 1450, held in a museum in Florence. On the left, underneath the wheel, we see the prophet Ezekiel. He is lying down by the Chebar canal.[2] On the right at the bottom, our preacher, Gregory, has joined Ezekiel by the river. Fra Angelico is a good Bible reader: he knows that Gregory too is somewhere there in the story. And then there is this wheel within a wheel. For Gregory, the outside wheel is the Old Testament. All the figures we see on the outside wheel are Old Testament prophets. The inside wheel is the New Testament. Gregory puts it this way in his sermon: "The Old and New Law are to be understood as a double wheel: The outside wheel is the covering one, while the second, covered wheel, is the wheel that does the uncovering."[3] What he means is simply this: the gospel, Jesus Christ himself, lies hidden inside the sacrament of the Old Testament. God doesn't want us to be struck dead when we see him, so he comes to us in sacraments.

Knowing that Christ is there, present in the chariot, is perhaps an unnerving idea. What if he shows up as our enemy rather than as our Savior? It is certainly possible for the flashing brilliance of God in Christ to blind us, to knock us out, perhaps even to kill us. But God's desire for us is not to have us dead, much as he didn't show

2. Ezekiel is also pictured toward the top right of the outer wheel.
3. Gregory the Great, *In Ezek.*, bk. 1, h. 7, n. 15 (*PL* 77.844–48), as quoted in Henri de Lubac, *Medieval Exegesis: The Four Senses of Scripture*, trans. Mark Sebanc (Grand Rapids: Eerdmans, 1998), 1:257.

Ezekiel the vision in order to put an end to him. The Lord is Savior to all. True, in this chapter he comes in judgment on his people. But later on, in Ezekiel 43, God rides his chariot back into the temple. God's light is the light of the gospel. "God is light, and in him is no darkness at all" (1 John 1:5). God is love, not hatred. The light that God shines in his incarnate Word, in Jesus Christ, is absolutely brilliant. To reject that light means to be blinded by it and so to end up in utter darkness. The love that reaches out to us in the gospel burns with fiery hot passion. To scorn that love is to find yourself out in the freezing cold of hell. "This is the judgment," John's Gospel reads, "the light has come into the world, and people loved the darkness rather than the light because their works were evil" (John 3:19). God's love is constant. It is unchanging. But when we reject his love in our lives, we experience God as a spurned lover, a jealous lover. The figure in the angelic chariot does not change. He is only love. The problem is not God and his desire to save his people. The problem is you and I, sitting by the Chebar canal.

When do the heavens open up? They open up when it's time for war. I'm not sure if you've ever thought of Christmas in that light. But at Christmastime the heavens open up. At Christmastime angelic messengers flash through the skies. At Christmastime the eternal warrior-Word arrives in human flesh. The gospel wheels are racing through the world. The divine warrior is coming to the rescue. We see the brightness of his light; we feel the burning of his love. And Christ is asking you and me, "Are you ready for the brilliance of my coming?"

Preacher's Notes

In this second sermon of the section on unveiled happiness, I put the word "unveiled" and the notion of happiness both under scrutiny. With regard to the former, in Ezekiel's vision the unveiling is unmistakable as Ezekiel sees the divine chariot and even "a likeness with a human appearance" inside the chariot (Ezek. 1:26). But God's unveiling isn't like human unveiling. God always shows himself in sacramental form, beyond which there are always greater depths of divine glory. As Hans Urs von Balthasar rightly explains, God's unveiling goes hand in hand

with an ever-greater veiling of his glory; the more of God's glory we
see, the greater the depth of his mystery appears.[4] Because God limits
the self-disclosure of his revelation to the form of a sacrament, we
are able to see him when he unveils himself to us. God's sacramental
unveiling is, therefore, an act of grace that ensures Ezekiel doesn't get
struck down as God comes to him in the heavenly chariot.

God's unveiling of himself in sacramental form means that Old
Testament theophanies such as this vision genuinely involve seeing
God himself, while at the same time they imply seeing God *in Christ*.
Some of the early church fathers, such as St. Irenaeus, were unwill-
ing to acknowledge that Ezekiel truly saw God.[5] Such reservations
stem from a laudable respect for the infinite greatness of God's glory,
which human sight cannot capture, not even in the beatific vision of
the hereafter. For this reason, many of the church fathers before the
Council of Nicaea (325) insisted that the visions of God were not
really visions of God; they were visions of Christ. The difficulty with
this idea is that it seems to introduce a ranking order between God
(the Father) and Christ—something the fourth-century Arians were
quick to exploit.[6] Rather than suggest that Ezekiel saw merely the
preincarnate Christ, it seems better to me to say that he saw God *in
Christ*. That is to say, all human seeing of God is limited to human
capacities, and God accommodates himself to those capacities by
providing sacraments—hence this sermon's language of Ezekiel's vision as a sacrament and of Christ as God's ultimate sacrament for us.
Here on earth God always reveals himself through sacramental means.

Although in this sermon I didn't raise the question of happiness
explicitly, it is nonetheless a topic of discussion. A literal or historical

4. Hans Urs von Balthasar, *Seeing the Form*, vol. 1 of *The Glory of the Lord: A
Theological Aesthetics*, trans. Erasmo Leiva-Merikakis, ed. Joseph Fessio and John
Riches (San Francisco: Ignatius, 1982), 441–62. Cf. Aidan Nichols, *The Word Has
Been Abroad: A Guide through Balthasar's Aesthetics* (Washington, DC: Catholic
University of America Press, 1998), 38–39.

5. Irenaeus, *Against Heresies* IV.20.10. Cf. Angela Russell Christman, *"What Did
Ezekiel See?" Christian Exegesis of Ezekiel's Vision of the Chariot from Irenaeus to
Gregory the Great* (Leiden: Brill, 2005), 69–70.

6. See Bogdan G. Bucur, "Theophanies and Vision of God in Augustine's *De
Trinitate*: An Eastern Orthodox Perspective," *St Vladimir's Theological Quarterly*
52 (2008): 67–93.

reading of Ezekiel 1 indicates—on my understanding at least—a message of impending judgment. God's appearance to Ezekiel in Babylon implies that he has abandoned his people because of their sin. This absence of God means the absence of happiness. I deal with this problem in three steps—three steps in the pursuit of happiness. In the first and largest part of the sermon, I give a contextual, historical exegesis of the chapter focused on the four living creatures (1:5–14) and on the wheels of the chariot (1:15–21). Consequently, I discuss God's departure from the temple. The veiling of God from his people and the misery this entails are the very opposite of the happiness that they believed to be as inviolable as God's presence in the temple.

In the second part, which is relatively brief, I turn from the people of Judah (and the exiles) to the prophet himself and look at what it meant for Ezekiel to experience the vision of God (1:22–28). Here I highlight both that human discourse cannot properly convey the reality of the vision of God and that in his self-revelation, God sacramentally accommodates himself to our capacities. This I follow by the third, christological section of the sermon, where I turn back to the chariot's wheels (1:15–21) to analyze Gregory's and Fra Angelico's reading of "a wheel within a wheel" (1:16). Their christological exegesis turns us back to the question of happiness. God intends only happiness for his creatures. When we don't receive it, it is because we spurn the love of God. Thus although God appears to his people in wrath, those who willingly accept his love in Christ recognize the warrior as the one who comes to rescue them. Happiness unveiled in Christ is God's purpose for us when the heavens open up.

I chose to introduce Christology in the last section of the sermon through a discussion of Gregory's and Fra Angelico's understandings of the wheels.[7] I do not mean to suggest this is the only entry point for a christological reading of the text. In some ways, it may be more in line with the literal exegesis of the text to see Christ as the occupant of the chariot, described as "a likeness with a human

7. For an excellent introduction to Gregory's sermons on the wheels, see Angela Russell Christman, "The Spirit and the Wheels: Gregory the Great on Reading Scripture," in *In Dominico Eloquio: In Lordly Eloquence: Essays on Patristic Exegesis in Honor of Robert Louis Wilken*, ed. Paul M. Blowers et al. (Grand Rapids: Eerdmans, 2002), 395–407.

appearance" (Ezek. 1:26), who Ezekiel clearly hints is God. (Fra Angelico depicts the essence of God in the gleaming metal in the midst of the fire [1:4] in the very center of his *Mystic Wheel*.) We could then see the self-revelation of God in Ezekiel 1 as a revelation of himself in Jesus Christ.

It is also interesting that, beginning with Irenaeus in the late second century and continuing throughout the Christian tradition (repeatedly reinforced in various kinds of artistic depictions), the four creatures have been interpreted as the four evangelists. For most of the tradition, the human face is Matthew, the ox is Luke, the lion is Mark, and the eagle is John. No doubt such allegorical exegesis stems in part from a desire to see the gospel as sacramentally present within the Old Testament. The chariot's speedy advance throughout the world may well have encouraged its association with the preaching of the evangelists. What is more, the distinct character of each of the Gospels was often thought to be appropriately reflected in the particular character of the creature associated with it.[8]

The understanding of a wheel within a wheel as a sacramental depiction of the relationship between the Old and New Testaments conflicts, of course, with my literal reading of the text, which sees the wheels as intercrossing. Obviously, Gregory the Great's exegesis—which he may well have adopted from the fourth-century preacher Ambrose of Milan[9]—isn't in line with the scientific, historical exegesis to which we are accustomed today. Just as ancient readers were apt to see the four evangelists depicted in the faces of the four creatures, so they were quick to recognize the relationship between the Old and New Testaments allegorically symbolized in the very words of the biblical text. But this does not mean it is carelessness or sloppiness that resulted in so many preachers interpreting the wheels as a reference to the sacramental link between the Old and New Testaments. More likely, they were interested in preaching the newness of the gospel

8. See, e.g., Augustine, *The Harmony of the Gospels*, I.6.9, in *Nicene and Post-Nicene Fathers*, series 1, ed. Philip Schaff (1888; repr., Peabody, MA: Hendrickson, 1994), 6:180–81.

9. For Ambrose's use of Ezekiel 1 in several of his works, see Angela Russell Christman, "Ambrose of Milan on Ezekiel 1 and the Virtuous Soul's Ascent to God," in *L'esegesi dei Padri Latini dalle origini a Gregorio Magno*, Studia ephemeridis Augustinianum 68 (Rome: Institutum Patristicum Augustinianum, 2000), 547–59.

and looked for places in the Old Testament that give expression to this truth. Whether this is a legitimate approach depends, I suspect, on what we regard as the task of biblical exegesis. I cannot see on what legitimate grounds we would reject it—though this collection of sermons probably makes clear that in my approach to the biblical text, I tend to be more restrained than many of my premodern precursors.

14

God of Change

2 Corinthians 3

2 Corinthians 3

¹ Are we beginning to commend ourselves again? Or do we need, as some do, letters of recommendation to you, or from you? ² You yourselves are our letter of recommendation, written on our hearts, to be known and read by all. ³ And you show that you are a letter from Christ delivered by us, written not with ink but with the Spirit of the living God, not on tablets of stone but on tablets of human hearts.

⁴ Such is the confidence that we have through Christ toward God. ⁵ Not that we are sufficient in ourselves to claim anything as coming from us, but our sufficiency is from God, ⁶ who has made us sufficient to be ministers of a new covenant, not of the letter but of the Spirit. For the letter kills, but the Spirit gives life.

⁷ Now if the ministry of death, carved in letters on stone, came with such glory that the Israelites could not gaze at Moses' face because of its glory, which was being brought to an end, ⁸ will not the ministry of the Spirit have even more glory? ⁹ For if there was glory in the ministry of condemnation, the ministry of righteousness must far exceed it in glory. ¹⁰ Indeed, in this case, what once had glory has come to have no glory at all, because of the glory that

surpasses it. [11] For if what was being brought to an end came with glory, much more will what is permanent have glory.

[12] Since we have such a hope, we are very bold, [13] not like Moses, who would put a veil over his face so that the Israelites might not gaze at the outcome of what was being brought to an end. [14] But their minds were hardened. For to this day, when they read the old covenant, that same veil remains unlifted, because only through Christ is it taken away. [15] Yes, to this day whenever Moses is read a veil lies over their hearts. [16] But when one turns to the Lord, the veil is removed. [17] Now the Lord is the Spirit, and where the Spirit of the Lord is, there is freedom. [18] And we all, with unveiled face, beholding the glory of the Lord, are being transformed into the same image from one degree of glory to another. For this comes from the Lord who is the Spirit.

Sunday, August 17, 2014

Change—how do we deal with it? We're often ambivalent toward it, aren't we? On the one hand, change happens all the time. Having recently become a grandpa for the first time, I am just astonished at how quickly a little baby changes. It's hard to believe that the child crawling all over the floor, grabbing hold of everything in sight, is the same baby who just months earlier lay peacefully in your arms, unable to move anywhere. Change is something we accept as just being part of life. On the other hand, we worship a God who does not change. The Letter of James says that God is "the Father of lights with whom there is no variation or shadow due to change" (James 1:17). If God changed in the same way a baby changes, it would be impossible to count on him. That God is *unchanging, immutable*, gives us the confidence that we are in safe hands. Creatures change; the Creator does not. So the question we face is this: Can change be a good thing? If God is *changeless*, how can we say that the rapid change we observe in a little infant is a good thing?

To be sure, not all change, even among creatures, is good change. Paul faces the serious accusation of being fickle, of changing at the drop of a hat. He had promised to visit the Corinthians but hasn't come through on his pledge. How can we count on a church leader who says one thing and does another? The change in Paul's plans was not a good one, many of the people in Corinth were convinced. In this second letter, St. Paul explains why he didn't come by to see the Corinthians even though he had promised them he would. His reason was not that he didn't feel like it. It was that a visit would've been too hard on the Corinthians.

Back in chapter 1, as Paul explains why he hadn't come to visit the Corinthians, he raises the question, "Do I make my plans according to the flesh, ready to say 'Yes, yes' and 'No, no' at the same time? As surely as God is faithful, our word to you has not been Yes and No" (2 Cor. 1:17–18). In other words, Paul is saying that he is not vacillating, changing back and forth, and his reason is that God doesn't change back and forth. In Christ, God never says "No"; instead, he always says "Yes." For, Paul comments, "all the promises of God find their Yes in him"—in Christ, that is. "That is why it is through him that we utter our Amen to God for his glory" (1:20). God doesn't change; he is utterly dependable. Paul knows it's important to be like God: changeless. It's Paul's changelessness that makes him dependable, much like God himself is dependable in Christ.

By the time we get to chapter 3, Paul is still defending himself against people who seem to be stirring up the congregation against his authority. So-called super-apostles is what he calls them (11:5). They have a high opinion of themselves, boasting and commending themselves to the Corinthians (10:12, 18) over against the apostle Paul. In contrast with their self-acclaimed status, Paul's résumé looks rather bleak, to say the least. All *he* can use to "commend" himself is a life of suffering and hardship: "calamities, beatings, imprisonments, riots, labors, sleepless nights, hunger" (6:4–5). This doesn't seem to be the best résumé to promote oneself. Paul seems to be a changeable, unpredictable character, someone whose letters of reference we don't want to look at too closely.

But Paul counters in chapter 3 by insisting he *does* have a letter of reference—and quite a good one too. "You yourselves are our letter of recommendation," he says in 3:2. Ironically, he's got one up on his opponents. They have to commend *themselves*. Paul has *others* speaking for him: the Corinthians are his letter of recommendation. They are a letter Christ himself wrote on Paul's behalf—not with ink but with the Spirit on their hearts. So Paul is pointing to the changed lives of the Corinthians; they are his letter of recommendation. Some change is good change. Paul's preaching has shone new light into the lives of these newborn Christians. The light of God's glory has utterly changed their lives. And it keeps changing them. That's what this whole chapter is about: God's glory changing lives. At the very end, in 3:18, St. Paul waxes eloquent about this change happening among the Corinthians: "We all, with unveiled face, beholding the glory of the Lord, are being transformed into the same image from one degree of glory to another." We're all being transformed, he says. We're all being changed from glory to glory. Paul's letter of reference is a bunch of people who have changed drastically and who continue to change in remarkable ways. God is a God of change.

So the apostle Paul puts forth a self-defense. But the beautiful thing about it is that in an important sense, it isn't a *self*-defense at all. It is not about him. It's about the people in the church. It's about you and me and the change *we* experience. Even the most difficult and debilitating of issues—a direct attack on his credibility as an apostle—St. Paul turns into an opportunity to preach to us about the marvelous change the Spirit of God works in our lives. What Paul is saying, in effect, is, "Don't look at me to see how fickle and changeable I am; I have no better defense than to ask you to look at yourselves, to see how you've changed." What an astonishing change it has been, and continues to be.

So God is a God of change. He is not, to be sure, a God who himself changes. But he is a God who changes you and me; in that sense, he is a God of change. We can see this, St. Paul points out, in Moses. The apostle takes us back in history, all the way to the founding events of the nation of Israel. They're at Mount Sinai. It should've been a celebration in worship of God—the very purpose of the exodus. But it turned into the disaster of the golden calf. Hot with anger, Moses throws down the tablets of the law and breaks them to pieces (Exod. 32:19). But despite everything that has happened, God is still willing to travel along with his people to the Promised Land. The Lord tells Moses to cut two new tablets of stone (34:1), and he comes down to Moses and talks with him on top of the mountain for forty days and forty nights (34:28). After that intimate meeting with God, Moses comes down the mountain, two new tablets with

Ten Commandments in hand. Although he doesn't know it, "the skin of his face shone because he had been talking with God" (34:29). Unbeknown to himself, Moses has changed.

At this point, the story gives us these two key verses—Exodus 34:34–35:

> Whenever Moses went in before the LORD to speak with him, he would remove the veil, until he came out. And when he came out and told the people of Israel what he was commanded, the people of Israel would see the face of Moses, that the skin of Moses' face was shining. And Moses would put the veil over his face again, until he went in to speak with him.

Talking with the Lord, standing in the tent of meeting, apparently Moses' face began to radiate with the glory of God's very own light. God's intimate conversation with Moses changed him; it made Moses ever more glorious, ever more like God. But after coming out of the tent, slowly but surely the glory would fade from Moses' face. Paul says in 2 Corinthians 3:13 that Moses "would put a veil over his face so that the Israelites might not gaze at the outcome of what was being brought to an end." The Israelites shouldn't see the outcome—Moses' regular face. Their focus should instead be on the initial shining of the glory on Moses' face.

This is a remarkable story of change. God is a God of change. Every time Moses would speak with the Lord, Moses would unveil himself (Exod. 34:34), and the glory of God would shine on him, transforming him, changing him so as to make him more like God— changing him, we could say, so as to make him more like the God whose Yes is always Yes in Christ. When God changes people, he makes them like himself—dependable, faithful, immutable people. What St. Paul does when he reads this chapter is to put the Corinthians—and to put you and me—in the position of Moses. What was happening to Moses is also happening to you and me. Second Corinthians 3:16 says, "When one turns to the Lord, the veil is removed." "Turns" is the word Paul uses. It's the language of change, of conversion. When we turn to the Lord, a change happens. The reason is: the veil is removed. And when the veil is removed, the glory of God shines on us so that we change more and more to become like God. God is a God of change.

We are like Moses. His turning speaks of our turning; his change of our change. But St. Paul is not looking just for similarities between Moses and us. The reason is that no matter how much we may be *like* Moses, we're much more *unlike* Moses. What happened to the glory that was shining off the face of Moses? Look at the second part of 2 Corinthians 3:7: "The Israelites could not gaze at Moses' face because of its glory, which was being brought to an end." The glory on Moses' face was *brought to an end*. Moses' face changed back; its glory was brought to an end. Without in any way being irreverent, we could almost say Moses' face was fickle; its glory didn't stay. St. Paul is emphatic on this point. He doesn't use the expression "being brought to an end" or "taken away" just in verse 7. He repeats it in verse 11, and again in verse 13, and one final time in verse 14. Moses' glory was, emphatically, glory that disappeared. It came to an end.

This change is apparently not a good change. And this change of Moses losing the shine on his face speaks not of any change in us. This change speaks of the end of a covenant. It says God's covenant with Moses is finished. It's had its day, and it's done. Here, Paul is not looking for similarities between Moses and the believers as he does in 2 Corinthians 3:16. Here in verse 7, he is looking for contrast. Moses' ministry, the old covenant, came to an end in sharp contrast to the glory of the new covenant, which, Paul says, is permanent. It doesn't change back. "If," he writes in verse 11, "what was being brought to an end came with glory, much more will what is permanent have glory." What he is saying is that the glory of the old is nothing like the glory of the new. The reason is that Moses' glory came to an end, while our glory—the glory of the new covenant—is permanent. This change is a permanent change. Once the veil is gone, it's gone forever. Much more than the glory beaming from Moses' face, the shine in believers has the permanence of the changelessness of God.

Paul's reading of this story about Moses is rather curious. On the one hand, Paul insists that the Corinthians are much *like* Moses: when they turn to the Lord, their faces begin to shine much like that of Moses whenever he would go in before the Lord (verse 16). On the other hand, they are much more *unlike* Moses: the new covenant is permanent, while that of Moses came to an end. Compared to the glory of the new covenant, the old one has no glory at all (vv. 7 and 11). So we are "*not* like Moses," Paul exclaims in verse 13. That's the upshot. We are *not* like Moses. Moses—and here we should think of his entire ministry, including the old covenant law—has been brought to an end. It's finished.

At this point, we may want to ask the apostle: If this is true, and if the change of the Corinthians is so much more radical and glorious than that of Moses, why continue reading Moses at all? But obviously this is not the conclusion Paul wants us to draw. He continues to read Moses, even in this chapter. The only thing is, Paul's reading of Moses changes. Not only do we have *people* changing in this passage, we also see changes in their *reading*. And the two are closely linked; they go hand in hand.

Throughout this passage, St. Paul talks about texts and about reading them. We already saw that he calls the church of Corinth his letter of recommendation, and he says this letter can be "known and read by all" (3:2). The Corinthians are a text—they're a letter of reference that speaks to Paul's career. They're a letter he wants people to read. Why is he so convinced that this letter can be read? The reason is that he has seen the Spirit transform their lives. The Corinthians read like an open book, both to Paul and to others. Their hearts are like tablets on which the Spirit has written his letter of recommendation for all to read.

It is the fact that the Corinthians have changed into a kind of text—a letter of recommendation—that makes Paul think of another text: the Ten Commandments. The letter of recommendation, he insists, has been written by Christ, with God's Spirit as his pen, "not on tablets of stone but on tablets of human hearts" (verse 3). At this point we have two texts: the Corinthians (as a letter of recommendation) and the tablets of the Ten Commandments. Paul contrasts these two texts when he says in verse 7 that the Ten Commandments were nothing but letters carved in stone. Moreover, because the people of Israel didn't stick to them, those letters carved in stone condemned them to death.

St. Paul comes back to the topic of reading texts one last time in verses 14 and 15. In these two verses he makes clear why he is still reading Exodus 34, why he is still reading Moses, even though the glory of Moses' face has been brought to an end. The reason is this: when veiled people read Moses, they see something different than what unveiled people see in Moses. When veiled people read Moses, all they see are those letters carved in stone, letters that condemn. But when unveiled people—people who have changed—read Moses, they see something else. What they see in Moses is glory, the glory of the Lord himself.

Why does the apostle still want us to read Moses? The reason is simple: he sees glory in the Books of Moses, even in the letters carved in stone. Not Moses' own glory, to be sure: that came to an end as soon as the people started looking at it. No, the glory Paul sees in the Books of Moses is the glory of Christ, the glory of the Lord. From then on, the only way to read the Old Testament is to see it marked from the outset with the newness of Christ, to see it marked with the changes that take place in the Christian life. There's a close link then for Paul between changed people and changed readings. The way we change has everything to do with the changed way Moses gets read. Only people who have been changed go deeper than the letters carved in stone. Only people who have been changed see the permanent glory of Christ shining from Moses' face.

St. Paul is deeply interested in reading texts. Christians have always been people of the book, captivated by reading texts. But Christians are never interested just in letters carved in stone, or letters on the page. Christians scour texts looking for the glory of Christ. And not only will we find Christ's glory in the text, but as we look at the glory of Christ in the text, its glory changes us—it changes us into itself. Christians, therefore, read for the sake of change. This is the astounding promise of the last verse of the chapter, that Christ changes us to become like him. When Paul speaks in verse 18 of the "image," when he says we are changed into the same image, he is talking about Christ. So he says this is what happens when you read Moses: you behold glory, and you become glory. You see Christ's image, and you become Christ's image.

God is a God of change. He always is. Long ago, he was a God of change for Moses. Then much more gloriously, he was a God of change for the Corinthians. Throughout history, God—our faithful, changeless God—has been a God of change. He still is. He is still a God of change, also for us. He is the God who says Yes to us in Christ. He is the God whose Yes means he is changing us into himself. That is the glorious promise of the gospel: when we *see* God's glory in Christ, we also *become* God's glory in Christ.

Preacher's Notes

It is not always easy to preach from the Pauline Epistles. For one, they have no obvious story line for readers to identify with. To be sure, the narrative redemptive historical context, emphasized by N. T. Wright and other proponents of the so-called New Perspective, does mean the preacher can point to a larger narrative flow from old to new covenant, and I highlight that flow in this sermon.[1] But the broad strokes of the story line of salvation history do not provide quite the kind of points of contact as does, say, a particular Old Testament character or a story from one of the Gospels. Further, the depth of theological reflection, along with the often nuanced and manifold references and allusions to the Old Testament, means that a sermon on a Pauline passage can easily turn into a rather abstract, intellectual exposition on the details of St. Paul's theology. While it is important for a sermon to do justice to the contents and the context of the passage under consideration, it is also important to appeal to the affections and to avoid turning a liturgical gathering into a dogmatic theology class. There are no obvious and easy ways to address these challenges. But the preacher may take encouragement from the fact that different genres—including the Pauline Epistles—legitimately allow for different homiletic approaches. Simply being aware that the Pauline Epistles pose distinct challenges for the preacher is already an important first step in establishing a connection with the congregation.

In this sermon, I try to deal with some of these challenges by focusing on the notion of change. This both narrows the focus and raises an issue with which everyone is able to identify. The choice of change as the topic of the sermon also has the advantage of allowing me (1) to draw in the broader context of the passage (the question of Paul's

1. See N. T. Wright, *What Saint Paul Really Said: Was Paul of Tarsus the Real Founder of Christianity?* (Grand Rapids: Eerdmans, 1997).

changeable or fickle character); (2) to discuss the heart of the passage (the change in believers through the glory of Christ); and (3) to discuss briefly the topic of divine immutability. I do not mean to suggest that my choice of change as the entry point into the passage is the only plausible one. It is quite possible, for example, to preach on this passage by focusing on the notion of glory, by speaking of life and death as they function in this pericope, by discussing the theme of ministry, or by making the notion of the vision of God key to the sermon.

It is not my custom to use sermons to explain doctrinal issues in great detail. At the same time, it will be obvious that, particularly from this sermon, several matters of theological significance come to the fore. The first one, to which I already alluded, is the question of divine immutability. The first requirement of the preacher is to be faithful to the text. Accordingly, my comments on divine immutability focus on the faithfulness of God's character in Christ. After all, this is the issue St. Paul discusses in 2 Corinthians 1: "For all the promises of God find their Yes in him" (1:20). The careful listener may notice that I use traditional theological language of divine *immutability*, and may perhaps wonder whether I limit the notion of immutability to God's faithfulness in Christ. I do not. It is important to affirm that God, in his very being, is not subject to change as human beings are prone to change, and that divine immutability and impassibility are essential to retaining divine transcendence.[2] But in the sermon, I am concerned both to stay in line with the focus on the text and to avoid entering too deeply into doctrinal matters.

A second key theological issue in this passage is the discontinuity between the old and new covenants, or between law and gospel. This issue lies, in some ways, at the heart of the passage, as it contains the much-debated line, "the letter kills, but the Spirit gives life" (3:6). I take a stance on this issue by arguing that "no matter how much we may be *like* Moses, we're much more *unlike* Moses." The theological stance underlying this statement is threefold. First, while there is discontinuity between old and new covenants, this is merely a *comparative* or

2. For further support of this position, see Thomas G. Weinandy, *Does God Change? The Word's Becoming in the Incarnation* (Still River, MA: St. Bede's Publications, 1985); Paul L. Gavrilyuk, *The Suffering of the Impassible God: The Dialectics of Patristic Thought* (Oxford: Oxford University Press, 2004).

relative discontinuity, which St. Paul grasps with the phrase "more glory" (3:8) and with words such as "exceed" (3:9) and "surpasses" (3:10). This relative contrast allows him then to insist that "the letter kills, but the Spirit gives life" (3:6), and that we are "not like Moses" (3:13). Only by taking these latter comments in isolation could we possibly arrive at an absolute contrast between law and gospel.

Second, it is clear Paul does not speak negatively about the law per se. He does not reject it in proto-Marcionite fashion. As elsewhere (e.g., Rom. 7:12), so here he affirms the goodness of the law by insisting that Moses genuinely participated in God's glory (2 Cor. 3:7, 9). The word "but" in 3:14 ("but their minds were hardened") makes particularly clear that for Paul the problem lies not so much with the law itself as with the blindness of the Israelites, a blindness he insists continues today when people read Moses with a veil over their hearts (3:15; cf. Rom. 11:7). The law as such was God's good gift for his people. As the fourth-century preacher John Chrysostom puts it, "Paul does not disparage the Old Testament but highly commends it, since comparisons are apt to be made between things which are basically similar in kind."[3] For Paul, the glory in old and new covenants is the same glory—that of God's self-revelation.

Third, Paul is not content merely to say that Moses (i.e., his ministry and covenant, including the law) has been "brought to an end" (2 Cor. 3:7, 11, 13). Even this comment is nuanced by Paul's insistence that in Christ Moses is reaffirmed. Toward the end of the sermon, I make this point by commenting that with veils removed, we see in Moses "the glory of the Lord himself." In 3:14–16, St. Paul appears to insist that our very reading of the law changes "when one turns to the Lord" and reads Moses with the veil removed. Indeed, according to the apostle, we see Christ's glory not just after the old covenant has been "brought to an end," but we see his glory also in Moses himself—provided we read him with veils removed.

3. John Chrysostom, *Homilies on Second Corinthians* 7.2; as quoted in Gerald Bray, ed., *1–2 Corinthians*, Ancient Christian Commentary on Scripture (Downers Grove, IL: InterVarsity, 1999), 220. Cf. Theodoret of Cyrus' illustration of the relative change that comes with the move from the old to the new covenant: "The light of a lamp shines brightly in the darkness of the night, but at midday it is barely visible and is not even thought of as light." *Commentary on the Second Epistle to the Corinthians*, 304, quoted in Bray, ed., *1–2 Corinthians*, 220.

We need to beware, therefore, of a false dilemma between what
we might call a "historical" and an "exegetical" reading of this passage, where the former reads Paul as talking about the change that
takes place in redemptive history through the coming of Christ, and
the latter understands the apostle as focusing on how as Christians
we should read the books of Moses. Paul presents both elements
alongside each other and interweaves the two. He brings to the fore
a historical contrast when he insists that Moses—that is to say, the
period of the old covenant—has been brought to an end now that
Christ engraves his will on people's hearts (cf. Jer. 31:31–34; Ezek.
11:19; 36:26–27). Historically, Christ is the fulcrum on which all of
history turns and through which the old covenant gives way to the
new. Paul highlights the exegetical implications of this change by
focusing throughout the passage on how to read texts—in particular,
how to read Moses. The coming of Christ and the gift of the Spirit
do not render the reading of Moses irrelevant or obsolescent. Quite
the contrary: St. Paul focuses on reading the old covenant (3:14–15),
and he explains that by doing so in the light of Christ one comes to
share in the glory of Christ (3:18). The historical change from old to
new covenant has immediate personal and exegetical implications.

Paul's insistence that we see the glory of Christ in the law of Moses
is based on a key doctrinal insight, namely, the identity of Christ with
the God who revealed himself to Moses. In 2 Corinthians 3:14, the
apostle decries the Israelites' hardened minds, which in the Exodus 34
narrative made it impossible for them to gaze on the glory of the Lord.
In 2 Corinthians 3:18, St. Paul applies the phrase "the glory of the
Lord" to Christ, and he maintains that when we behold his glory, we
are transformed from glory to glory (or in the ESV, "from one degree
of glory to another"). Thus while the Israelites were unable to "gaze"
or look intently (*atenizō*) on Moses' face, even though its glory was
being brought to an end (3:7), believers of the new covenant *are* able
to behold (as in a mirror; *katoptrizō*) that same glory of the Lord.[4]
For Paul, Christ is the Lord who showed himself long ago to Moses.

4. Albrecht Oepke makes the point well: "For Paul . . . there is no doubt that the
redeeming God of the OT and the NT is one and the same. Hence the glory of Christ
is to be seen also in the OT covenant when this is properly understood (v. 18: δόξα
κυρίου [glory of the Lord] referred to Christ)." "Κάλυμμα," in *Theological Dictionary*

All this implies that our continuous transformation into the life of God is grounded in Christ's identity as God or Lord. When we see God, we see him in Jesus Christ. God makes it possible for us to see him without us being put to death because we see him in Christ. Already in this life—already in our reading of the law of Moses—we see God and are transformed in and through our vision of his glory. Our vision of God is possible, and increases in clarity, inasmuch as God continuously changes us into his own divine glory. The vision of God, along with the divinization of believers, centers on our participation in Christ as our Lord. Once this point is made in the sermon, any application is redundant. The application, as usual, lies in the glorious gospel message itself.

---

of the New Testament, trans. Geoffrey W. Bromiley, ed. Gerhard Kittel (Grand Rapids: Eerdmans, 1965), 3:560.

Epilogue

Nostalgic for Love

*T*his book of sermons is intended to be a work of retrieval. I have tried to show that the sacramental exegesis of the church fathers is worth recovering. I am not the first to engage in such a project of retrieval. Since the mid-twentieth century, much has been written about theology as retrieval. The French Catholic movement of *nouvelle théologie* self-consciously engaged in a *ressourcement* or retrieval of the church fathers, of biblical theology, and of ancient liturgical elements.[1] Increasingly, Protestants too recognize the need for a retrieval of the tradition in order to nourish and sustain the church's future.[2] The notion of retrieval implies that some sort of interruption has occurred, attenuating the link between the present

---

1. See Hans Boersma, *Heavenly Participation: The Weaving of a Sacramental Tapestry* (Grand Rapids: Eerdmans, 2011).

2. See, e.g., John Webster, "*Ressourcement* Theology and Protestantism," in *Ressourcement: A Movement for Renewal in Twentieth-Century Catholic Theology*, ed. Gabriel Flynn and Paul D. Murray (Oxford: Oxford University Press, 2012), 482–94. The Baker Academic book series "Evangelical *Ressourcement*: Ancient Sources for the Church's Future," edited by D. H. Williams, is further evidence of Protestant interest in retrieving the tradition. See D. H. Williams, *Evangelicals and Tradition: The Formative Influence of the Early Church* (Grand Rapids: Baker Academic, 2005).

and the past. The notion implies a kind of forgetfulness in the more recent past, a neglect of a rich, earlier past that is worth recovering. In short, projects of retrieval assume that riches of a more distant memory have been covered over by neglect (or, in some cases, deliberate obfuscation), and our task is to blow off the dust so that the ancient treasures can shine in renewed glory.

It is hardly surprising that those who put forward projects of retrieval are sometimes accused of nostalgia. Brad Gregory, in his much-debated book *The Unintended Reformation*, attempts to forestall this type of criticism by titling his conclusion, "Against Nostalgia."[3] Paul Tyson, who advocates a return to a Christian Platonist understanding of reality, anticipates the same objection in the introduction to his book: "Immediately I hear someone cry, 'ah, nostalgia!,' as if it is my intention (*per impossibile*) to take us back to the life-world of the Middle Ages."[4] And, of course, I too was careful to remark in the introduction to this collection of sermons that I don't recommend to my students that they simply imitate patristic or medieval interpretive approaches in their own exegetical work. Jumping back over centuries of wrestling with the text in an attempt to recover the pure gold of patristic exegesis would surely warrant the label of nostalgia.

We must roundly acknowledge that the Christian tradition cannot be radically discontinuous. While it may be possible genuinely to discern periods of decline, presumably even during those times, the decline is limited in some ways. The promise of Christ that "the gates of hell shall not prevail" (Matt. 16:18) against the church asks from us a high view of divine providence and a strong trust in the Spirit's guidance of the church throughout history. Attempts at retrieval, including the present collection of sermons, should not project the notion that God was asleep at the wheel for most of the time following the patristic era.

The term "nostalgia" appears to have first been used (in a rather negative way) by the Swiss doctor Johannes Hofer in 1688 to describe

3. Brad S. Gregory, *The Unintended Reformation: How a Religious Revolution Secularized Society* (Cambridge, MA: Belknap Press of Harvard University Press, 2012), 365.
4. Paul Tyson, *Returning to Reality: Christian Platonism for Our Times* (Eugene, OR: Cascade, 2014), 6.

a medical diagnosis. Nostalgia was a disease producing "erroneous representations," which in turn caused patients to "lose touch with the present. Longing for their native land became their single-minded obsession."[5] In her book *The Future of Nostalgia*, Svetlana Boym gives an interesting overview of the various characteristics of the ailment and its development. However, she also points out that the longing inherent in the modern epidemic of nostalgia goes back all the way to the mythology of Homer. Odysseus' return home from Troy and from Hades lies at the root of the modern preoccupation with this sickness—the Greek term *nostos* meaning "homecoming," and the word *algos* meaning "pain" or "ache."[6]

Perhaps we don't have a high view of the truthfulness of Homer's myths. And despite the shortcomings of late seventeenth-century medicine, Hofer and his colleagues were certainly right that the longing for a long-lost home can be irrational and has the ability to immobilize us so as to prevent us from moving forward on our journey. Some forms and expressions of nostalgia are less than salubrious and should be actively resisted. For some, therefore, the label of nostalgia is enough to repudiate any foolhardy attempt at a theology of retrieval. But there is little reason to trust in a kind of myth of progress that regards each and every historical development as a positive step forward. History is made up of periods of progress *and* decline, and attempts to correct decline seem to me to evidence sharp-wittedness, not feeblemindedness. Depending on what is at stake, nostalgia may be a type of longing we should foster rather than disparage. Nostalgia for patristic exegesis is, in some sense, a good thing.

It is important to ask, therefore, *what* precisely we are nostalgic for. In these sermons I have attempted to retrieve something I believe lies at the heart of the patristic sensibility: the recognition that Christ is present in the historical realities depicted in the Old Testament Scriptures. As I tried to retrieve this central element, several other aspects came to the fore as well. In all, the preceding sermons have broadly highlighted three themes: (1) the hidden, sacramental presence of new covenant realities—Christ himself, the church, and our

5. Svetlana Boym, *The Future of Nostalgia* (New York: Basic Books, 2001), 3.
6. Ibid., 7–8.

eschatological future—in the events depicted in the Old Testament; (2) the believers' ascent to heaven, based on God's gracious decent in Christ; and (3) the beatific vision of God as our ultimate goal: unveiled happiness.

Nostalgia can sometimes lead to an undue sense of isolation. In our yearning for a long-lost age, we ignore that this age has left its traces—perhaps deeply imprinted at times—throughout history. I am convinced that the three themes to which I just alluded can be found not only in the church fathers. To varying degrees they are constants throughout the Christian tradition—though admittedly, modern, historical methods of exegesis have made it difficult for Christians to regard them as central to the way we read the Bible.

We witness some of this constancy in the theology of the seventeenth-century English preacher from Bemerton, George Herbert (1593–1633). At the time of writing this epilogue, I am teaching a seminar at Regent College that focuses in part on *The Temple*, a collection of Herbert's poems. I cannot help but be struck by the presence of each of the three themes in Herbert's poems. Herbert's continuity with the great tradition of the church comes to the fore in a number of ways, and it may be worthwhile to have a brief look at some of his poems—both by way of caution against a one-sided type of nostalgia that erroneously assumes that the sacramental cast of patristic exegesis disappeared along with the era of the church fathers, and also to give the reader some glimpse into the beautiful world of Herbert's poetry, to which I have become a recent convert.

"The bunch of grapes" is a poem in which the speaker identifies with the Israelites as they have seen the grapes of the Promised Land but have backed down from entering Canaan. God punishes them with forty additional years in the wilderness: "I did toward Canaan draw; but now I am / Brought back to the Red sea, the sea of shame" (449).[7] This is the episode of Numbers 13 and 14, which I depict in sermon 8 ("God's Own Rest"). Herbert unapologetically allegorizes the narrative, speaking straightforwardly of the Christian's spiritual

---

7. My quotations come from George Herbert, *The English Poems of George Herbert*, ed. Helen Wilcox (Cambridge: Cambridge University Press, 2007).

life by using the terms "Canaan" and "Red sea." In the second stanza, he explains how the journey of the Israelites is also that of every Christian:

> For as the Jews of old by Gods command
> Travell'd, and saw no town:
> So now each Christian hath his journeys spann'd:
> Their storie pennes and sets us down.
> A single deed is small renown.
> Gods works are wide, and let in future times;
> His ancient justice overflows our crimes. (449)

For Herbert, each Christian's pilgrimage is "spann'd" or matched by the exodus of the Israelites. Their stories write about us. Although Herbert does not elaborate at length, it appears that minor historical events ("A single deed is small renown") are able to contain or "let in future times" that are far greater than the original events. The sacramentality of time to which this line alludes allows the life of the church (and of "each Christian") to be present in the earlier events of Israel's narrative:

> Then have we too our guardian fires and clouds;
> Our Scripture-dew drops fast:
> We have our sands and serpents, tents and shrowds;
> Alas! our murmurings come not last. (449)

Notwithstanding the direct identification of the speaker with the Israelites, Herbert also recognizes that the New Testament reality far outshines the ancient sacrament. Although the first three stanzas have the speaker pining for the cluster of grapes that the spies brought from the Promised Land, the final stanza opens with the recognition that in Christ a much greater reality is found: "But can he want the grape, who hath the wine?" (449). When "future times" are "let in" to enter the Old Testament narratives, it becomes clear that the latter are mere sacraments of a reality that far exceeds them in glory.

In "The Pearl. *Matt. 13*," Herbert reflects on the parable of the pearl of great value, in which Jesus compares the kingdom of heaven to "a merchant in search of fine pearls, who, on finding one pearl of great value, went and sold all that he had and bought it" (Matt. 13:45–46). In three subsequent stanzas, the speaker reflects on the relative worthlessness of learning, honor, and pleasure—seeing as he is intimately familiar with each of them. "I know the wayes of learning," he exclaims at the beginning of the poem (322). In the next two stanzas he reiterates, "I know the wayes of honour," and "I know the wayes of pleasure" (322–23). And he summarizes at the beginning of the fourth and last stanza, "I know all these, and have them in my hand" (323). Nonetheless, after the lengthy descriptions of the "wayes" of the world in the first three stanzas, the speaker ends each of them with the comment, "Yet I love thee" (322–23). The love of God appears to win out, in each case, against the knowledge of earthly goods. Or, to put it in the terminology of this book, sensed happiness gives way to heavenly happiness.

The poem's conclusion describes the speaker's ascent to God:

> Yet through the labyrinths, not my groveling wit,
> But thy silk twist let down from heav'n to me,
> Did both conduct and teach me, how by it
> To climbe to thee. (323)

The various "wayes" turn out to be a labyrinth. The only way to climb out of it is to "climbe to thee." But it is a journey of ascent made possible only by the descent of a thread, "thy silk twist let down from heav'n to me." The "silk twist" is an allusion to the ball of thread that, in the myth of Theseus and the Minotaur, Ariadne gave to Theseus so that after killing the Minotaur at the heart of the labyrinth, he would be able to find his way back. The speaker in the poem places himself in the position of Theseus. And it is hard not to see in the "silk twist" a deeper, allegorical reference to Jacob's ladder and to Christ—much as I try to articulate in sermon 12 ("The Gate of Heaven").[8] Herbert recognizes Christ as Ariadne's thread, as Jacob's ladder, as the one whose gracious, divine descent enables our ascent back to God.

8. For helpful analyses of the poem, see Anne-Marie Miller Blaise, "'Sweet-nesse Readie Penn'd': Herbert's Theology of Beauty," *George Herbert Journal* 27 (2003–2004): 1–21; and Christopher Hodgkins, "'Yet I Love Thee': The 'Wayes of Learning' and 'Groveling Wit' in Herbert's 'The Pearl,'" *George Herbert Journal* 27 (2003–2004): 22–31.

Finally, in a number of poems, Herbert speaks of the beatific vision of God—unveiled happiness—that awaits the believer in the heavenly future. In doing so, he draws on a theme that was also important to the church fathers and to many in the later medieval tradition. This theme permeates the sensibilities of many Puritan divines of Herbert's time. And although he would not have identified as a Puritan, certain elements of Calvinist spirituality (such as the descriptions of inner turmoil and anxiety) permeate his poetry. Herbert, much like the Puritans, combines allegorical exegesis with recognition of the limited value of sensed happiness and with the aim of seeing God in the hereafter. Herbert's recognition of the centrality of the beatific vision puts him in line with a long tradition of theologians for whom the unveiled happiness of the eschaton was their ultimate aim and desire.

The speaker's sense of unworthiness of seeing God comes through in the first stanza of the well-known poem "Love (III)": "Love bade me welcome: yet my soul drew back, / Guiltie of dust and sinne."[9] Herbert depicts the speaker as a dusty traveler arriving at a roadside inn where Love as the host wants to serve him:

> But quick-ey'd Love, observing me grow slack
> From my first entrance in,
> Drew nearer to me, sweetly questioning,
> If I lack'd any thing. (661)

The contrast between God's "quick-ey'd Love" and the traveler's "dust and sinne" continues into the second stanza:

> A guest, I answer'd, worthy to be here:
> Love said, you shall be he.
> I the unkinde, ungratefull? Ah my deare,
> I cannot look on thee.
> Love took my hand, and smiling did reply,
> Who made the eyes but I? (661)

The poem's first two stanzas speak both of God's "quick-ey'd Love" observing the speaker and of the speaker's inability to "look on

9. Herbert, *English Poems*, 661. The themes of beauty and vision play a role in each of Herbert's three "Love" poems. Cf. Blaise, "'Sweetnesse Readie Penn'd,'" 11.

thee"—a problem remedied by Love's insistence that he is the maker of the eyes. God, in other words, not only has eyes but is also the maker of eyes. Or put differently, the creaturely eye has its archetype in the Creator's eye. In every way, he is the one to be trusted when it comes to the possibility of the beatific vision.

When in the final stanza the speaker still objects to the invitation to eat in Love's presence ("Truth Lord, but I have marr'd them: let my shame / Go where it doth deserve"), Love points him to Christ as the one "who bore the blame" (661). This leads to the poem's conclusion with the speaker accepting the host's condescension in serving him: "You must sit down, sayes Love, and taste my meat: / So I did sit and eat" (661). The eucharistic overtones of the last lines—reverberating back onto the entire poem—are obvious. For Herbert it is in the Lord's Supper that he is in the presence of the host and finally dares to look on him. It is in tasting Love's meat that, for Herbert, we accept the Creator ("Who made the eyes but I?") and Redeemer ("Who bore the blame?") as the one who renders us worthy to be served. For Herbert, God's sight transforms us as we allow our own vision to be healed by his.

Each of these three themes—the sacramental presence of Christ in the Old Testament, human ascent by means of divine descent, and the eschatological hope of the beatific vision—connects the world of the church fathers with that of the seventeenth-century poet George Herbert. The presence of these three themes bespeaks an approach to Scripture that treats its words as sacraments. They are the manna of "Scripture-dew"—our present-day desert gift according to Herbert's "The bunch of grapes"—that makes present to us the heavenly, eternal Word and so gives us a glance into the heart of Love. The sacramental presence of Christ, both in Scripture and in the Eucharist, is the real presence of Love. In recollecting those places where we have seen eternal Love come down—patristic exegesis, Herbert's poetry—the response of nostalgia is both right and just. It expresses our desire to taste Love's meat. Sacramental preaching aims to make us nostalgic for Love.

Subject Index

adultery, 45
allegory. *See* exegesis: allegorical
Ambrose of Milan, 180
angels, 85, 89–91, 135, 162, 170–71
  and Jacob, 155, 157–58
  and Joseph, 70, 75
  and Philip, 4
  and the Sadducees, 129
Aquinas, Thomas. *See* Thomas Aquinas
ark of the covenant, 85, 91, 173
ascension, 82–85, 88–93
Athanasius, 87–88, 93
atonement, 92–93
Augustine, xviii, 51, 112, 147, 180n8
  on Isaiah 53, 8–11
  on Psalm 1, 114 15, 121–22
  on the Sermon on the Mount, 141

Balthasar, Hans Urs von, 177–78
baptism, xx, 10, 133, 176
beatific vision, xxiv, xxv n10, 38, 136–37,
  160, 174, 178–79, 192, 195, 200,
  203–4
Bernard of Clairvaux, xviii, 44, 50, 52
Bible. *See* Scripture
biblical interpretation. *See* exegesis;
  Scripture
blessedness, xxiv, 119–20, 140, 144

Calvin, John, 112. *See also* Puritan
canon, 50–51, 162
Childs, Brevard, 23
Christology, 148n4, 164, 179
Christus Victor. *See* atonement
church, the, xx, 5–6, 9–11, 40, 147
  and Israel, 201
  and the Song of Solomon, 43–45, 50
  unity of, 16–18
Communion. *See* Eucharist
covenant
  new, 71, 104, 188–89, 192–94, 199
  old, 188–89, 192–94
creation, xx, 57–58, 61–65, 80, 92, 102
  and grace, 61–65
Creator, 29, 37, 67, 92, 175, 184, 204

Daniélou, Jean, 65n5, 89n2, 163–64
deification, 105. *See also* participation
De Lubac, Henri, 25n5, 122n18, 163
  on patristic and medieval exegesis, 164
desert. *See* wilderness
desire, 30, 35, 39, 44–48, 75–76, 83,
  112–14, 151, 204
  erotic, 42–43, 49–50
  God's, 104, 176–77
  natural, 63
  spiritual, 67

Scripture Index